Notorious Identity

Notorious Identity

*Materializing the Subject
in Shakespeare*

Linda Charnes

Harvard University Press
Cambridge, Massachusetts
London, England
1993

Copyright © 1993 by the President and Fellows of Harvard College

Printed in the United States of America

This book is printed on acid-free paper, and its binding materials
have been chosen for strength and durability.

Library of Congress Cataloging-in-Publication Data

Charnes, Linda.
  Notorious identity: materializing the subject in Shakespeare /
Linda Charnes.
    p. cm.
  ISBN 0–674–62780–6
  1. Shakespeare, William, 1564–1616—Knowledge—History.
  2. Shakespeare, William, 1564–1616. Antony and Cleopatra.
  3. Shakespeare, William, 1564–1616. Troilus and Cressida.
  4. Shakespeare, William, 1564–1616. King Richard III.
  5. Historical drama, English—History and criticism. 6. Identity
  (Psychology) in literature. 7. Legends in literature. 8. Fame in
  literature. I. Title.
PR3014.C43 1993
822.3'3—dc20
93–9755
  CIP

For my mother and father

Acknowledgments

I began to articulate the concerns of this book in a dissertation on Shakespeare. My acknowledgments therefore must begin with my teachers. As an undergraduate at the University of California, Santa Cruz, I was encouraged to pursue graduate study by Harry Berger, Jr., and Michael J. Warren. In the doctoral program in English at the University of California, Berkeley, I studied early modern literature and culture with Janet Adelman, Joel Altman, Stephen Booth, William Bouwsma, Joel Fineman, Donald Friedman, and Stephen Greenblatt. I learned as much from the differences between and among their approaches as I did from their wonderful scholarship and teaching. There is no way to talk about anything (and especially not about Shakespeare) without ventriloquizing the voices and appropriating the labors of others; but however fantasmatic (and symptomatic) the desire for one's own voice may be, I am grateful to Joel Altman (my dissertation director) for supporting my efforts to pursue that fantasy. From 1987 to 1989 I was a Berkeley-Harvard Exchange Scholar. Marjorie Garber and the Harvard English Department graciously hosted my stay, giving me the opportunity to benefit from seminars and lectures at Harvard's Center for Literary and Cultural Studies.

While working on this book as an assistant professor at Indiana University, I've been fortunate in the support I've received from colleagues and friends, at Bloomington and elsewhere. Peter Stallybrass, Catherine Belsey, Lena Cowen Orlin, Paul Strohm, and David Bevington read the manuscript in full or in part at different stages of its development; and I am deeply indebted to them for their criticisms, encouragement, and engagement with my work. I've also benefited in many ways from conversations with Judith Anderson, Harry Berger, Jr., Michael Bristol, Jonathan Elmer, Sheila Lindenbaum, Carolyn Mitchell, Louis Montrose, Michael Warren, Lindsay Waters, Stephen Watt, Don E. Wayne, and

Richard Wheeler. Louis Montrose provided valuable advice and moral support as I worked on the final details of manuscript preparation.

The Indiana University English Department and the College of Arts and Sciences have given me generous support: specifically, research funds to attend conferences, summer faculty fellowships, and leave to work on this book. In particular I thank Patrick Brantlinger, Mary Burgan, Susan Gubar, Kenneth R. Johnston, Christoph Lohmann, and Paul Strohm for helping me pursue and receive grants. I was fortunate to be able to teach graduate seminars on some of the material in this book to an extremely intelligent and engaged group of students. I thank especially Elizabeth Kuhlmann, Jeffrey Martinek, Nebila Romdhane, Donya Samara, and Stephen Weiskopf for their energy, challenges, and insights.

Sections of Chapter 2 are taken from " 'So Unsecret to Ourselves': Notorious Identity and the Material Subject in Shakespeare's *Troilus and Cressida," Shakespeare Quarterly* 40 (Winter 1989), and I thank Barbara Mowat and the Folger Shakespeare Library for permission to use them. A short section of Chapter 3 appears in "What's Love Got to Do with It? Reading the Liberal Humanist Romance in Shakespeare's *Antony and Cleopatra," Textual Practice* 6 (Spring 1992). I thank Terence Hawkes and Routledge for letting me revise and use this section here. I have Helen Deutsch to thank for sending me a postcard from Florence of the wonderful Michelangelo Cleopatra, and Elizabeth Taylor (and Twentieth Century Fox) for permission to accompany it with her version on the book jacket.

Lindsay Waters at Harvard University Press enthusiastically supported this book from its earliest stages. I thank him in particular for his well-timed "Coraggio!"; Alison Kent for cheerfully and patiently answering all my questions about protocol; and Jeffrey Martinek for helping me compile the index. My gratitude goes especially to Maria Ascher, of Harvard University Press, for her wonderful manuscript editing, fine ear, and attentive eye.

The sojourn is long—subjectively if not always chronologically—between entering graduate school and publishing one's first book; and the support of family and friends is crucial to the completion of both. For the sustaining gifts of their friendship along the way, I thank Catherine Belsey, Patrick Brantlinger, Curt Breight, Mary and Bill Burgan, Emily Charnes, Dorian Gossy, Susan Gubar, Charles Hayse, Julia Michael, Carolyn Mitchell, Roger Mitchell, Louis Montrose, Cornelia Nixon, Edwina Norton, Peter Stallybrass, Paul Strohm, Dean Young, Stephen

Watt, and Barrett Watten. Finally, it gives me the deepest pleasure to thank Alec Norton for his generosity, encouragement, and love; and my parents—James Charnes and Helga Hayse—for all of the above, as well as the force that through the green fuse drives the flower.

Contents

Notorious Identity

Introduction

I have no more made my book than my book has made me.
Montaigne, "Of Giving the Lie," trans. Donald Frame

This book is concerned with an old and well-known phenomenon: fame. And with the most famous of playwrights: Shakespeare. But it is not about Shakespeare's fame, although what it has to say about notorious identity in Shakespeare's plays will have implications for the notorious figure Shakespeare has become. Rather, it is about the representational politics, strategies, and fantasies that make a certain kind of fame culturally productive in a certain way. It is also necessarily concerned with the relationship between fame and history, for the same technologies that produce the former produce the latter. In fact, the two are inseparable from each other: "history" is what the "record" of persons and events becomes, and these in turn become famous by virtue of the particular roles they are assigned in the narratives of "history." But fame and history are the results not only of cultural inscription but of reinscription. Fame by its nature is redundant. Like history, it condenses meaning around—and *as*—both persons and events "after the facts." Always constituted retroactively, famous figures and historical events exist as representations, as well as effects, of their own *belatedness*.

The three plays that I will consider here each involve figures who are, and were in Shakespeare's day, indisputably "notorious." Richard III, Troilus and Cressida, and Antony and Cleopatra are legendary figures who mean—and mean intensely—in the Renaissance, long before Shakespeare takes up the task of giving them life on the stage. But when he does, he seems concerned less to merely reproduce cultural mythography than to demonstrate what's involved, for the *figures* of such notoriety, in the experience of being reiterated. These plays explore what it is like to be subjected to and by the extraordinary determining force of infamous names.

The kind of fame this book explores, however, is not of the garden

1

variety. For there is nothing "natural" about being famous. Like other cultural fabrications, it takes many forms—fame, legend, infamy, notoriety—each enabling the figuration of particular ideologies and deploying a particular politics of reproduction. In order to evoke what's peculiar about notorious identity, as well as the represented relations of its production in Shakespeare's plays, it is necessary to distinguish it both from what could be considered a historically "earlier" version of fame and from a less ideologically "charged" kind.

What Leo Braudy has characterized as "the frenzy of renown" had for many centuries been based on fame (whether simple or infamous) as moral paradigm: the extent to which it underwrote, by positive or negative exemplum, the dominant political and social ideologies of a particular time and place.[1] Figures such as Aeneas, Ulysses, Augustus Caesar, Caligula, Alexander, and Joan of Arc, to name only a few, functioned as exemplary icons whose names compressed narratives of duty, adventure, empire, perversion, ambition, and religious activity (subversive or patriotic). In other words, these figures' "stories," whether fictional or historically "real," were conveyed by their names alone; and retelling their stories was useful in consolidating authorized and particular versions of "history."[2] With reiteration, such figures became legends: reliable fixtures in the apparatuses of European historiography and mythography. For a legend is a cultural product which depends upon the naturalizing or "forgetting" of its own history as a manufactured thing. Always read as a paradigm for some authoritative reality, the legendary elides the space that originally existed between its own constructedness and that "reality" to which it refers, imposing both its values and its authority as *originary* rather than derivational.[3] (In this way a legend could be regarded as a precapitalist prototype of the commodity fetish, insofar as its value or significance is "misrecognized" as inherent rather than as produced by an accretive and laborious cultural process.)

But even a legendary figure does not necessarily have notorious identity. In order for a figure to have notorious identity, he or she would have to be significantly dis-figured by fame, or, as I will argue, would have to be displaced by a notoriety that subrogates figuration with citation. A notorious name, I wish to suggest, is the object of a cultural desire not for what it signifies but, rather, for *signification itself.* Juliet's question "What's in a name?" could, in this context, be answered with "What's not?" At stake in the problem of notorious identity is the way it positions its designated objects as subjects in relation to the conditions that generate such a desire: conditions in which a particular kind of notoriety emerges both as an effect—and as a symptom—of an emergent capitalism, of textual and theatrical reproduction, and the influences that both are exercising on the changing conditions of identity in early modern England.

Playing on all meanings of "notorious" (noted, annotated, indicted, widely and overly known, obsessively talked and written about), I wish to invoke in the term "notorious identity" not merely well-known historical and/or literary figures, but *infamous* figures. With the emergence of a new kind of "symbolic economy" in early modern England—one starting to organize around pecuniary relations and the concept of the market as a social process—another kind of fame (which is not merely "exemplary") becomes thinkable, one that represents the *symptomology* of its new conditions of production and dissemination. Notorious identity, I shall argue, is the *pathological* form of fame, insofar as pathology means "deviations from the normal that constitute disease or characterize a particular disease."[4] If we regard fame as the "normal" counterpart to notoriety (insofar as it attaches to the persons it represents), "notorious identity" can be considered a peculiarity of fame which causes "dis-ease" by detaching itself from, and thereby rendering immaterial, irrelevant, or redundant, the persons or figures it "originally" designates. To say this is not to fall into an essentialist opposition between "real" persons and "mere" representations. Rather, it is to observe a slippage between famous figures and their famous names—names that, like the money form itself, become commutable because they are no longer attached to designated objects or "things." And yet, in splitting off from the figures they designate, notorious names cannot be entirely dissociated from their significations in earlier modes of the process of symbolization. They drag along, as Jean-Joseph Goux has argued, as a form of neurosis:

> To each mode of production there corresponds not only the "contents" of a dominant ideology but a characteristic mode of neurosis, as effect and reflection of its socioeconomic structure, as the effect of its mode of production and exchange, of its relations of production . . . The progress of civilization, leaving beneath and behind it the signifying modes of production which it outmodes and interdicts, produces a neurotic succession . . . For the idea repressed by neurosis is the ideology of a superseded period, and the neurotic individual becomes the symptom of the era left behind . . .

> Neurosis is the effect of a missing social enactment of a significant social conflict; the subject is obliged to act it out privately, thus deforming what used to be a collective task.[5]

Since a legend is always constructed through a mode of symbolization that is a "collective task," and since it is also always constituted as legend "after the fact," the social enactment of the original significant social conflict is always already superseded. To be "a legend in one's own time" is to be the "neurotic individual" *whose own life* is the "era left behind." In this symptomology, the notorious name—and not what it designates—becomes the thing "itself," and the subject of notorious identity becomes his or her own belated "other": the effect of what notorious identity both produces and represses, a haunting and haunted symptom of his or her own notorious name.

Notorious identity, then, emerges as a function of the commodification of the desire for signification itself. It is what happens when names become the objects of such desire—the property of a cultural marketplace in which they serve as commodities in the political economies of history, legend and the versions of "legitimate" authority they authorize. The notorious subject is constituted by its own simultaneous placement (the identifying name) and displacement (the lost "signified") in the mode of symbolic and material production. The subjects of notorious identity may or may not desire that their names be so minted. But like other forms of currency, names—like coins that bear the images of emperors, queens, and presidents—can be deployed in ways and transported to places not under the control of the figures they represent.

We live in a culture that fetishizes names: "name brands" (Calvin Klein, Gucci, Oscar de la Renta), names associated with brands (Elton John for Diet Coke, Michael Jackson for Pepsi, Ray Charles for Diet Pepsi, Michael Jordan for Nike), brand names that replace the generic names for the things they designate (Kleenex, Band-Aid), names that over time seem to require a reconfiguration of the bodies to which they attach (Cher, Michael Jackson, Madonna). Even within academic culture the existence of the "citation index" signals the extent to which the number of times a name appears—regardless of what is attached to it— provokes desire and secures profitability. We live in a culture in which material interest accrues to names the more they are kept in circulation.

But there is another use of names that leads not directly to material gain (although it tends to get there eventually) but to that ideological form of surplus value known as cultural "legitimacy" or "authority." It is this form of "profit" that can be linked more directly with that being both manufactured and interrogated in Shakespeare's plays and in early modern England. Notorious figures are deployed differently from the "merely" famous in the marketplace of cultural meaning. The difference can be thought of as that between a James Earl Ray and a Willie Horton (or, to locate the distinction within one now "notorious" figure, the pre- and post-Anita-Hill Clarence Thomas). Both Ray and Horton bear names that are famous; but whereas Ray is famous for what he did and to whom he did it (the murder of Dr. Martin Luther King), Willie Horton's notoriety is of a fundamentally different nature. The difference is in what the fame produces, how it is produced, and who benefits from its effects. Willie Horton is "notorious" for the way his name has been circulated in a politics that, finally, has nothing whatsoever to do with him per se or even with his particular crime. His name—completely detachable both from him and his actions—is an instantly recognizable marker or "coin" that contributes to a particular ideological economy—in this instance an antiliberal, anti-Democrat, and "tough on crime" conservative stance. Whereas no one circulated James Earl Ray's name as a deflectionary marker for some "other" agenda (he was himself a racist and not just a manipulable "sign" for the racism of others), Willie Horton is notorious for the *commutability* and appropriability of his name in multiple and competing ideological arenas.

In early modern England, the use of "legendary" figures and materials was inseparable from how England's cultural identity was formed by writers in every mode of literary and historiographic production. Put to the service of a deeply self-conscious cultural mythography, the matter of legend provided a body of usable fictions from which historiographers could cull the associations and values deemed "appropriate" to England's desired identity, whether these materials were produced directly to authorize a particular regime (as in the Tudor development of the Richard III "legend"), or used less directly to foster a more diffuse (yet more pervasive because less obviously polemical) sense of British identity. Few historians regarded this mythography as "fact," just as few regarded Homer's and Virgil's stories as factual history. Whether or not such narratives were "true" was less important to Renaissance writers than what they chose to appropriate and apply to England's "history."

But the project of historiography, like that of the theater and other forms of cultural production, had to adjust its strategies and tropes to the shifting material conditions and social relations of a new market economy. If, as Jean-Christophe Agnew argues, "the new liquidity of mercantile relations, like the growing fluidity of social relations in general, made itself most vividly felt in those literary genres devoted to social description and moral instruction," I would argue that nothing registered the impact of the "new liquidity" more than literary representations of fame, that most socially descriptive and morally instructive of cultural genres.[6] Wresting fame from the realm of moral and exemplary discourse, Shakespeare resituates it squarely within the marketplace of these new relations (however symbolically they may be represented), laying bare the fact that fame *always* operates as a form of symbolic capital in ideological struggles and negotiations—that it secures particular versions of history because of its purchasing power as a form of social "currency." "The Prince with his subjects, the master with his servants, one friend and acquaintance with another, the captain with his soldiers, the husband with his wife, women with and among themselves, and in a word, all the world choppeth and changeth, runneth and raveth, after marts, markets, and merchandizing" (John Wheeler, *A Treatise of Commerce*, 1601).[7]

In early modern England, as Agnew points out, the social antagonisms produced by the subversive as well as productive mechanisms of the market foregrounded a society "groping to envisage a social abstraction—commodity exchange—that was lived rather than thought" (*Worlds Apart*, pp. 8–9). As the notion of the market was shifting from that of place to that of process, of movable, fluid activity, there arose with the transition from a land-based to a money-based economy a pervasive and uneasy sense that all social relations were becoming market relations (and not just those which had long explicitly been so, such as the property exchange effected through kinship and marriage; and not just those necessarily recognized as such under the notion of financial "gain"). The conjuncture of material and symbolic exchange became less cordoned off socially because less cordoned off spatially, less immediately visible on the surface of social interactions, yet more deeply imbricated in ways of *feeling* about one's interactions with others. Attempting both to figure and to figure out "a problematic of exchange," Britons, Agnew tells us, "were putting forward a coherent and repeated pattern of problems or questions about the nature of social identity, intentionality, accountability, transparency, and reciprocity in commodity transactions—the who, what, when, where, and why of exchange" (*Worlds Apart*, p. 9). Agnew's detailed analysis of the pervasive effects of the market as social abstraction as well as financial structure provides a useful material basis for understanding much of the anxiety (also persuasively elaborated in other terms by Norbert Elias, William Bouwsma, and Walter Cohen, among others) in the texts of early modern England. Observing that efforts to understand the nature of these social anxieties were complicated by the fact that "these confusions included serious questions about the character and authority of the 'self' on whose behalf [they] were to be expressed," Agnew makes the crucial point that such efforts were "structured around problems of *representation*" (*Worlds Apart*, p. 10, italics added). In his view, such representations—and especially those "literary" genres that gave voice to the anxieties—figured the extent to which "individuals [were coming] to see themselves in the likeness of commodities" (*Worlds Apart*, p. 12).

This last formulation, as insightful as it is, can more fruitfully be applied to this study if we rearrange its order. Since Shakespeare's notorious figures already function as those cultural commodities known as legends, it would be more accurate to say that, in the three plays I consider here, Shakespeare represents not individuals who come to see themselves as commodities but rather *commodities that come to see themselves as individuals*. Failing in various ways and to different degrees to recognize the extent to which they are signed into the indentured servitude of a representational marketplace, Shakespeare's notorious figures are simultaneously overdetermined and represented as experiencing their textual existence as a *first-time occurrence*—one in which contingency is fantasized by the subject even as it is prohibited by the social. Inhabiting dramatic texts that are linguistically saturated with their prior textual histories, these figures nevertheless act out a sense that there may still be something undisclosed about themselves, something that will not "merely" be reproduced, something that exceeds the containment of their own citationality.

With uncanny prescience, the plays figure both the longing for and the consequences of such a "mistake." As Bruce Robbins has evocatively pointed out, "There is to every text that reproduces a legendary figure a Lacanian unconscious—both to text and to figure, if by that term we understand Lacan's view of the unconscious as 'sedimented linguistic history.'"[8] Shakespeare's peculiar construction of notorious identity, as both paradigmatic condition and effect of legendary reproduction, inevitably builds into its represented figures these sedimented traces of the figures' own *intertextual* "linguistic history." Each had notorious existence in earlier texts. Each carries into the plays this history, a knowledge of which is shared by the audience. These three plays, more than any others in the Shakespearean corpus, foreground the extent to which their notorious figures must negotiate, like a ghostly obstacle course, relationships to their own belatedness; and each play reconstitutes (in senses both iterational and mutational) its notorious figures by making this negotiation the very *material* of subjectivity "itself." Moving through textual terrains that relentlessly confront them with what is always already "known" or disclosed about them, these figures *symptomatically* enact the desire to be, in Coriolanus' words, "authors of themselves."

Before proceeding any further, I should clarify how I am using the terms "identity" and "subjectivity." "Identity," as the OED tells us, is from *idem:* to make identical, to treat, consider, or regard something or someone as "the same." To identify is to determine to be the same with something that is already known, to establish what a given thing, or who a given person, *is.* Thus, to "identify" someone is to attempt to secure meaning, to erase multiplicity and eliminate indeterminacy—to "fix" that person, so to speak. But there is a paradox built into the term, since it is also always citational, insofar as it depends upon comparison: to render something "the same as" something else. I wish to evoke the paradoxical and contradictory nature of a concept that etymologically collapses two into one—that takes two terms of a comparison and makes them *the same thing.* When I refer to the notorious identities of the figures in these plays, I shall mean the way they are "fixed" by their legends: the way they are determined—by a prior textual history, by the audience, reader, other figures within the plays, and finally even by Shakespeare—to be "the same as" their legends make them. Their "identities," then, will connote the extent to which they are historically encoded and entrapped by their famous names.

Apart from (but in crucial relation to) this, I will use the term "subjectivity" partly in Althusser's sense of being "subjected" to determining ideologies, but without the absolute fixity this sense implies.[9] In other words, while "subjectivity" does mean being subjected to determining forces, it also implies the experience of negotiating a relationship to these forces. "Subjectivity," as I will use it, means the subject's *experience* of his or her relationship to his or her "identity." Hence, a necessary space is opened up between "identity" (which is the artificially constructed "thingness" of self as it has been constituted in the past) and "subjectivity" (which is the relationship to that "thingness" as it is experienced in the present). In this space the possibility of indeterminacy, of dis-identification, as well as a fantasy of autonomous choice in thought, action, or emotion, becomes thinkable. It means resisting being signed into permanent inscription—resisting being "legends."

It has been argued that "drama is not the literary mode best suited to embody subjectivity."[10] In terms of my definition of notorious identity and the subjects it produces, I will argue exactly the opposite: that in the Renaissance, drama is the dominant mode in which the provisional, performative, and contingent nature of subjectivity can literally be embodied. Alterity to textual identity is an inevitable condition of dramatic representation. The figures in these plays may be permanently "identified," insofar as their names encode their legends. But as dramatic figures, they exist as versions of themselves. Drama, as written script that is repeatedly performable, embodies a principle of multiplicity, since it takes figures from narrative genres and "translates" them into dramatic figures, who are multiplied again by the actors who perform them, and yet again by subsequent performances with different actors. Consequently, Shakespeare's notorious characters are both finished and unfinished, absolute in what they "mean" yet multiplicitous in how that meaning is reproduced. It is precisely the destabilizing aspects of drama and the theater that enable Shakespeare to explore the relationship between "identity" as that which fixes meaning (both personal and political) and "subjectivity"—the unstable heterogeneity that simultaneously constitutes and unfixes even the most fixed of names.

My central argument is that identity in these plays is aligned with the representational politics of narrative historiography and its policing role in the official technologies that consolidate "legitimate" authority. Identity is that which carves "characters" in stone, forcing them to correspond to earlier textual versions of themselves. Against this fixity, these figures express and enact a desire to be their own "originals": a fantasy that uses "playing" and theater as a way to stage a subjectivity in which something "secret" about an overly known "self" might still materialize. This embattled dynamic (which sets the mimetic possibilities of theater against the reinscriptive force of legendary narrative) generates a set of conditions in which subjectivity appears as a diacritical effect of its own relationship to identity. In these plays, subjectivity is represented *only* in those moments that threaten to destabilize—or even to shatter—identity. Shakespeare's notorious subjects, then, materialize as their own "alter egos"—always as "other" to the ideological forces that constrain and determine meaning in the machinery of textual, theatrical, and cultural reproduction.

Throughout this project I will play with the term "materialize," drawing upon all meanings of "materiality," from the sense of "matter" as "building material, timber, hence stuff of which a thing is made" (OED), to the more abstract sense of the subject of discourse or consideration (OED). The paradoxical nature of these multiple definitions evokes the problem of notorious identity, insofar as "matter" is used to signify concrete, unimpeachable substance, as well as the matter of discourse, that materially based but ultimately symbolic figuration produced by linguistic process. The fusion (and confusion) of these applications gives us a term that has its own deconstruction built into its definition, an epistemological term that at once aims at securing the determinate (the proverbial "last instance"), yet is also necessarily a function of language, which is indeterminate and subject to conflicting interpretations. The "matter" of any "thing itself" is, strictly speaking, *questionable*. In the Aristotelian and scholastic sense, matter is "that component of the essence of any thing or being which has a bare existence, but which requires the addition of a particular 'form' to constitute the thing or being as determinately existent" (OED). To materialize the notorious subject, then, is to take that "essence" or "bare existence"—in this case, a citation—and give it the "addition of a particular 'form' that will constitute it as "determinately existent."

I would add for the purposes of this project a more modern definition as well. To materialize is to render something that is absent present in a specifically visual way. Of course, as legends, Shakespeare's notorious figures already possess the "particular form" of the name. But as dramatic figures, they must be given another kind of particular "substance." To posit a "material subject" that oscillates between these definitions of "matter" is to raise the hoary specter of essentialism. But it is to raise it as *the plays themselves* raise it: as a function of the protagonists' fantasies of selves that might exist apart from the mandates of cultural notoriety. These plays explore the relationship, and the fundamental antagonism, between notions of "essential" selfhood and "originary" texts, revealing both to be diacritically *constitutive* fantasies—structures that are at once necessary and epistemologically insupportable.

What gives these plays their extraordinary power (despite their reiterative material) is the way the playwright builds his own representational difficulties with these overdetermined stories and figures into the plays themselves. Rather than trying to make these figures "new" to an audience that "knows" them only too well, Shakespeare's strategy is to portray their desire, and inability, to be new *even to themselves:* to represent their efforts to produce subjective self-representations that can in fact be realized only at the *expense* of their notorious identities. The "frenzy of renown" is already, in Shakespeare, becoming something substantially different: the frenzy of the name, or fame and its symptoms.[11] Like streakers across the stage of their own legends, Shakespeare's notorious figures transgress their own textual identities by disrupting smooth reiteration, making simple "reproduction" impossible. Notorious identity in Shakespeare is absolute identity at once secured and disrupted by the very subject it engenders. Belated arrivals on the scenes of their own legends, Shakespeare's notorious subjects exceed the reputations that always already precede them.

Chapter 1 ("Belaboring the Obvious: Reading the Monstrous Body in *Richard III*") considers the way Shakespeare resurrects the "deformed" last Plantagenet, whose overthrow ushered in the Tudor reign and upon whose putative physical and moral monstrousness rested the justification of the new dynasty. At once reiterating Tudor myth and revealing its dependency on the manufacturing of a monstrous body to meet the requirements of an ideologically overdetermined history, the play makes us undergo the experience of *being* Richard III, of being "singled out" as the "individual" exception that proves the social rule. Literally made to embody the imprimatur of his own legend, Shakespeare's Richard attempts the doubly impossible: to be an exception to the exception that he already is—to be a monster of his own making. Seeking the crown as a way to subrogate one set of symbolically overdetermined structures (the significance of physical stigmata and its deployment within the Tudor myth) with another (the "King's Body," with its social centrality and exemptions from physical and temporal flaws), Richard attempts to inscribe himself anew within the process of social symbolization, a process, the play reveals, that requires the production of monstrous waste in order to secure sacred authority. An example of what Lacan calls the "extimate," Richard is the lynchpin, the nodal point, of the first tetralogy, that *thing* that has to be both inside and outside—central and marginal—in order for an antagonistic social formation to secure "consent" and close ranks around its incorporative exclusion.

If *Richard III* embodies notorious identity in the deformed "person" of Richard, *Troilus and Cressida* embodies the monstrous in the form of the play itself. In Chapter 2 ("'So Unsecret to Ourselves': Notorious Identity and the Material Subject in *Troilus and Cressida*") I examine the way the famous figures who inhabit this play act out, through the staging of perverse misrecognitions, a rebellion against a coercion and oppression of subjectivity that cannot be openly confronted or directly challenged because of the massive cultural authority of the story of Troy and its "epic" protagonists. This rebellion takes the form of what I call "neurotic nostalgia"—a nostalgia which rewrites originary absence as if it were loss, and leads to a kind of neurotic symptomology (not only enacted by the figures but embodied in the formal structure of the play as well) in which the characters are forced to be and not be "themselves."

The various divisions in the play (the "this is and is not" paradigm) symptomatize the figures' simultaneous resistance to and realization of their infamous roles. Deeply exhausted and disillusioned by their own story even as the play begins, these figures must be tricked into continuing to fight, tricked into reproducing their notorious identities. Through the production of myths of "private" desire, "motivations" are fabricated for other kinds of social, political, and textual operations. The play actively thematizes how desire (both public and "private") is not only appropriated by social production but becomes its dominant form, motivating "legendary" behavior in figures who might otherwise want nothing so much as to roll over and play dead.

If notorious identity in *Richard III* involves a claustrophobic fusion of bodies and texts, and if *Troilus and Cressida* exhibits the schizophrenic disjunction of their confusion, the playwright offers another possibility in *Antony and Cleopatra*. Of all the legendary figures Shakespeare treated, Antony and Cleopatra achieve the highest degree of alterity to their prescribed roles. Chapter 3 ("Spies and Whispers: Exceeding Reputation in *Antony and Cleopatra*") addresses the relationship between visual and discursive modes of representation and the different structures of subjectivity produced by each. Although Egypt is established as an alternative site to the center of Roman historiography, the play is crosshatched with messengers and "reporters" who continually translate Antony's and Cleopatra's theatrical existence into material for the Roman discursus. If any Shakespeare play explores the relationship between staging spectacle and "controlling the press," this is it. *Antony and Cleopatra* choreographs the representational technology of manufacturing legends, even as the two "legendary lovers" work to avoid the conscripting effects of the legendary machine. The play deconstructs, even as it stages, the possibility of a "private" subject of greatness that is not destined for public consumption as legend. Simultaneously, it reveals that no matter how much Antony and Cleopatra may seem to want to dodge the coercions of notoriety, it is their own investment in themselves as legends that both subsidizes their fantasies of individual autonomy and makes them answerable to the spies and whispers of others.

Antony and Cleopatra reveals that no matter how "positivist" legendary narratives may be, their effects are finally determined by what happens at the site of consumption, effects which can be neither predicted nor contained by "authoritative" texts. The play demonstrates how different representational apparatuses produce subjects—discursive or histrionic—whose capacity to appropriate social structures for their own use depends upon their ability to evade absolute "identity." It also reveals that in the struggle and symbiosis between theater and hegemonic cultural texts, there are no such things as definitively enclosing acts.

Before turning to Shakespeare's plays, I should say something about my theoretical orientation, methodology, and aims. This book is in no way a "source study": I shall not be concerned to compare Shakespeare's treatment of his legendary figures with the earlier versions of More, Holinshed, Caxton, Chaucer, Pliny, Plutarch, and others. That ground has been well and thoroughly covered. Rather, I will be looking at how the politics of standing in a belated relation to one's own cultural priority is negotiated, thematized, foregrounded, suppressed, and otherwise represented—directly and indirectly, advertently and inadvertently—within the plays themselves.

Throughout this study I work across theoretical fields, using the insights of Louis Althusser, Jacques Lacan, Jacques Derrida, Pierre Bourdieu, Georges Bataille, Michel de Certeau, Jean Baudrillard, Roland Barthes, Jean-Joseph Goux, Eve Sedgwick, Gayle Rubin, Gilles Deleuze and Félix Guattari, and Slavoj Žižek—to name only those whose work is most influential here. I have found that each provides powerful tools for analyzing the relationship between subjectivity and the social.[12] There are, of course, contradictions within and among the histories of these discourses: most notably those of Marxism, feminism, and psychoanalysis. Over the last decade there have been many fine studies about the respective and internal contradictions, histories, purposes, mutual contributions, ideological politics, conflicts, strengths, and shortcomings of each methodology. It is neither my goal nor my desire to rehearse the positions outlined in these studies or to attempt to reconcile the fissures and incommensurabilities—some real and some imagined—between them.

Rather, throughout this project I will tease out the complementary and mutually constitutive insights shared among feminism(s), materialism, historicism, psychoanalysis, social and political theory, cultural anthropology, and deconstruction. And while such an approach may at first glance seem "merely" eclectic, my choice of materials is guided throughout by a conviction that a sum of certain aspects of these approaches lends greater insight than any of their constituent parts. I do not believe that synthesizing is fully achievable or even desirable. For this reason, I will resist the apotropaic impulse to declare my allegiance to a particular critical or theoretical camp and hope that the extent to which my approach is successful—by which I mean persuasive and evocative rather than prescriptively reiterable—will be achieved by interpretive accretion rather than by programmatic formula. Like Žižek, whose style I admire, and like Polonius, whose style I do not, I think that with the peculiar, the uncanny, the pathological, one only by indirection finds direction out.

Having said this, however, I recognize that a little apotropaism sometimes goes a long way; and it may be helpful to state the particular paradigms central to my investigation of notorious identity, along with a few of my theoretical "first principles." I take it as axiomatic that identity is socially constituted; that subjectivity is indefeasible from the representational structures and politics of social identity; that social structures structure "psychological" structures; and that subjective structures also reconstitute and inflect social structures. I am persuaded that the unconscious is structured like a language and, like language, its forms and representations of desire depend upon its relation—subversive, conformist, or both simultaneously—with modes of material and cultural production; that there is an unconscious to texts and to social formations as well as to persons; and that "pathology" in individual subjects is always organized around (and even authorized by) misrecognition, displacement, and denial in the social.

I qualify these axioms, however, with a belief that persons are not merely the "effects" of social formations; that although in Western culture gender is a socially constructed patriarchal category which mandates "acceptable" forms of desire, it does not always predict, control, or even anticipate the range of forms desire might take; that although ideological structures necessarily inflect the unconscious by determining the representational *particularities* of repression, hysteria, displacement, misrecognition, and desire, they are not fully capable of managing or recognizing all their representational forms and operations; that the subject/object distinction, with its construction of "unique individuals," is a culturally productive fabrication of Western metaphysics and that subjects are continuous with the social in literally indiscernible ways; but that while they are indefeasible, subjects are *not identical to* the social—where "interpellations" fail, where identities dis-integrate, where desires do not conform to social production, this is where the "real" can be said to erupt. I take as axiomatic the importance of historical specificity in being able to speculate on the range and limitations of the "thinkable"; but I take as axiomatic that whatever its specific historical forms, an unconscious is always detectable in every representation and is always relevant to any effort to understand both the designs of history and the designs of persons.

Too many scholars of Renaissance culture read, in the important injunction to "always historicize," an injunction to *only* historicize; and while historicity is important because it enhances the legibility of the grammar of any given set of representations, we must also recognize that it is impossible not to *fantasize* our relation to what we reconstruct as the past. Historicism, as its best practitioners understand, is never unmediated by ideology; but it might be well to add that it is also, therefore, never unmediated by subjectivity—and subjectivity is never "identical" to ideology. Historicism—"new" or otherwise—offers responsive and responsible speculations only if it remembers that its own practices are neither epistemologically "authoritative" nor reiterably secure.

This project, then, will take as equally important and mutually constitutive the ideological, the material, the psychological, and the historical. As I have said above, anyone familiar with these approaches will readily see that there are contradictions between them. What they share, however, is a powerful awareness of the diacritical relationship between subjects and the social. Each methodology can be usefully qualified in ways that conform to a growing conviction (with useful political applications) in postmodern critical theory that desire is about flows and relations rather than "inherent" drives, irreplaceable objects, and biological organs. Which brings me to some final words about my methodology vis-à-vis the post-Marxist, post-psychoanalytic radicalism of Gilles Deleuze and Félix Guattari.

In their critique of subjectivism in *Anti-Oedipus* and *A Thousand Plateaus,* Deleuze and Guattari argue for the radical exteriority of social relations and of desire.[13] The unconscious is an exterior form—a site produced by the social—in which desire operates through flows and not through "organs," and maps relationships between pulsive sites and not body parts. In describing the way we can "unhook ourselves from the points of subjectification that secure us, nail us down to a dominant reality," they posit the cultivation of a "body without organs" (BwO) and argue for a creative desire that can be produced only by "dismantling the organism." Such "self-destruction," however, has "nothing to do with the death drive." Rather, it means "opening the body to connections that presuppose an entire assemblage, circuits, conjunctions, levels and thresholds, passages and distributions of intensity, and territories and deterritorializations measured with the craft of a surveyor" (*A Thousand Plateaus*, p. 160). This is not to be confused with anarchism, for it is actually a subtle and skillful process of "looking for the point at which [one] could patiently and momentarily dismantle the organization of the organs we call the organism" (p. 162). It can, as they warn, be "botched" if one doesn't exercise the art of caution:

> You have to keep enough of the organism for it to reform each dawn; and you have to keep small supplies of significance and subjectification, if only to turn them against their own systems when the circumstances demand it . . . Mimic the strata. You don't reach the BwO, and its plane of consistency, by wildly destratifying . . . This is how it should be done: Lodge yourself on a stratum, experiment with the opportunities it offers, find an advantageous place on it, find potential movements of deterritorialization, possible lines of flight, experience them, produce flow conjunctions here and there, try out continuums of intensities segment by segment, have a small plot of new land at all times. It is through a meticulous relation with the strata that one succeeds in freeing lines of flight, causing conjugated flows to pass and escape and bringing forth continuous intensities for a BwO . . . You have constructed your own little machine, ready when needed to be plugged into other collective machines. (pp. 160–161)

It is just such a process that I have attempted to perform with the conjunction of theoretical materials in this project: at once to lodge myself on the organized strata of particular theories and to experiment with the opportunities they afford, the flows that are contingent upon whatever can be made to materialize, advantageously, in specific moments. This is not the same as "synthesizing," nor is it devoid of organizing principles. To deterritorialize is not necessarily to deconstruct. It is to form contingent organisms and to look for small plots of new land upon which to set them in motion. There is a logic between theoretical fields which, like the BwO, have their own flows as well as stratic "organs." To theoretically "deterritorialize," then, is neither to "syncretize" nor to make decathected conciliatory gestures toward *discordia concors*. Rather, it is to recognize the way theoretical fields continually reterritorialize their relations to each other only by being deterritorialized. Consistencies can be established without the intellectual policing of methodological self-sameness—and they can form new strata that enable "intensities" to "flow" across the "organs" of dominant theoretical codes.

Therefore, throughout this project I assay a Theory without Organs, and attempt to construct significant intensities rather than intensive signifiers: to poach strategically, with caution as well as craft, on the possibilities and opportunities offered by multiple systems without reifying the stratic structures that block and hypostatize new meanings based on movement. I believe that this is precisely the negotiation Shakespeare's plays themselves both problematize and perform as they stage—in dramatic form—figures at once overdetermined by, and "other" to, their intertextual histories. In each chapter I "re-organize" my theoretical materials around the particular manifestations of notorious identity represented in each play. To impose an identical formulation on each play would be to subject them to the same kind of identificatory violence that their legends impose on their protagonists. It would be to enact as critical practice the very identity politics the plays interrogate.

This book is concerned with what materializes at the ruptures or fissures between identity and heterogeneity in Shakespeare's legend plays, in early modern England, and by speculative extension in postmodern Western culture. I look at how Shakespeare represents the forms of cultural neurosis and subjective displacement produced by the master trope of Identity: the way that the notorious subject is produced as that which *will not, yet must* be made to conform to "the program." I wish to stress that this is not to reiterate the theoretically stalled trope of "subversion yet containment." The Foucauldian paradigm of power, no matter how it is formulated, fails to believe in the power of resistance in its particular readings of cultural texts because it can only detect the ways in which neurosis is produced and coopted by the structures and functions of power "itself."[14] I suggest that the Foucauldian model fails to uncover such evidence because it does not believe in the transformative signifying power of symptoms—either in the social or in the subject.

All forms of cultural and psychological resistance, however, are not created equal. Unlike neurosis, which does frequently lend itself in productive ways to the operations that necessitate it, hysteria offers another possibility. I agree with Avital Ronell that hysteria can be an "inherently revolutionary power: it intervenes, breaks up continuities, produces gaps . . . refusing conformity with *what is*."[15] Hysteria is what the system produces and then excludes, what breaks off to wander, in multiple forms, through the organism—whether individual, social, historical, or theoretical—whose "integrity" of identity depends on its suppression. The symptom may be continually displaced, but it cannot be kept from talking back. Since the deepest aim of this project is to critique the way a culture, through iterational strategies, produces notorious identity for a traffic in names as commodities, I do not wish to produce a critical methodology that will behave like a good fractal, picking up and laying back down its own tracks as it goes along, or that will provide easy structures for its own iterability. However, since I do wish, through my "meticulous relation with the strata," to construct my own "little machine" that can, when advantageous, be "plugged in" with other collective machines, I invoke what is productive and *constructive*—rather than merely disruptive, merely abreactive—about hysteria. Abreaction can never be productively revolutionary because more often than not it leads to reinforcing the very constraints that necessitated it in the first place. Therefore, by constructive "hysteria," I will mean something that disrupts whatever system is repressing it, as well as producing it, not through the sheer force of attack, rejection, or expulsion but by wandering between systems, between encodings, at once trespassing upon, inhabiting, and mutating established and policed tropes of systematicity.[16] Insofar as I am reorganizing insights that appear along the lines of demarcation, the territorial overlap, and the mutual displacements among cultural materialism, new historicism, feminist psychoanalysis, deconstruction, and social and political theory, my approach can be labeled, should anyone wish to do so, New Hystericist.

This is, of course, only partly tongue-in-cheek. For a new hystericism would in fact aim to exploit the subjective inconsistencies within any "identified" critical methodology. Against the prescriptive and proscriptive imperatives of narrative versions of *historia*—"new" or otherwise—one could profitably pose the destabilizing imperatives of *hysteria*. Implicitly challenging the misogynist history built into a term which conflates unstable, "illegitimate," untrustworthy, "irrational," and "inappropriate" forms of response with female voices and bodies, such an approach would reclaim and reevaluate those modes of enunciation that resist, disrupt, or intervene in dominant modes of organizing "knowledge," both social and subjective. With the emphasis on the "new," I can envision a disciplined redeployment of a hystericism that would operate not as negative critical reaction but as affirmative critical practice: not just as a force that breaks down conformities but as one that reconvenes them, bringing into contingent arrangements structures that have theoretically segregated themselves from "other," "unidentical" structures. A new hystericist practice would not only perform readings of cultural texts with an eye toward its own situatedness within *symptomatic* critical narratives, but would by definition challenge the imaginary forms of "mastery" critical methodologies fantasize for themselves. It would, appropriately, o'erflow the measure.

In this way I hope that my "methodology" will replicate what Shakespeare is doing in his legend plays, which produce their new figures precisely by materializing, as theatrical practice, the symptoms of what's repressed in the reproduction of the known.

1

Belaboring the Obvious
Reading the Monstrous Body in *King Richard III*

Many questions were troubling the explorer, but at the sight of the prisoner he asked only: "Does he know his sentence?" "No," said the officer, eager to go on with his exposition, but the explorer interrupted him: "He doesn't know the sentence that has been passed on him?" "No," said the officer again, pausing as if to let the explorer elaborate his question, and then said: "There would be no point in telling him. He'll learn it on his body."
Franz Kafka, "In the Penal Colony," trans. Willa Muir and Edwin Muir

We live at a moment when the name "Freaks" is being rejected by the kinds of physiologically deviant humans to whom it has traditionally been applied: Giants, Dwarfs, Siamese Twins, Hermaphrodites, Fat Ladies, and Living Skeletons. To them it seems a badge of shame, a reminder of their long exclusion and exploitation by other humans, who defining them thus have by the same token defined themselves as "normal." Like all demands on the part of the stigmatized for a change of name, this development expresses itself as a kind of politics.
Leslie Fiedler, *Freaks*

If the explorer in Kafka's story had elaborated his question, he might have asked about the purpose of an apparatus that inscribes on the subject's back, without enunciating to his face, his *sentence*, the executive failure of which in this story constitutes the crime. "Honor thy superiors" is the mandate which conflates sentencing with punishment: the subject "learns" his sentence as it is written on his body.[1] Around the sixth hour "enlightenment" comes, as he realizes the inevitability of the terms of his sentence and finally submits to the absolute subjection the Harrow demands. What makes this punishment so fitting is the way it literalizes the subordination of the prisoner's body to the inscriptive condemnation of his "superiors": the way it demonstrates their right to write on the "wrong" and therefore to right them by rewriting them, making their persons fit their sentences. In this collapse of distance between subject and sentence, we can see how powerful ideologies and their technologies of discursive reproduction organize subjectivity in terms of what bodies can be made to mean.

Although the term "Freaks" has been rejected by those persons who do not want to render "normalcy" to others by virtue of their own strangeness, the "demands of the stigmatized for a change of name" are not a particularly recent phenomenon.[2] The naming of deviants has always simultaneously been a process of giving them a local habitation. But this local habitation has also been a peripheral habitation, a space in which they can be at once safely contained and available for use by a culture that measures its own normative acceptability in terms of what it excludes. Physical difference and "deformity" have long been used to establish and reinforce dominant political and cultural standards, as Erving Goffman has pointed out:

> The Greeks, who were apparently strong on visual aids, originated the term *stigma* to refer to bodily signs designed to expose something unusual and bad about the moral status of the signifier. The signs were cut or burnt into the body and advertised that the bearer was a slave, a criminal, or a traitor—a blemished person, ritually polluted, to be avoided, especially in public places. Later, in Christian times, two layers of metaphor were added to the term: the first referred to bodily signs of holy grace that took the form of eruptive blossoms on the skin; the second, a medical allusion to this religious allusion, referred to bodily signs of physical disorder. Today the term is widely used in something like the original literal sense, but is applied more to the disgrace itself than to the bodily evidence of it . . . The term *stigma,* then, will be used to refer to an attribute that is deeply discrediting, but it should be seen that a language of relationships, not attributes, is really needed.[3]

Fiedler and Goffman raise two points crucial to any consideration of Shakespeare's *Richard III:* the political nature of the language of deformity and conformity in the process of naming; and the fact that the signifier is simultaneously dependent on and independent of the relationship between bodies and texts.

Nature as Symptom

In Renaissance texts the term "monstrous" is applied to anything that is regarded or asserted as "unnatural" in virtually all discursive categories. Deriving from the Latin *monére* (to warn or admonish) and *monstrare* (to show or demonstrate), the term was deployed both as descriptive and as polemical device. Significantly, its etymology produces an essentializing conflation of nature and politics; and asserts as obvious or *self-evident* the warning that questionable objects or occurrences are taken to be.

But in early modern England physical deformity was not conceptualized solely in terms of the body. Rather, the "tricks of Nature" that beset the human frame were articulated as part of a broader set of relationships between and among different kinds of "phenomena," physical and metaphysical. The body was one signifier in an elaborate network of signification in which God's "signature" could be read in the physical world, and strange occurrences—earthquakes, floods, volcanoes, comets, and "monstrous" animal and human births—were frequently regarded as immanent warnings of divine judgment and political disaster.

This view however, as many scholars and historians have noted, was far from static; and by the sixteenth century the writings of Copernicus, Nicholas of Cusa, Giordano Bruno, Galileo, Kepler, and, in England, of Bacon, Harvey, Burton, and Dee, were starting (however indirectly) to alter an earlier, more unilaterally theological view of the universe, a view that was still largely operative in Elizabethan England. These theories further destabilized ideologies of hierarchical "arrangement" in ways that produced anxiety and debate about the epistemological and authoritative bases of discourses of order, "natural" hierarchy, and "degree," as well as the nature—boundaries, possibilities, limitations—of nature itself.[4] In many texts, from sonnets and masques to prose narratives and plays, from ballad books and conduct manuals to scientific and political treatises, the terms "nature" and "natural" appear repeatedly in vexed contexts, demonstrating a growing lack of consensus and confidence regarding the physical world and how to read its signs.[5]

The early modern belief in monsters and marvels arose at least in part as a "natural" extension of theological belief (although not without much disagreement, as evidenced by the escalating debates over the existence and operations of "witches"), from the "knowledge" that there were supernatural forces at work in the world. And yet, even this sense was unstable; and the exact forms and range of the supernatural were

never precisely defined. Discussions tended to record "symptomology"—manifestations of phenomena that were forever mutating in
their forms. Extravagant speculations and varied "theories" appear in
numerous tracts cataloging bizarre omens and eyewitness encounters
with all manner of demons. As for how to regard such "beliefs," one
could argue that in so aggressive a universe the study of these things
was not merely the province of the crazed fanatic, but rather the necessary task of vigilant men living in a world infested with spirits. But at
the level of social symptomology, this literature signals an epistemological crisis around the very notion of *categories*. The endless cataloging of
the scholastics (which, as William Bouwsma has argued, probably
channeled all kinds of obsessive anxiety) can be regarded at least in part
as a buttress against a growing sense of nature as morphological peri-
phrasis: a phenomenology in which things "express" their significance
in continually shifting, indirect, and potentially treacherous ways.[6]

Like all forms of anxiety management, vigilance requires *creating*
symptoms that can then be brought under control. In the demonizing of
women in witchcraft persecutions, we see how patriarchal anxiety un-
dergirds religious, sexual, and political concerns about "unruly" or
"perverse" women and their bodies, as again and again women become
the designated symptoms of social, political, and theological anxieties
that required a discernible (and ultimately controllable) local habitation. If reading omens and portents in comets, floods, and "late eclipses
of the sun and moon" meant becoming a "sectary astronomical," reading texts in the bodies of women and men required less specialized
skills. The human body, like the "bodies" of the state, Nature, and the
universe, wore signal marks of moral predisposition. Since bodies *could*
signify, it followed that if they can be construed as deviant they *must*
signify. Not only were women's bodies most easily and readily available as "other," but they are morphologically "deviant" from men's
bodies and consequently could be constructed as preinclined to demonic perversity.

Although witch persecutions undoubtedly had more to do with the
patriarchal politics of displacing onto, and terrorizing and dominating,
women than with keeping communities "free" from satanic influence,
women were not the only ones whose bodies were appropriated for textual signification. God's warnings could also be read in the deformities
of a town cripple, dwarf, leper, or hunchback. In the late fifteenth and
early sixteenth centuries, such conditions were almost always regarded
as *stigmata*, or the scourge of God. As the French surgeon Ambroise

Paré claimed, "It is certain that most often these monstrous and marvelous creatures proceed from the judgement of God, who permits fathers and mothers to produce such abominations from the disorder that they make in copulation, like brutish beasts, in which their appetite guides them, without respecting the time, or other laws ordained by God and Nature."[7] There were, however, other strains of thought woven into the discourses of deformity. Among peasants and villagers, as well as in much popular literature, the body may still have been a tablet for the inscription of God's judgment, and the deformed were still to be avoided (especially, as Goffman says, "in public places") as objects of God's wrath or the ritual pollution of witchcraft. But the increasingly "scientific" and secularized attempt to understand the formations of the body produced treatises in which surgeons and natural philosophers (one thinks here of Montaigne as well as Bacon) saw monsters more as "natural wonders—signs of nature's *copia* rather than of God's wrath."[8] It also became possible to think monsters as entertainments; and, in an emergent capitalist economy, to imagine displaying them for profit (witness Stefano and Trinculo's fantasy, in *The Tempest*, of showing Caliban for silver).

Perhaps more important even than the theological or quasi-scientific view of deformity as a moral semiology that "reveals a person's 'inner depths'" was a growing attention to the "hygienic" importance of "rectitude" or posture: the appropriately "straightened" body of the nobility and the socially aspiring. Extraordinary attention was paid to precisely formulating and implementing the "proper" lines of male and female bodies, and—for men especially—the performance of courtly activities such as dancing, swordplay, display riding. The disposition of body members was laid out according to elaborate, even mathematical, grids and trajectories. Enforcement occurred in infancy and youth through swaddling, binding, and corsets; and in adulthood the *trompe l'oeil* effects of clothing remapped the visual surfaces of the body. What Georges Vigarello has characterized as "the new insistence on a 'well proportioned' posture" concentrated largely on how the body could be shown or displayed in the social sphere:

> The distinctly Platonic reference occasions a translation of the stiffening rules concerning physical uprightness. Not only does "bad" posture pose a permanent threat to physical appearance, but the "good" one, because of the symbolism of the relations here at play, requires strengthening. The sixteenth century's enthusiastic belief

in proportion is the justification for new requirements concerning physical bearing. The body's microcosm must evoke, by the subtleties and wealth of measures and relationships among its parts, those of the world at large . . . Sartorial culture changed in one way by granting privilege to rigidity and rectitude, as well as to geometric shape . . . Deportment has become more rigorous. To the social process is added a passionate discussion of the principles which revealed measures and proportions, even though they might be very theoretical and, in fact, more verbal than verifiable.[9]

This "passionate discussion," "more verbal than verifiable," mystified even as it elaborated strategies for achieving "rectitude." But the important point to make is that the religious fear provoked by those who didn't "measure up" seems, by the late sixteenth century, to have been less pervasive than the class fears such codes of uprightness were meant both to produce and to alleviate.

If in theological semiology the blatantly "deformed" were portentous of political disaster, in court semiology even normal bodies that would not hitherto have been considered "deformed" had to be rendered, at least in how they were regarded, "bent" or curved so as to permit the nobility to reproduce its "distinctiveness" through ever more strenuous models of physical "straightness." The "hunchback" was a figure to whom was attached a special stigma, one that was socially useful because of its obviousness as the antithesis of noble physical bearing. A curved back was the sign that one's trajectory—moral, religious, and, perhaps more crucially, social—was "meant" to be downwardly mobile. In England, the religious anxieties of the Reformation were, by the late sixteenth century, equaled by the class anxieties inflicted by a "monstrous" blurring of "proper" boundaries and distinctions between competitive mercantile and aristocratic classes and how they represented themselves in social space.

Thorough studies of the social and political history of teratogenesis in early modern England and Europe have been conducted by others; but I invoke it in broad strokes here as a way of introducing a particular kind of relationship between subjects and signifying practices, one that will be central to this chapter. In and through this relationship, narratives of descriptive signification—what I will call the *tropics of evidence*—reproduce in other forms the pathology that prompts their operations and that they seek to describe. It is clear that the emergent ideology of empirical observation is undermined by the renewed attention of Renaissance "scientists" to alchemy and astrology; and by the frequent mendacity of many "scientific" accounts. Paré's journals, for example, are full of "observations" and illustrations that could only have been fictitious. "A Monster, half man, half swine" (p. 70), "Marine monster having the head of a Monk" (p. 109), and "Figure of a monster with the face of a man and the body of a goat" (p. 69) are just a few of the many bizarre entries one finds. The rational tone of the text contrasts sharply with the images, which are at once outlandish and polemical—a fish with the "head of a Monk," for example. In reading the head of this strange creature, what Paré "sees" cannot materialize outside the political and theological culture in which he sees. Such an "authoritative" text substitutes its own kind of monstrousness—in the sense of both showing and admonishing—for the "popular" lore it presumably aims to supplant by demonstrating its inability fully to separate rationalist and "popular" modes of observation.[10]

In Paré's "medical" text we can see what Hayden White has identified in comparing the processes of historiography and psychoanalysis: the "overemplotment" of a culture's (or a patient's) *traumatic* events. According to White, this happens when the culture/patient "has charged them with a meaning so intense that, whether real or merely imagined, they continue to shape both his perceptions and his responses to the world *long after they should have become 'past history.'*"[11] Overemplotment saturates Paré's text to the extent that he, like the historiographer (and the analyst), can make "sense" of strange events only by "shar[ing] with his audience general notions of the forms that significant human situations *must* take by virtue of his participation in the specific processes of sense-making which identify him as a member of one cultural endowment rather than another" (p. 86). Whether Paré cynically sensationalizes what he sees, or "believes his eyes" as he looks through the lens of the "general notions of the forms" of significance in his particular cultural endowment, is beside the point. His text exemplifies the way ideologies of observation, whether in natural philosophy, in historiography, or in individual subjects, betray themselves in practice. Like witchcraft prosecutors, as well as Tudor historiographers, Paré could not advance his case without also producing in his own way the monstrosity he purports to report. Constructing bodies in "scientific" discourse, then, is as overemplotted as constructing "persons" and events in historiography. Both involve endowing things with "a meaning so intense" that they continue to determine perceptions and responses to what is, in fact, past history.

Shakespeare's first tetralogy ends with a play constructed from a series of historical accounts of "traumatic" cultural events—civil wars, infighting within and among powerful families, competing claims to a throne. These are exactly the kind of events that would trigger "overemplotment," accounts which in their invested repetitions and revisions produce a cultural symptomology not unlike the "traumatized memory" of an individual patient. And like the patient of psychoanalysis, a culture must find a way to *re-emplot* its traumas. "Historians," as White argues, "seek to refamiliarize us with events which have been forgotten through either accident, neglect, or repression. Moreover, the greatest historians have always dealt with those events in the histories of their cultures which are "traumatic" in nature and the meaning of which is either problematical or overdetermined in the significance that they still have for current life, events such as revolutions, civil wars, etc." (*Tropics*, p. 87). Obviously Shakespeare was neither a historiographer nor a psychoanalyst. And yet the last play of the first tetralogy seems, in an extraordinary way, simultaneously to perform and deconstruct the activities of both. As Phyllis Rackin has recently pointed out, "the history play in Shakespeare's hands was clearly an experimental genre."[12] However, while Rackin is right in saying that because "contradictory notions of historical truth and changing conceptions of historiography inform those experiments . . . it is impossible to derive a single, coherent theory of history from those plays" (*Stages of History*, p. 27), it is inaccurate to say that *Richard III* "resolves the problems of historical causation and dramatic structure in a conventional providential moral and a conventional dramatic plot" (p. 28). While the play does end on a "clearly providential" note, its "conventionality" is so foregrounded that, like Baudrillard's *hyperreal*, it becomes monstrous in its own right. Like Richard's deformed body, it advertises too obviously its use in the politics of signification.

Shakespeare, like the historians White describes above, is dealing with the traumatic events of his culture, the meanings of which are both "problematical and overdetermined in the significance they still have for current [Elizabethan] life." The issue, however, is where the playwright locates the trauma and how the play interrogates its inevitable symptomology. For although it is true that by the end of *Richard III* the events of the first tetralogy funnel into Tudor providentialism, it is not true that the play's most overemplotted traumas are resolved. On the contrary. What is extraordinary about *Richard III* as the end of the first tetralogy is not the "conventional" way it wraps up historical process as "the working out of a clear providential plan" (*Stages of History*, p. 27) but, rather, what that wrapping up *materializes*. For in the "ingenious" figure of Richard there is something more than "the rise and fall of a single strong character" (ibid.). There is a remainder, an excess thrown off by his physical presence, a signification that is concretized in his person and body and that at the same time casts its own shadow, implicating the surround. Shakespeare's *Richard III*, unlike that of More, Rous, Hall, Holinshed, or Morton, stages the *subjectivation* of cultural "overemplotment" by producing Richard as the subject of traumatic cultural memory, the figure who is forced both to embody and to experience its symptomology. The play explores what happens when symptoms that properly belong to systems become constitutive of persons. Shakespeare's play exploits the "portentousness" of monsters as a truth of another kind, one that reveals how persons are produced to fit the requirements of history's "traumatic events." Richard III is, I shall argue, the first tetralogy's designated symptom. And like other cultural symptoms, he must be produced in order to enable and justify the "cure" that, at least in terms of historiography, has always already preceded him.[13]

II

Richard III is the most "notorious" of all the historical kings Shakespeare chose to represent. This notoriety is twofold: Richard's defeat ushered in the Tudor monarchy, and he was widely reputed to have been a physical and moral monster. Richard II, Henry IV, Henry V, Henry VI—all had existence in the histories and chronicles, all were "identified" by the place they occupied in English history and politics; but as dramatic figures, none were (or had to be) as politically and peculiarly "invested" as Richard III. None carried the almost mythic imaginative weight that the deformed Last Plantagenet had for the Elizabethans. But Richard is important for another reason as well. He is arguably the first subjectively "dense" figure to appear in Shakespeare's plays. By this, I mean that he is the first figure in the corpus for whom the requirements of social identity produce a thematized disjunction or alterity: simultaneously a nexus of identification and a barred Otherness. Richard is "identified" by his portentous and overdetermined positioning in Tudor historiography; yet the play maps Richard's desire for *disidentification,* his efforts to evade a taxonomy that is always used to enforce his alignment with this textual history. Why is it that

Shakespeare's representation of a notoriously "known" figure produces such a pronounced "subjectivity effect"?[14]

Critics have often said that Shakespeare's Richard III is memorable because of the pleasure he takes in his villainy. Like the medieval Vice (the clichéd Renaissance figure of the Machiavel) with which he is frequently aligned, Richard seems to embrace with relish and bravado the "stock" role of villain that Tudor history has cast him in. But the case has also been made that Richard is "psychologically complex," a reading most frequently advanced by psychoanalytic critics who see in his misogyny and murderous aggression the effects of extraordinary narcissistic wounds (a reading that Freud performed on the figure in his famous essay on the "exceptions," and that feminist psychoanalytic critics have since rendered more subtle and convincing by their attention to gender politics, the social and historical construction of the patriarchal family, and the role of the mother within it).[15]

The apparent divergence of these views—Richard as stock figure versus Richard as narcissistically disturbed—is, however, revealing of a more general difficulty critics have negotiating the relationship between social and subjective structures. This difficulty is evident when critics argue that Richard represents Shakespeare's movement away from "stock" dramatic figuration—Richard's "inwardness" (read out of his morose soliloquies about his sense of disenfranchisement) demonstrates Shakespeare's "evolution" toward a more "realistic" kind of character with whom the audience is meant, presumably, to identify.[16] The problem with this approach, as I see it, is that it opposes "figurativeness" to "realism" in a binary economy that fails to recognize their inherence in each other. Such a "choice" is in fact a false one. Whatever complexity the representation of Richard achieves is diacritically produced *only in relation* to the reified conventions that also and simultaneously hypostatize him as "historical" Vice.

In other words, whatever "inwardness" Shakespeare achieves with Richard depends precisely upon his construction as stock villain. There is in the play an overwhelming apparatus, a kind of Tudor "Harrow," that demands that Richard be the Vice; and this brooding, inexorably structural habitus becomes for Richard what Slavoj Žižek has called "the big Other": the "other presumed to know" against which subjectivity strains and out of which strain emerges the *effect*—both for the subject and the audience—of "inwardness" and complexity.[17] It isn't that Richard is either the Vice or the Psychological Individual. Rather, Richard is subjectively convincing precisely to the extent that the historical, textual, political, and dramaturgical necessity to "prove a villain" materializes him as a certain kind of subject: one who is strung out between demands that he be at once the pathological individual and the general sign of a politics gone wrong.

What Shakespeare does is make his project Richard's project: the task of producing another "version" of Richard that will stand "apart" from that of official Tudor historiography. This is not to say that Shakespeare gives Richard "conscious" knowledge of his textual reiteration: nowhere does Richard directly refer to the Tudor chronicles. But the language of the play is full of references to and images of those accounts in the ways other figures talk to and about Richard, and in the ways Richard narrates himself. Richard's notorious identity constitutes the play's ontological habitus, within which Richard is forced to partake, however anamorphically, of a "sense"—denied at the level of knowledge, expressed at the level of symptom, and realized at the level of practice—of his prior textual existence. His subjectivity, then, is a paradoxical effect of his alienation from an identity that always already precedes him: the signification system that determines the ideological environment of the play and provides the materials for subjectivity within it. Composed largely of the language of omens and portents, it is voiced through the figures who read in them the ineluctable signs of historical "destiny."

The three parts of *Henry VI* depict the increasingly violent and depraved actions committed in the name of royal ambition and political power. In *Richard III*, all the political monstrosity developed in the first tetralogy is "embodied" in the deformed figure of Richard. Shakespeare's audience would immediately have recognized Richard's physical deformity and moral depravity as a synecdoche for the state; and there are frequent references in the play to the "unnatural" state of political affairs and their connection to the monstrous and unnatural Richard. Such charges are explicit in Anne Neville's lament over Henry's death and her choric diatribe against Richard in Act 1, scene 2:

> Foul devil, for God's sake hence, and trouble us not;
> For thou hast made the happy earth thy hell,
> Fill'd it with cursing cries and deep exclaims.
> If thou delight to view thy heinous deeds,
> Behold this pattern of thy butcheries.
> O gentlemen! See, see dead Henry's wounds
> Open their congeal'd mouths and bleed afresh.
> Blush, blush, thou lump of foul deformity,

For 'tis thy presence that exhales this blood
From cold and empty veins where no blood dwells;
Thy deed inhuman and unnatural
Provokes this deluge most unnatural. (50–61)[18]

While I will consider this scene in detail later, I want to call attention
here to the four references to sight in these lines: "If thou delight to view
thy heinous deeds," "Behold this pattern of thy butcheries," "O gentle-
men! See, see dead Henry's wounds." The tropics of evidence are adumbrated in what will develop in the play as a full-blown competition
over what constitutes on the one hand the most *effective,* and on the
other the most *authoritative,* kind of evidence.

Anne's appeal is to the "natural" eye, which in this context is inseparable from the play's relentlessly visual moral iconography. In making
a plea for "plain" vision, Anne implores the lords to read Richard as the
obvious. If we remember the importance of keeping a vigilant eye toward the signs of the cosmos, these lines affiliate themselves with a politics of vision—with the cultural "belief" that physical bodies, physiognomies, and morphologies are invested with an *inherent* discursive
significance. In a play (and culture) obsessively concerned to establish
the grounds of authority and therefore political legitimacy (and all that
it appropriates), the power to attach meaning to things—and especially
to things that don't automatically "speak for themselves," such as body
parts, physical features, wounds that bleed afresh, and so on—to determine what counts as evidence, interpret it, and administer that interpretation, is precisely what constitutes political power. It is not surprising,
then, that efforts to personify Evil should seek the most obvious figures
in whom "difference" can be productively harvested.

In Shakespeare's *Richard III,* as in the authorized Tudor histories,
Richard's identity is inseparable from his physical "difference." So long
as this identity is perceived by others within the play as corresponding
to that of Tudor legend, so long as his body is regarded as "evidence" of
his identity, he can have no "legitimate" authority. In order to acquire
it, however briefly, Richard must combat the play's politics of vision
with an alternative strategy, one that negates the ideology of the visual
by realigning the significance of his body with an ideology of the *invisi-
ble* body. There are, both within the medieval setting of the play and in
sixteenth-century England, ideological structures available that Richard (and Shakespeare) can appropriate to replace an *obvious* body with
one that is implied, one not necessarily determined by physical charac-

teristics. In seeking the crown, Richard seeks no less than a new body: the body implied by "the King's Body," which, according to medieval political theology, admits of no flaws and is the highest manifestation of God's grace on earth.[19]

Shakespeare's play diverges most clearly from its sources when it takes that most "sublime object of ideology," the English crown, and sublates it to another desire. For gaining the crown is not Richard's ultimate aim; his underlying aim is to use the King's Body to transform "handicaps" of his own. Gaining the crown will enable him to effect a kind of trade in which he imagines that he can exchange his misshapen, half made-up body for the "King's Body" and its divine perfections. With the success of this exchange, Richard will remove himself from the periphery (where his disharmonious parts place him) and relocate himself at the center.[20]

The fascination Richard holds for the audience lies in his attempts to resist and escape the deformed and deforming signification the play insists upon—his attempts to counteract the Richard of Tudor legend, which I will henceforth call "the play's Richard," with his own version, or Richard's Richard. The play's Richard is the figure inherited from John Rous, Morton, Polydore Vergil, More, Grafton, Halle, and Holinshed; his deformity was deployed as "evidence" of moral and political depravity. This identity is continually referred to by others, particularly the women, including Anne Neville, Margaret, Elizabeth, and his mother the duchess; and it is characterized by a language of dehumanization: he is a "bunch-backed" toad, a bottled spider, a mad dog, a devil, a foul stone, a lump of foul deformity. Since Richard's experience of himself is inseparable from how he "reads" the signs of his own body as a signifying text, his entire course of action can be seen as directed toward gaining control over the social construction, perception, and manipulation of bodily signifiers. Richard knows he cannot replace the perception of monstrosity with that of normalcy; but he can subrogate, by means of inversion, one ideology of exception with another. He can sublate his deformed body to the perfect "Body" of the king.

This is not to say that gaining the crown is a "psychological motivation" for Richard. At least, it's not psychological in the sense of individual pathology. Overdetermined by a habitus in which bodies *must* signify, Richard's "desire" for the crown is both an objective compulsion toward the only alternative structure available for him to inhabit that equals, in its own symbolically mandated weight, his portentous body; and a desire to replace stigma, and its shameful sense of social exclusion, with charisma—the symbolic value attributed to someone who is perceived as being "near the heart of things."[21] It is, as Bourdieu evocatively puts it, a desire to substitute one kind of "distinction" for another:

> Charm and charisma in fact designate the power, which certain people have, to impose their own self-image as the objective and collective image of their body and being; to persuade others, as in love or faith, to abdicate their generic power of objectification and delegate it to the person who should be its object, who thereby becomes an absolute subject, without an exterior (being his own Other), fully justified in existing, legitimated. The charismatic leader manages to be for the group what he is for himself, instead of being for himself, like those dominated in the symbolic struggle, what he is for others. He "makes" the opinion which makes him.[22]

It is just such a symbolic struggle that Shakespeare's Richard is engaged in: that of attempting to exchange status as the absolute object of Tudor historiography for that of the "absolute subject without an exterior," of his own making and regard. Richard's ontological project is to be for the group what he wishes to be for himself, rather than being for himself what the group always already knows that he is. This is how stigma operates: it deprives the subject of any inhabitable self-image that is not determined by others. The play, then, charts not so much Richard's "progress" toward the crown as his progress toward a fantasy of absolute subjecthood—a subjecthood that he will, paradoxically, lose *precisely by materializing it* when, like Bourdieu's charismatic charmer, he finally "'makes' the opinion which makes him."

III

It is because subjects do not, strictly speaking, know what they are doing that what they are doing means more than they know.
Pierre Bourdieu, *Outline of a Theory of Practice*

This, therefore, is the basic paradox we are aiming at: the subject is confronted with a scene from the past that he wants to change, to meddle with, to intervene in; he takes a journey into the past, intervenes in the scene, and it is not that he "cannot change anything"—quite the contrary, only through his intervention does the scene from the past *become what it always was:* his intervention was from the beginning comprised, included.
Slavoj Žižek, *The Sublime Object of Ideology*

What we regard as "history" is always "mediated through subjectivity": it becomes history only by the process of repetitive inscription in and through the symbolic. Consequently its "Truth arises from misrecognition"—whatever it signifies in the social formation necessarily routes through the misrecognition of consciousness (what Žižek calls "the opinion of the people"—*Sublime Object*, p. 61). "If we want to spare ourselves the painful roundabout route through the misrecognition, we miss the Truth itself" (p. 63). And this Truth is that the significance of history is consolidated only retroactively, like the "truth" of the analysand who has come through psychoanalysis and assigned his symptomology its place in the narrative. The very grammar of history, therefore, is proleptic: it puts later things first (just as Shakespeare chronicles later historical events in the "first tetralogy"). In this way, what was once profoundly contingent is reconstituted as "inevitable." *Richard III* maps the function of repetition for the subject who wants to "spare himself the painful roundabout route," who will not know what he knows, who refuses to read the signs, as if they were external to him and he could choose *not* to read them. In the figure of Richard we see the subject who will not identify with the symptom, who does not "believe" in omens and therefore secures his function as the symptom and omen of others. By rejecting his own portentousness, Richard "intervenes" and in his illusion of contingency ends up confirming "providential" history. This illusion is figured in Richard's denial of the language of intertextuality, his mistaking of his existence as *a first time occurrence*, as if he had no prior textual existence which had already constituted his own "symbolic necessity." This in itself would not be remarkable if the habitus of the play (within the larger habitus of Elizabethan England) weren't structured around this "necessity," if it weren't full of other figures who continually speak Richard's deformed frame as the advertisement of an overdetermined historical frame.[23]

The centrality of Richard's physical deformity is clear from the play's opening lines, and contemptuous self-regard is the first position the play engages. Richard begins by referring to the late wars, as we are reminded of the preceding plays in the first tetralogy:

> Now are our brows bound with victorious wreaths,
> Our bruised arms hung up for monuments,
> Our stern alarums chang'd to merry meetings,
> Our dreadful marches to delightful measures. (5–8)

Centered in emblems of the battlefield, this language charts a move from one kind of public space—the overtly political male space violently choreographed by war—to another, less overtly political space of the gender and class relations practiced in courtly "leisure," now made possible by a temporarily stable disposition of state power. In Althusser's terms, these lines translate the openly repressive apparatuses exercised when political power is fought for by martial means into the ideological apparatuses that interpellate the subjects of "legitimate" redistributions and delegations of that power. Such a change is, however, metonymic rather than substitutive. The gap between these two kinds of activities—the naked aggression of warfare and the social and sexual aggression of court life—is increasingly compressed as Richard's language moves "indoors" into the realm of aggression he envisions as the erotic:

> Grim-visag'd War hath smooth'd his wrinkled front;
> And now, instead of mounting barbed steeds
> To fright the souls of fearful adversaries,
> He capers nimbly in a lady's chamber,
> To the lascivious pleasing of a lute. (9–13)

The conflation of war and eroticism is here condensed into a narrative troping that becomes increasingly claustrophobic, as it moves from the outdoor space of the battlefield to the socially elite space of "merry meetings," and then to the privatized space of "a lady's chamber," until finally it reaches the personalized space of bodies:

> But I, that am not shap'd for sportive tricks,
> Nor made to court an amorous looking glass;
> I, that am rudely stamp'd, and want love's majesty
> To strut before a wanton ambling nymph:
> I, that am curtail'd of this fair proportion,
> Cheated of feature by dissembling Nature,
> Deform'd, unfinish'd, sent before my time
> Into this breathing world scarce half made-up—
> And that so lamely and unfashionable
> That dogs bark at me, as I halt by them—
> Why, I, in this weak piping time of peace,
> Have no delight to pass away the time
> Unless to spy my shadow in the sun,
> And descant on mine own deformity. (14–27)

Lacking a battlefield in which to "pass away the time," Richard knows that he has not been fashioned to participate in the "sportive tricks" of erotic courtship. The language Richard uses to describe the facets of war—bruised arms, dreadful marches, wrinkled fronts—metonymically links his body to Grim-visag'd War. He, too, has bruised arms, a dreadful march; he, too, will smooth his wrinkled front as he manipulates others. For Richard, the absence of an opportunity openly to exercise violent aggression forces him into a position of self-regard, in which he must behold his own image and establish a relationship to his "person." The soliloquy is rhythmically propelled by rhetorical self-reference: "I that am not shaped for sportive tricks," "I that am rudely stamp'd," "I that am curtail'd of this fair proportion." These lines clearly assert Richard's "I" as the issue at stake; and the imbrication of self-regard in the social is immediately foregrounded.

Since Richard claims he cannot "prove a lover" (a claim he will, significantly, disprove later) his alternative is to "spy my shadow in the sun, / And descant on mine own deformity." To "descant," as the OED tells us, is to enlarge upon a theme. Enlarging upon his deformity would mean establishing a perspective in relation to it. Ernest Gilman, in discussing the emergence in the sixteenth and seventeenth centuries of perspective painting, points to the centrality of the human body in contriving contingent perspectives:

> Perspective, like music and mathematics, was seen to be based on a satisfying system of proportions—between the objects to be painted and their images, between the *braccio* and every figure in the painting, and between the distance of the observer's eye and the entire construction. It embodied and revealed the substratum of the harmonious order of nature, and put the painter, no less than the philosopher, in touch with the intelligible world. At the center of this order is man. The proportions of the human body provide the basic unit of perspective measurement, and the painting is organized around the viewpoint of the individual spectator.[24]

If we imagine for a moment Richard as spectator to his own shadow, he becomes at once the individual viewer Gilman describes above, and the object that provides the proportions of the image he witnesses. Richard's awareness of his deformity, reflected back at him by his shadow, can lead him to two possible perspectives. In the first, he can perceive the deformed shadow as a perverted structure in an otherwise harmoniously ordered world. But this would require detaching himself from the image of his shadow (figuratively speaking), regarding it only as an external image to which he is the spectator, the "other." In the second, however, we might imagine that he sees his shadow on the ground (rather than, say, against a wall); in this instance the shadow is visibly connected to him (presumably at the feet) and such a detachment is impossible—he is positioned as both spectator to and represented object of the deformed image. In such an orientation there could be no clear distinction between spectator and spectacle. Richard, however, "incorporates" both perspectives; that is to say, he knows he has been "curtail'd of this fair proportion," but at the same time his perspective is itself overemplotted: the place from and through which he looks is fixed by his deformed proportions. It is this straddling that leads him to attempt to "dispossess" his deformity. But such a dispossession can be no mere denial; rather, it requires a restructuring of the world according to his own proportions: the creation of a world in which all behavior, values, and perceptions are extensions of his body image. A world—according to Richard—in which the misproportions of his body provide the "normal" perspective from which all ways of seeing are derived.

In his opening soliloquy Richard speaks of himself as the victim of a surround—alternately conceived as maternal, natural, social—that is assigned mysterious agency: he is "rudely stamp'd," "curtail'd" of fair proportion, "cheated of feature." Contrary to the rumors others have generated about his remaining too long in the womb and being born with teeth and hair, Richard claims to have been "sent before [his] time," "unfinish'd" and "scarce half made-up." The discrepancy of versions of Richard is apparent even here; and the emotional significance of his sense of being born before he was ready will permeate his relations with the play's female figures. Richard replaces a language of overgestation, of prodigious *belatedness,* with one of underdevelopment, of rude and untimely *prematurity,* and in doing so speaks a fantasy of preceding his own legend. By literally reconceiving himself, this time as "unfinish'd," "scarce half made-up," he speaks a fantasy of arriving early at the scene of his own story, with the possibility of "making up" the rest himself. However, Richard's fetal self-revisionism denies the conditions that compel the activity in the first place; and his efforts to reorganize the relationship between his body and the social becomes the driving impetus toward a status in which he will be not excluded (because he is not shaped for sportive tricks) but at the very center.

> I do mistake my person all this while!
> Upon my life, she finds—although I cannot—
> Myself to be a marvellous proper man.
> Richard III (1.2.252–254)

After Richard's acknowledgment of his deformity in the first scene, it is others, and most notably the women, who repeatedly refer to his body in the most scornful and degrading terms. The project, then, of reorganizing the relations of social perception begins properly with Richard's courtship of Anne Neville. In this scene, and *apparently* against all odds, Richard produces himself as an object of libidinal attraction. I say "apparently" because however preposterous his success may seem, it reveals as much about the play's libidinal structures and affective investments as it does about Richard, and possibly more. Although critics diverge in their views of the courtship—its success, its apparent absurdity, its "psychological veracity" (or more commonly its lack thereof), most tend to fall into one of two camps. Either they find it unbelievable that Anne capitulates, or they see Richard's "genius" and his success as a function of rhetorical skill.[25] Although Richard must (and did) marry Anne as part of his progress toward the crown, this scene does far more than just establish the requisite "traffic in women" necessary for the disposition of property and lineage. The reach of its effectiveness, however—what Richard calls his "secret close intent"(1.1.158), cannot be understood by appealing to notions of psychosexual "health" or "normalcy." On the contrary. It is precisely its preposterousness that renders the scene dramatically successful, erotically convincing, and centrally revealing of the rest of the play's social and libidinal relations. The scene works by revealing the socially productive fascination that always underlies revulsion, and by demonstrating the discursive and libidinal identities between contempt and desire, revulsion and attraction, political obsession and sexual fixation. Richard's "genius" in this scene may be rhetorical; but its force issues from the way he both manipulates and sets in motion around himself the affective power of the object of sexual disgust.

As Jonathan Goldberg has recently argued about the "preposterous" (with its rhetorical origins in the classical figure of *hysteron proteron*), it etymologically and epistemologically reorganizes sexual economies by treating ends—anatomical as well as teleological—as beginnings.[26] To understand the preposterous eroticism of this scene in particular (and its links to Richard's success in reorienting public perception in general), we must first consider how its identities are visually invoked and then discursively appropriated.

As I've already noted above, when Richard enters in Act 1, scene 2, Anne is performing a ritual lament over Henry's body and railing against Richard:

> Foul devil, for God's sake hence, and trouble us not;
> For thou hast made the happy earth thy hell,
> Fill'd it with cursing cries and deep exclaims.
> If thou delight to view thy heinous deeds,
> Behold this pattern of thy butcheries.
> O gentlemen! See, see dead Henry's wounds
> Open their congeal'd mouths and bleed afresh.
> Blush, blush, thou lump of foul deformity,
> For 'tis thy presence that exhales this blood
> From cold and empty veins where no blood dwells;
> Thy deed inhuman and unnatural
> Provokes this deluge most unnatural. (50–61)

Richard's "foul deformity" is yoked to his "heinous deeds," and both are connected to the political by their ability to draw forth blood from the dry wounds of the dead king. Anne's rhetoric verges here on the excessive; and Richard properly reads in its "excess of affect" her vulnerability to a fundamentally "perverse" courtship. Anne's hatred and public volubility provide Richard with a store of discursive materials already charged with appropriable affective energy. When she says "Avaunt, thou dreadful minister of hell!" he replies "Sweet saint, for charity be not so curst." She calls him a "Foul devil," and he returns: "Lady, you know no rules of charity, / Which renders good for bad, blessings for curses." Anne escalates her indictment: "Villain, thou know'st no law of God nor man, / No beast so fierce but knows some touch of pity." Richard inverts her sense: "But I know none, and therefore am no beast." Anne, recognizing his strategy, replies, "O wonderful, when devils tell the truth!"; and Richard counters with "more wonderful, when angels are so angry." These flip-side tosses of the same rhetorical coinage continue, as Anne calls him a "diffus'd infection" and a "hedgehog," and he calls her "Fairer than tongue can name thee" and "gentle Lady Anne."

Drawing Anne into a libidinal economy that trades on the tensions and identities that link binaristic oppositions, Richard's inversions produce erotic effect even as they escalate antagonistic affect. In fact, they do so precisely by underscoring such antagonism. Speaking the language and gestures of courtly gentility, Richard provides a new epistemology for the revulsion Anne feels, taking an emotional intensity surrounding one kind of history and substituting for it another:

> Your beauty was the cause of that effect:
> Your beauty, that did haunt me in my sleep
> To undertake the death of all the world,
> So that I might live one hour in your sweet bosom. (125–128)

Here Richard claims that the desire for Anne's beauty motivated his violent actions, a claim that forges a link between her beauty and his "monstrosity." In perhaps the scene's most "perverse" lines, Richard makes another remarkable juxtaposition:

> Anne: And thou unfit for any place but hell.
> Richard: Yes, one place else, if you will hear me name it.
> Anne: Some dungeon?
> Richard: Your bedchamber.

Assertions of personal desire are proffered to occlude those of providential history, as Richard realigns political with sexual ambition, murder with sexual desire, dungeons with bedchambers, and the erotic with violence, entrapment, and damnation. In the courtship scene, Richard is able to sustain a perfectly balanced inversion that works partly because, as David Holbrook has pointed out, "to substitute hate for love has what Polanyi calls 'the logical appeal of the apparent stability of the total inversion of values.'"[27] But its logic is stabilized not just by the structural homologies that support ideological inversions but also by the particular kind of metonymy inversion produces: one that renders radical opposites "alike." Richard cunningly personalizes as sexual desire political actions and ambitions that are shared by most of the other figures in the play. For Richard, the political *is* the personal, as he fabricates sexual subjectivity as a usable fiction. By rhetorically substituting sexual for political desire, Richard insinuates an interactive ground on which he can compete with his fellow men *as if he were no different* from them.[28] After claiming that he is not "shap'd for sportive tricks," Richard nevertheless deploys them; and in doing so, counters others' view of him as prodigious object with a version of himself as a social subject—of desires, emotions, and physical drives. By courting Anne, he includes himself in the social.

But Richard's rhetorical skill is not the only influence at work in this scene. The success of the courtship is underwritten by the mise-en-scène. Just as the play uses Richard's body to make its "point," Richard requires a body through which to run his rhetorical legerdemain. Richard "woos" Anne not in some pleasant garden or lady's chamber, but over the dead Henry's corpse and its gaping, bleeding wounds. After Anne succumbs, Richard himself is stunned by his success:

> Was ever woman in this humour woo'd?
> Was ever woman in this humour won?
> I'll have her, but I will not keep her long.
> What, I that kill'd her husband and his father:
> To take her in her heart's extremest hate,
> With curses in her mouth, tears in her eyes,
> The bleeding witness of her hatred by,
> Having God, her conscience, and these bars against me—
> And I, no friends to back my suit at all;
> But the plain devil and dissembling looks—
> And yet to win her, all the world to nothing!
> Ha! (232–243)

That Richard is baffled signals not the absurdity of the scene but rather its deep logic: no matter how "perverse" Richard believes himself to be, there is something familiar about what has transpired. Something happens at the level of the visual that prompts Richard to imagine that he can transform the perception of physical *evidence*, can make it mean differently. The "bleeding witness of her hatred" underscores the scene's (and the play's) violent scopophilia; but it is Anne who initiates the recoding of Henry's wounds by the very *copia* of her terminology. First she calls them "these wounds," then "these windows," then "these holes" (1.2.11–13), and finally, these "congeal'd mouths" (1.2.56). Henry's wounds, windows, holes, and congealed mouths, detached from the rest of his body by their *obviousness* as targets of the gaze (by what they "show" in the Lacanian sense, in which the object of the gaze shows itself showing itself), are assigned a kind of agency in which they literally *express* the excessive force of Richard's presence, the power the play gives him to mobilize that which should be congeal'd (whether blood or hatred or desire or line of succession). As multiple signifiers, however, they also provide materials for contesting the significance of this force—what it means in a *particular* representational lexicon. According to conventional Renaissance lore (which Anne enunciates), the wounds bleed in the proximity of the murderer, and thus are claimed as part of the play's arsenal of Tudor propagandistic devices which code Richard as political portent or monster.

But their very "detachability" also makes them available for Richard's use. Richard picks up the prurient threads which run through Anne's (and the audience's) engagement with Henry's wounds by openly respeaking them as sites of fetishistic scopophilia: loci of sexual rage and jealousy, as well as substitutive objects / causes of desire, in a libidinal economy which Richard structures around *penetration*—the transgression of political, social, personal, and gender boundaries. As the agent of such "seduction," Richard himself need not experience "sexual" desire. As Baudrillard has argued, "Seduction is not desire. It is that which plays with desire, which scoffs at desire. It is that which eclipses desire, making it appear and disappear . . . Such is the attraction of the dark body of seduction. Things seem to follow their linear truth, their line of truth, but they reach their peak elsewhere, in the cycle of appearances. Things aspire to be straight, like light in an orthogonal space, but they all have a secret curvature."[29] Richard transforms Henry's corpse and its wounds into this dark body of seduction. This "secret curvature," this appearance and disappearance, describes the way Richard's language reorganizes the discursive habitus according to the signifying trajectory of his own misshapen body, with its less-than-secret curvature. Richard, too, aspires to be "straight" (considers himself cheated by dissembling Nature); but for him there is no movement—whether toward the sexual or toward the royal—that does not reach its peak elsewhere, in the cycle of appearances, that does not veer from its target.

When Richard appears at the beginning of the scene and Henry's wounds bleed afresh, Anne immediately claims them for the play's portentous version of Richard as historical monster. Richard advances his own version of the portentous by recoding the wounds as portents of desire—signs, in Bourdieu's terms, of his own "absolute subjecthood"—put forward to counter the absolute objecthood affixed to him by Tudor history. Henry's wounds will no longer testify for Henry against Richard: now they testify for Richard and his desire. The bleeding witness for the prosecution becomes a witness for the defense.

But this shift isn't libidinally effective with Anne until Richard offers his own breast and sword to her (or pretends to), proclaiming his willingness to take his "wounds" at her hand. In this move, Richard's body becomes identified with Henry's and Anne's with Richard's; and even while Anne remains rhetorically unconvinced ("Arise dissembler," she says in 1.2.189), there is something powerfully persuasive about this shifting of bodies and gender roles, as Richard gives Anne the same phallic instrument used to enter Henry's body, and offers up his breast to her. By giving Anne the opportunity (however disingenuously) to penetrate his body with the same "tool," Richard positions her within the *structure* of his desire (however dissembled), mimetically doubling not only Henry but an "Anne" who now *invites* penetration. This shift of gendered subject positions enacts a process of mimetic triangulation in which Anne and Richard are identified in a variation of the "homosocial" in which Henry's body, with its cuts of "desire," simultaneously provides a feminized medium for which these two opponents can compete (in terms of how it signifies) and through which they can meet.[30]

This kind of identification/triangulation has links, however, to an older theatrical tradition enacted in medieval Corpus Christi celebrations and play cycles: the practice of contemplating Christ's wounds. Throughout the first tetralogy, Henry is frequently aligned with the figure of Christ: loving, pacific, politically ineffectual but morally pure, helpless against the cunning manipulations of the more "worldly." Anne clearly equates Henry's wounds with Christ's (as she equates Richard with Satan, who "has made this happy earth a hell"); and her lamentation over his body on the stage solicits what Peter Travis has called "ocular communion": a joining in and with the spirit and meaning of Christ's Passion by contemplating representations of his mortified body, a ritual designed not only to foster religious desire but to reinforce communal bonds through the "magic" of sacred identification—with Christ, and, through him, with fellow observers.[31] Such plays were meant to produce a kind of affective inhabitation of the figure of Christ, in which the mysteries of the Eucharist and transubstantiation were "realized" by gazing at graphic representations of his wounds—by entering, as it were, his body with one's eyes.

But such representations became increasingly lurid in the late Middle Ages and focused more and more on the graphic physical humiliations imagined to have been inflicted by the "tortores," especially in the Chester cycles, in which there is also much fascination with the exchange of bodily fluids—"spittle and mucus" (Travis, "Social Body," p. 28, quoting Rosemary Woolf). The intensity of physical language, image, and display in these performances is part of a larger set of representations that has generated much work on the fascination the body and its apertures were provoking apart from explicitly theological concerns.[32] As Travis says, "Scholars have told us about late medieval affective piety, the increasing realism and sensationalism of the religious arts, and the attendant psychology, rather like violence in pornography, of heightened shock to envigorate desensitized feelings" (p. 29). Shakespeare's *Richard III* draws upon and "perverts" this tradition, as Anne's exhortation to "behold" Henry's wounds recalls the convention of "ocular communion," here evoked to ratify political and social homogeneity (through a sacralized object) against a common enemy. In this invocation, Henry's wounds are sanctified like Christ's. But unlike Christ's body in the medieval cycles, Henry's sexual status as a *male* body, a body with a penis, is drastically effaced. Travis points out the "unwavering attention given to Christ's penis during two centuries of Renaissance art" ("Social Body," p. 19), noting how concerned church authorities were to assign him his "full manhood," concerns "generated by the horror of lack" (p. 20). In the late medieval plays, the attention paid to Christ's wounds, to his physical subjection, was always accompanied by "attention"—arguments, gestures, or images—designed to dispel anxieties that he might be "nonsexed" (as those without a particular kind of representation of the phallus have, until very recently, always been designated) and therefore "less than perfect."

But as Sarah Stanbury has also argued, part of the controversy around Christ's masculinity in these representations of the Passion had to do with who was doing the gazing, whose eyes were palpating the limp and punctured male body. Anxiety over potential emasculation is initially engendered by the fact that it is women, and Mary in particular, who tend to direct the gaze of the viewers, both within the representations (in a painting or among a group on the stage) and outside it as well. The viewer's/audience's gaze is circuited *through* a female gaze, one that is disallowed in virtually every other cultural arena. Women do look in medieval narratives and poems; but when they do, it is almost always coded as erotic transgression, insofar as looking repositions women within subjectivity, and frequently (and more threateningly) in authority.[33]

Such transgression and the erotic aspect that I would argue is always present in the gaze are even more directly provoked in drama than they are in painting or lyric, since the viewer confronts the materiality of bodies on a stage. In *Richard III* (as in other scenes of sacralized violence in Renaissance drama), the transgressive erotic potential of the medieval paradigm makes its way into the semisecular tableau of Anne's lament, as she boldly exhorts others to "behold," "behold." Her speech seems less grief-laden (although she sheds tears into Henry's wounds, a *literal* ocular communion in which her tears enter his body) than warrior-like. Positioned in rhetorical equilibrium with Richard, her language is powerful, confrontative, and aggressive, like her ocular decorum. Her visual assertiveness, however "socially legitimized as a gesture of grief" (Stanbury, "Virgin's Gaze," p. 1087), as well as her position as designated mourner, appropriates Henry's body, arrogates it to herself, and consequently, by way of exactly the kind of imaginative empathy and identification such ritualistic mourning is designed to foster, reconstitutes it as an extension of herself. Anne's sensationalistic attention to Henry's "holes," and lack of corresponding attention to his more "manly" parts, pre-pares (if one might be forgiven the pun), Henry's body for what will be Richard's transsexual repairing which, rather like the violence in pornography, achieves its "heightened shock" by gendering all wounds as female (and conversely, by regarding all females as wounded).

Rhetorically recoding Henry's dead body and its wounds as the "effect" (penetration) of "that cause" (sexual desire), Richard transforms political wounds into sexual ones: simulacra of the deflowered maidenhead. Accordingly, Henry's death is translated from a political-theological sacrifice into a sexual one. Henry's "Passion" becomes Richard's. Like the sexuality pornography claims to "express," Richard's penetrations of Henry's body are passed off as sexual, rather than political, in nature; and correspondingly, so is the bloody "deluge" that issues from the wounds. Thus, Henry's body becomes, *pace* Baudrillard, the "peak" that is "reached elsewhere": the *actual* target of the secret curvature of Richard's political desire, dissembled by Richard as the *deflectionary* target of his sexual desire.

In this circuitry, then, "ocular communion" over Henry's body becomes a kind of staged communal voyeurism, in which a body that cannot look back (now visually and discursively coded as female) is "probed" by the gaze of others for its significance. Such activity has long been aligned (as Foucault has argued about the Inquisition, witchcraft interrogations, and the history of confession) with sadistic erotic pleasure, the pleasure afforded (by definition almost exclusively to men) within patriarchal Western culture by exercising scopic and discursive power over bodies with less or no power.[34] Despite their differences in this play as male and female figures, and however vitriolic Anne may seem in relation to Richard, they enact a shared voyeurism, a perverse ocular communion over and through a shared body that they have both "entered" and appropriated in their respective ways. In terms of the rhetorical symmetry of their verbal intercourse, as well as the symbolic symmetry of their intercourse with Henry's body, the courtship is staged, however temporarily, between *equals*; and it is partly this suspension of sheer phallic prerogative that allows for the kind of "friction" that in Shakespeare's courtships frequently constitutes the erotic.[35]

This is not, however, to say that it is only friction between antagonists that constitutes the erotic in this scene, nor is it to claim that the political—either in terms of royal politics or in terms of gender politics—has even for a moment been suspended. On the contrary. The scene critiques the very conditions of the eroticism it stages. No matter how much moral authority Anne is allowed to exercise in this scene (as the voice of Tudor providentialism and judgment), she is still finally reigned back into the confines of her female body. She has looked aggressively and spoken aggressively and therefore transgressed "proper" feminine decorum; but in doing so, she has also opened herself. A woman's look not only violates but renders her vulnerable to violation. A woman with open eyes, open mouth, and open ears is no longer the *hortus conclusus*, no longer the "body enclosed," no longer safely contained, in terms of how she might either mislead or be misled.[36] That Anne's eyes and mouth are so very open in the courtship scene means that her ears will not be far behind. The woman who spits at Richard and says that he "infect[s] [her] eyes" (1.2.152) is signaling that he has already somehow gotten inside. It is through her ears that Richard will secure his success; and he rams his tidings fruitfully.

In revising the epistemology of Henry's death in terms of sexual desire, Richard draws upon a long tradition in which women's bodies and beauty are the putative cause of war, murder, and betrayal; and his success in this scene includes him within this conventional tradition. But it also demonstrates his awareness of it as a form of *preposterous displacement,* in which the outcome of aggression between men is proleptically installed in the bodies of women as originary cause. Anne, like many other female figures, is simultaneously positioned as the object/cause of violence and as the recipient of that violence as a sacrificial tribute. Richard reinfuses the cold relic of Henry's corpse with the hot life of the sacred gift:

> Your beauty, that did haunt me in my sleep
> To undertake the death of all the world,
> So I might live one hour in your sweet bosom.

Proclaiming his willingness to pay everything, Richard's declaration of prodigality of expenditure (to undertake the death of all the world for an hour in Anne's "sweet bosom"), like Satan's, inverts Christ's (who undertook to save the life of all the world) and matches in its profligacy the vehemence of Anne's language. This is no offer of sonnets, undying love, or eternal worship. Here is a dead king (along with a dead husband and promise of even more murderous tributes) served up on the trencher of sexual desire. Reading in Anne's will to sight and speech a will to a certain kind of knowledge (like Eve listening to the serpent), Richard insinuates a desire for her that matches her own in its excessive vehemence and renders its bearer perversely appealing.

That Anne, near the scene's end, goes, within twenty-one lines, from wishing Richard's death (188) to wearing his ring signals the erotic force of the scene's visual and discursive choreography. But this has, I suggest, more to do with the structural operations of transgression than it does either with Richard's "genius" or with Anne's sudden credulity. Rather than attributing it to "characteristics" of Richard or Anne, one might better approach the eroticism of this scene by looking at how the play maps the homologies between excesses of violent ambition and sexual desire. The distinction Bataille has drawn between the "homogeneous" and the "heterogeneous" worlds is illuminating here. The "homogeneous" is that which works conservatively to affiliate social and economic elements with a predictable, reproducible, and conventionally recognizable mode of social production: it is that which excludes contradiction in the social formation. The "heterogeneous," however, "concerns elements that are impossible to assimilate," including notions of the sacred and the taboo.[37] According to Bataille, "the heterogeneous thing is assumed to be charged with an unknown and dangerous force"; and "the heterogeneous world includes everything resulting from *unproductive* expenditure (sacred things themselves form a part of this whole). This consists of everything rejected by homogeneous society *as waste or as superior transcendent value*" (*Visions of Excess*, p. 142, italics added). Including cadavers, human bodily waste, body parts, and "persons, words, or acts having a suggestive erotic value," Bataille establishes an identity between "waste" and "superior transcendent value." To posit them as general equivalences is to describe the ideological structure that constitutes the play's overarching structure of desire. For the play sets up an opposition between the ideology of "divine right," transcendently bestowed by God on the Tudor monarchy, and the "waste" that it must make, under such overdetermined historiography, of Richard. Coded as waste from the very beginning of the play, by himself as much as by others, and belonging to the realm of the "heterogeneous" because of his withered arm, crook-back, deformed, abortive, and lumpish person, Richard is nevertheless a vitally productive element in the Tudor politics of providential transcendence. For while both waste and superior transcendent value may *seem* to exist outside productive expenditure, *it is precisely this appearance* that is socially productive. More important, both are capable of generating the same kind of affective response: "Heterogeneous elements will provoke affective reactions of varying intensity, and it is possible to assume that the object of any affective reaction is necessarily heterogeneous (if not generally, at least with regard to the subject). There is sometimes attraction, sometimes repulsion, and in certain circumstances, any object of repulsion can become an object of attraction, and vice versa" (*Visions of Excess*, p. 142). Richard's courtship of Anne, as well as the rest of the play, generates those "certain circumstances" Bataille describes by foregrounding the constitutive identities between waste and transcendent values, between curses and blessings, devils and saints, "proper" and improper men, loathing and attraction—all the identities Richard extracts from Anne's language. And her response unarguably demonstrates the intensity of her affective reaction to the play's most heterogeneous object.

This scene works by undermining the pretenses of distinction between high political, and therefore moralized, discourse (which Anne speaks)—the ideology of royal authority and its "universal" signification (also linked to "high" tragedy, which Anne attempts to make of this scene as she laments Henry's death in Senecan style); and Richard's equally ideological but more pragmatic discourse of personal desire and the body: lust, scopophilia (his actions the result of gazing at her beauty and wanting an hour in her sweet bosom). Henry's "corse" and its wounds become the site of articulation between two discursive strategies: one public, "official," and "moral," the other private, unsanctioned, and "base." These narratives, propelled by Anne's and Richard's respective gazes, converge in Henry's bleeding wounds, which are translated from a political sacrifice (the iconology of high tragedy) into a transgressive erotic gift. To borrow from Lewis Hyde, who speaks of the transformative power of gifts, "It is this element of relationship which leads me to speak of gift exchange as an "erotic" commerce, opposing eros (the principle of attraction, union, involvement which binds together) to logos (reason and logic in general, the principle of differentiation in particular."[38] By insisting that Henry's

death was the result of his desire for union with her, Richard underscores Anne's "involvement" *with* him in those wounds, one which
binds them together; and in doing so, counterposes the principle of eros
to Anne's logos, her rhetorical efforts to differentiate, in absolute terms,
not only herself from Richard, but Richard from all humanity. Henry's
body becomes this transformative gift, and the bleeding wounds become a sign not of accusation but rather of the *plenitude* of Richard's
desire.

Whether Anne perceives herself to be repositioned by Richard's
"gift" inside an erotic commerce or to be the recipient of a Maussian
"prestation" is not clear.[39] But the scene works in the way that prurience
always works: by running ideological misrecognition through an object
of affective fixation. Involving repeated exhortations of the gaze, the
scene requires the audience's fetishistic scopophilia: its investment in a
politics that constructs "that which shows" (the object of the gaze showing itself to the gaze) as that which *wants to be seen showing itself,* and
consequently sees in the hysterical symptom the "will" of the "other."
What is actually most "perverse" about this scene is not Richard's love
suit but rather its foregrounding of Henry's body, which becomes the
obscene, the too-much-exposed, too visible, too ob-vious object. If, according to T. S. Eliot, the "problem" with *Hamlet* is the "excess of affect," the problem in *Richard III* is the excess of *objects.*[40] Richard's power
in this scene derives from a knowledge he bears in his own body: an
understanding of the way bodies can be made to mean more than they
say. It is (to paraphrase Bourdieu) precisely because bodies do not,
strictly speaking, speak for themselves that what they mean is always
more than they say. And that meaning transposes the political and the
libidinal through the power relations, whether conducted on the battlefield or in a lady's chamber, that organize both fields. As Peter
Stallybrass and Allon White have pointed out about the symbolics of
the sewer in nineteenth century Paris, "The melodramatic coercion of
extreme opposites into close intimacy here becomes the ultimate truth
of the social. For indeed the signs of the sewer could not be confined
'under the surface.' The sewer—the city's 'conscience'—insisted, as
Freud said of the hysterical symptom, in 'joining in the conversation.'"[41]
Henry's body and its "sewage" "join in the conversation" that
Richard's body has already set in motion; for Richard has turned
Anne's hyperbolic monologue into dialogue, and has made the wounds
speak, as it were, out of both sides of their mouths. Henry's body provides the material for two discursive trajectories—moral/political and

sado-erotic—in which these apparently "extreme opposites" are co-erced, melodramatically to be sure, "into close intimacy." The question to be addressed now is: How does this "become the ultimate truth of the social"?

The "attraction of repulsion" arises from a confrontation with a plea-sure that cannot be "legitimately" owned (Stallybrass and White, *Transgression*, p. 144). This pleasure, refracted through the ritual disavowals of prurience, may particularize an individual's history or may be gen-eral—the "ultimate truth of the social." But the truth of the subject is also always a representation of the ultimate truth of the social. Henry's corpse functions in the courtship scene the way Richard's body func-tions in the rest of the play. For just as Henry's wounds "speak" him as portentous object without his "consent," so is Richard's body made to enunciate a discourse that doesn't originate in his own utterance.

Richard's sense of what's at stake in bodies is foregrounded when, comparing himself to Edward, he says Anne will nevertheless "debase her eyes" on him. Anne exclaims earlier in this scene that Richard "in-fects" her eyes. But ocular "infection" is the demonic form of ocular communion: penetration that threatens rather than reinforces structural integrity. That Richard can sway a woman who begins by pleading for "proper" vision, a woman who at one point tells him to get "out of [her] sight," does seem to enable Richard to creep into a new kind of favor with himself. And yet, it is unclear which side of his mouth he speaks out of when he says,

> I do mistake my person all this while!
> Upon my life, she finds—although I cannot—
> Myself to be a marvellous proper man.
> I'll be at charges for a looking glass,
> And entertain a score or two of tailors
> To study fashions to adorn my body:
> Since I am crept in favour with myself,
> I will maintain it with some little cost. (252–259)

Richard realizes that he does have a kind of power to transform the way others regard him; he is clearly stunned by the success of his courtship. But we can also see a desire for a different kind of self-regard, as he says, "Shine out, fair sun, till I have bought a glass, / That I may see my shadow as I pass." These lines are no doubt ironic, and we can imagine Richard capering facetiously as he says them. But if we recall his earlier remarks which are echoed here, it is apparent that his successful courtship has given him a perspective in which he is willing to "descant" on his deformity. Richard begins to find more habitable an image partly of his own making, or at least to envision the possibility of eliding his monstrousness from public perception, demonstrating how rhetorical success reorganizes bodily subjectivity. Richard's achievement in the erotic signals the possibility that language can reconstruct his "person" in terms of how it shows itself showing itself; and that he might revise his status as the object of public gaze in other arenas. If he can translate ocular "infection" to ocular communion with Anne, perhaps he can do so elsewhere.

IV

When the community is attacked from outside at least the external danger fosters solidarity within. When it is attacked from within by wanton individuals, they can be punished and the structure publicly reaffirmed. But it is possible for the structure to be self-defeating.
Mary Douglas, *Purity and Danger*

It is a sign of superstition to place one's hopes in formalities; but it is a sign of pride not to conform to them.
Blaise Pascal, *Pensées*

Shakespeare's *Richard III* figures structural self-defeat. But the route to that defeat, its journey through individual and social misrecognition, involves a mapping of the two other circumstances Douglas describes above. Structural self-defeat in this play requires both the external danger which fosters solidarity within and the internal attack of the "wanton individual" who must be punished. But in the play both roles are played by Richard, who externalizes the danger by realigning himself within the social formation and simultaneously produces himself as the wanton individual whose punishment will presumably reaffirm the structure. Now that Richard is equipped with a wife, the next step in his project to alter the social perception of his deformity is to locate its *origins* outside himself, to create a new epistemology for his own bodily signifiers, one in which he is the afflicted rather than the teratogenic. Positioning himself within social structures from which he has been (and feels himself to be) excluded, Richard turns to a kind of self-splitting in which even he can deploy the "monstrous" Richard—but now as a function of others' plotting rather than the allegory of his own.

If at the end of the courtship scene Richard says he "mistakes" his person, he reclaims it differently in Act 3, scene 4, by declaring to Hastings that he has been the victim of witchcraft. This demonstration is ostensibly meant to put Hastings in an impossible position and thus give Richard "grounds" to murder him; but it is also, significantly, the last time in the play that Richard calls public attention to his physical deformity. Speaking as if he has only just noticed his "affliction," Richard asks his council:

> I pray you all, tell me what they deserve
> That do conspire my death with devilish plots
> Of damned witchcraft, and that have prevail'd
> Upon my body with their hellish charms? (3.4.59–62)

Implying that he wasn't born with his deformity, Richard claims it is the recent work of Elizabeth and Mistress Shore and their "hellish charms." Unveiling his arm as if revealing its twisted shape for the first time, Richard makes his own ludicrous plea for vision, calling upon the lords to "witness," "see," and "behold" his deformity:

> Then be your eyes the witness of their evil.
> See how I am bewitched! Behold, mine arm
> Is like a blasted sapling wither'd up!
> And this is Edward's wife, that monstrous witch,
> Consorted with that harlot, strumpet Shore,
> That by their witchcraft thus have marked me. (67–72)

Whether or not these lines are meant to be comic they are so, for they display as a revelation what was, as Thomas More bitingly put it, "a weryshe wythered arme & small as it was never other."[42] Richard knows, as do the others, that he is not unveiling some hitherto unnoticed marvel. The point is not whether anyone is actually fooled by the display. What is important is how it adumbrates Richard's strategy of consolidating political power. Relying on the misogynist tradition of blaming male infirmity on "monstrous" female power, Richard's displacement of monstrosity onto "that witch" and "that harlot, strumpet Shore" is, like his courtship strategy, preposterous because it exchanges consequences with origins. But it also productively conflates the attack from within with the attack from outside. In calling upon the lords to behold his withered arm, he rallies them around their newly constituted "common enemies" Elizabeth and Mistress Shore. But he also performs a breach of decorum that stuns the men into silence: a performance in which anyone who dares to regard his deformed body as *proper to him* is a traitor to the new solidarity that has been rhetorically fostered around complicitous misogyny. Richard eclipses his "difference" from the other men by invoking the "differences" of gender. Now "one of the boys," Richard can posit his deformity as something leveled against him (and by extension against all men) by dangerously conniving women. Selectively dispossessing and deploying his deformity, Richard speaks it in terms that he purports to control by displaying himself as the target, rather than the origin, of malignity.

If Richard cannot alter his body in reality, he can acquire enough political power to implement his politics of vision, a perspective based on preposterous revisionism—of history, of physiognomy, even of ontogeny. Rejecting a version of himself in which he presumably spent two years in the womb and was born with teeth and shaggy hair, Richard's prenatal revisionism is pushed to an absurd limit when he instructs Buckingham, in Act 3, scene 5, to "infer the bastardy of Edward's children." In his most audacious call for deformed perspective yet, Richard commands Buckingham to tell the mayor and his men:

> . . . when that my mother went with child
> Of that insatiate Edward, noble York
> My princely father then had wars in France.
> And by true computation of the time
> Found that the issue was not his-begot;
> Which well-appeared in his lineaments,
> Being nothing like the noble Duke, my father. (86–92)

Richard revises two of his mother's pregnancies and, in this latter revision, alters his father's role as well. It follows, of course, that Richard's lineaments are like those of his father the duke. And for anyone to protest otherwise would be to malign not only Richard but the memory of "noble York."

Moving under a cloud of *paranoia* (because it apprehends danger even as it misrecognizes the source, direction, and nature of the threat), Richard's sense of his deformity does seem initially to arise, as Janet Adelman has forcefully argued, from a sense of impeded birth, a driving need to "hew his way out with a bloody axe" and thus be free of a strangling and claustrophobic maternal power. And yet, Richard's apparent obsession with the conspiracy of the "triad of female powers—Mother, Love, and Nature"—which "all fuse,"[43] *itself reproduces* the epistemological *displacement* the play's prophetic discourse rhetorically enacts, one that structurally replicates Richard's reassignment of the source and agency of his deformity to Elizabeth and Mistress Shore. In other words, Richard's construction of his personal history mimics the play's revision of his political history. In both it is women who are readily available—to Shakespeare as much as to Richard—as the displacement vehicles for a prophetic claustrophobia that is, for the playwright as well as his protagonist, ultimately textual and political in nature.

The real source of Richard's paranoia originates not in his mother's womb but rather in the historiographic "womb" of textual reproduction under a century of Tudor reign—a carapace which has kept the historical figure of Richard gestating repeatedly and too long, and against which Shakespeare's Richard launches a compensatory fantasy, a paradigmatic reaction-formation, of being sent "before [his] time" into the world. Richard's problem is not that he has been sent prematurely into the world, scarcely half made-up, but precisely the opposite: he has been overlong in the world, sent too often, too made-up, overdetermined by repeated *textual* births that have rendered him too readable and his body too legible. Overwritten into monstrosity by a century of overemplotted historiographic gestation, Shakespeare's Richard is subject to a textual history that underwrites the legitimacy of a Tudor queen while at the same time figuring the pervasive male dread of and contempt for the female body and female power.

Richard's disgust for female sexuality in general and maternal power in particular constitutes, at least in part, his painful route through misrecognition, his misprision in the locus of individual origin of a political oppression that continually embeds itself in bodies, whether the demonized bodies of devouring mothers and "harlots" or the deformed bodies of bunchbacked portents. Richard's disposition toward women, then, replicates the play's disposition toward Richard: it abreactively locates in discursively marked bodies (in this case the sexually reproductive bodies of women) what properly belongs to the invested politics of *social* reproduction.

In fact, one might even say that the intensity of Richard's contempt for women, and theirs for him, is based on a painful *identification* that must be disowned on both sides. For if Richard exhibits an "excessive" misogyny (excessive in relation to the mean of misogyny in Shakespeare's plays), that antipathy is fully reciprocated. Throughout the play the voices that have not lent themselves to Richard's efforts to pervert the public perspective have been primarily (although not entirely) the women's voices—from Anne Neville to Elizabeth to Margaret to the Duchess of York. Nowhere are the play's identity politics more fiercely articulated than in the voices of its female figures. Richard's language of self-loathing is remarkably like the language the women use to vilify him; and it is their prophecies, curses, and dehumanizing contempt that he must work the hardest to discredit, both to himself and to others. One of the play's many ironies is that the very category of persons who have themselves been relentlessly constructed in terms of their "flawed" bodies by centuries of misogynist discourse should level it most forcefully against Richard. Like the female figures in the play, Richard is marked as other, as the antithesis of "marvellous proper men."

While these female figures are consistently locked into roles that are powerless directly to affect the political infrastructure (except as vehicles in the "traffic in women" that fosters familial and political alliances through marriage), they are endowed with accurate political vision where Richard is concerned. Even Anne admits to Elizabeth, in Act 4, scene 1, that it was her ears, and not her eyes, that succumbed when "[her] woman's heart/ Grossly grew captive to his honey words" (78–79). None of the play's male figures (other than Richard himself) are as aware of what bodies can be made to mean; and this is because misogynist discourse—from patristic exigesis to courtesy manuals—locates female identity first and last in a body that is inferior to or less than the "perfect" or "complete" male body. The price of the women's clarity of vision is their intolerable identification with the identity politics enforced by their subjective inhabitation—their "women's hearts" "grossly captive"—in "lesser" bodies.

Relegated to the proverbial sidelines, the play's women serve as prophetic commentators—paradoxically as morally empowered by their socially stigmatized morphology as Richard is disempowered by his. The real power of their voices, however, has less to do with the moral truth of prophecy than it does with the play's interrogation of the intensely coercive and political relationship between words and things, between "objective" designation and subjectivation. If, as Madonne Miner has argued, Richard's impulse with regard to all women is "the impulse to silence, to negate," it is an inevitable consequence of Richard's desire to efface the portentous signification of his own body.[44] In his efforts to supply new signifieds to signifiers, Richard must silence the women. If Richard's political and personal agendas require that he efface the "character" that is literally etched onto his body and the social and subjective significance of those monstrous signs, it is the women who repeatedly reassert his physical deformities as stigmata. The female figures may be deprived of direct political effect within the play, but they purvey its metadramatic voice—the voice that "properly" names, that "correctly" connects seeing and speaking. This is the crucial link that Richard is intent on severing. The women must be silenced because they are a constant and intolerable reminder of the confluence between thing and name. Giving the women the power to prophesy proleptically, Shakespeare has "authorized" them to refer, if only in roundabout ways, to the same "historical" texts that serve as his own sources. For Richard, who wants to alter his status by becoming a royal "exception" rather than a monstrous one, female voices revive the barely repressed knowledge that any achievement of his own version of identity can be only temporary. That in this nightmarish Cratylitic universe which he seeks to rewrite, Richard Plantagenet, by any other name, will still be a monster.

By vilifying women for their sexual conduct, Richard draws from and adds to the rich store of male anxiety about patrilineage and women as property, and produces a viable public perception, however fragile and policed, of himself as *ipso facto* a "proper man" in relation to the women he designates as monstrous. The social recoding and redeployment of his deformity depend upon the motility of public misogyny. But to anchor himself in his new public body, Richard needs another set of ideological coordinates that will not only reinforce his difference from women but also reestablish his difference from other men. Richard knows that he cannot eradicate his "exceptionality"; he can only alter how its representational politics are perceived and interpreted. The presumed heterogeneity that locates Richard outside the bounds of homogeneous society offers him a hierarchic as well as a lateral possibility. Waste (to return to Bataille's lexicon) can be recycled into "superior transcendent value" (as Renaissance theatrical costume and property managers knew), since both are only diacritically constituted by their relationship to "legitimate" objects of representation.

To complete this substitution, however, Richard must attempt to redeploy the sacred status of kingship, a status that his own actions as well as the actions of other male figures throughout the first tetralogy have dangerously undercut. Exhibiting the same canny awareness of the power of public ritual and performance that Elizabeth Tudor relied upon to produce her "prince's body," Shakespeare's Richard enacts a series of set pieces that stage his induction into this rarefied state. When

Buckingham returns after carrying out orders to praise him to the mayor and his men, Richard is furious to learn that when bade to cry "God save Richard, England's royal King,"

> . . . they spake not a word,
> But like dumb statues or breathing stones,
> Star'd each on other, and look'd deadly pale. (3.7.24–26)

Richard replies, "What, tongueless blocks were they? Would they not speak?" In order to achieve *objective* existence, Richard's revisionist politics requires a corroboration that only public enunciation makes possible. When the mayor and the men seek Richard's audience in Act 3, scene 7, this recognition fuels Buckingham's advice to Richard to "Be not you spoke with but by mighty suit" (46). After the citizens' earlier reticence, it is crucial that they now implore Richard to be king and that he "be not easily won to [their] requests" (49). Sought and woo'd by the mayor, his men, Catesby, and Buckingham, Richard appears above the crowd propped "'tween two clergymen," "two props of virtue for a Christian Prince." Overtly these "props" help stage Richard's observance of the Machiavellian dictum that a Prince "appear to be all religion."[45] But they also bespeak a new set of referents for Richard's person, a new context in which his "parts" may be outlined and interpreted. This Richard is a figure suffused with divine grace, a man whose humility is matched only by his greatness:

> Definitively thus I answer you:
> Your love deserves my thanks, but my desert
> Unmeritable shuns your high request.
> First, if all obstacles were cut away,
> And that my path were even to the crown
> As the ripe revenue and due of birth,
> Yet so much is my poverty of spirit,
> So mighty and many my defects,
> That I would rather hide me from my greatness—
> Being a bark to brook no mighty sea—
> Than in my greatness covet to be hid,
> And in the vapour of my glory smother'd. (3.7.152–162)

Richard answers "definitively" because definition is precisely what's at stake. Invoking his "defects" in this new context, Richard alters their "nature," implying "poverty of spirit" rather than murderous aggression as their source. Deflecting attention from his portentous physical "defects" by calling attention to self-asserted defects of "character," Richard "owns" only defects of his own design. His body human is now flawed only relative to the king's body (as any man's would be) and not in relation to the rest of mankind.

But like so much of Richard's language, this passage refracts the truth it misspeaks. Richard the sign will not be permitted to sever the connection between signifier and signified. It is because he at once "covets to be hid" and desires to be "obvious" or visible in a new way that he has sought the crown to begin with. He does indeed desire to be "smother'd" in this vapor of glory, this smokescreen of ideological rhetoric generated around the crown. It is only royal power that can smother the other Richard, the monstrous object of scorn. And it is only by maneuvering others into thrusting greatness upon him that Richard can anchor himself in the social center of power and perchance believe, if only briefly, in his own fiction. By "acquiescing" to the supplication of others, Richards binds them into an agreement that implicates all who are involved:

> Attend the sequel of your imposition.
> Your mere enforcement shall acquittance me
> From all the impure blots and stains thereof:
> For God doth know, and you may partly see,
> How far I am from the desire of this. (231–235)

The "sequel of [their] imposition" is the fiction of Richard's Richard, reauthored in fantasy by himself and ratified publicly by others. Throughout *Richard III* royal power is spoken of as *vestiture,* as magical raiment that alters the person who wears it. In 4.2.4–5, Richard, prodding Buckingham toward the elimination of Edward, asks, "But shall we wear these glories for a day, / Or shall they last, and we rejoice in them?" And in Act 4, scene 4, Elizabeth tells him to "Hid'st thou that forehead with a golden crown / Where should be branded, if that right were right, / The slaughter of the Prince that ow'd that crown" (140–142). And it is no wonder that Richard conceives his new role as a disguise, when his own mother calls him "Thou toad, thou toad" (4.4.145). Becoming king figures for Richard a fantasy in which he believes he can eclipse the deformed Richard of Tudor legend with his own version of himself, one in which his lineaments are like those of his father, noble York; and one in which he has, if not "love's Majesty," Majesty's love. In a discursively revised habitus where power has been "imposed" upon him, Richard can sustain a sense that the "portentousness" of his defects has been "acquitted." He has, at the exhortation of others, traded his body human—with its "impure blots and stains thereof"— for a body royal. If Richard's project with regard to the play's female figures has been to break the connection between seeing and speaking, his project now is to reconnect them in a new way, around a new kind of "evidence." Bearing official witness to this social transformation is the mayor, who seals Richard's politics of vision with a ritual utterance: "God bless your Grace: we see it, and will say it" (235).

To elaborate on the problem of belief, however, it should be said that the lords, the mayor, and his citizens need not necessarily *believe* Richard's claims, or at least need not believe them in the sense of personal "conviction." Rather, what is required is a set of ideologically viable structures powerful enough to support Richard's new performance of himself, and the coercive power of men like Buckingham, who stand to gain from Richard's usurpation as well. As in all forms of collective misrecognition, whether or not Richard's audience is convinced by his performance matters less than how effective it is as a social ritual within the play's representational politics. For there is a kind of externalized, functional belief that is not dependent upon individual belief—in fact, one that bypasses it altogether and is generated *only by* social performance. We might call this "social belief," or the "belief *effect*." As Žižek points out in his analysis of belief under conditions of late capitalism, "belief" becomes increasingly depersonalized and embodied in "the social relations between things." In other words,

> It is belief which is radically exterior, embodied in the practical effective procedure of people. It is similar to Tibetan prayer wheels: you write a prayer on a paper, put the rolled paper into a wheel, and turn it automatically, without thinking . . . In this way, the wheel itself is praying for me, instead of me—or more precisely, I myself am praying through the medium of the wheel. The beauty of it all is that in my psychological interiority I can think about whatever I want, I can yield to the most dirty and obscene fantasies, and it does not matter because—to use a good old Stalinist expression—whatever I am thinking, *objectively* I am praying.[46]

Arguing that in feudalism social relations circulate through "a web of ideological beliefs and superstitions" (p. 34), Žižek points out that in capitalism (even, I would add, an emergent capitalism), subjects increasingly perceive themselves "as free from medieval superstitions, when they deal with one another they do so . . . guided only by their selfish interests" (p. 34). The transition in England from a feudal to a capitalist economy and its ensuing social relations occurred over several hundred years. Shakespeare's play represents positions which straddle the overly formulaic distinction Žižek makes above partly because its conditions of production are situated in a long transitional phase that included, variously, the ideological operations of both systems (witchcraft trials *and* Baconian "rationalism," for example); and partly because the degree to which belief could or could not be embodied in rituals was one of the cruxes of Reformation theology. But the play also *dramatizes* a conflict between two kinds of belief. For while Richard manipulates and treats the "fancies" of others with a contempt that anticipates individualist rationalism—the subject "free from medieval superstitions"—other figures in the play fetishize "omens" and "portents" precisely by regarding them as such: by displacing synchronic *social* relations in paradigmatic objects, in things that "express" those relations *for* persons. Richard's person is that object; and his mistake can be located in the fact that he fails to take seriously enough his own status as fetish, as that *thing* the significance of which, like the monstrous itself, is at once socially constructed and presumed to be inherent.

In the play, as in the figure of Richard, we see a confrontation between two different species of historical fetish, both of which exercise influence in the objective conditions (in Bourdieu's sense of what operates as and passes for the Real in the social formation) of early modern England. The first is *textual:* the narrative reinscription during the fifteenth and sixteenth centuries of Richard as monster accretes around his figure until it becomes that most reified of textual commodities—a legend. The second is *theatrical:* the sixteenth and early seventeenth centuries elevated the role, importance, and artfulness of social performance. The influence and sophistication of Renaissance drama coincided with, and was constitutive of, a heightened theatricality in everyday life. A "new histrionicism" profoundly shaped careers and crafted identity; and performativity—on royal progresses, in court society, on deathbeds as well as scaffolds—had enormous power to influence social and political perceptions.[47]

There is, as Mary Douglas has argued, a socially persuasive force generated post hoc simply by virtue of a successful performance of itself: a kind of "institutionalized admiration" effected only through rituals—an effect "which does not belong to the formal political structure, but which floats between its segments."[48] It may validate the status quo when used effectively by those with cultural authority, "but it also has the potentiality of disrupting ideas about authority and about right and wrong, since its only proof lies in its success." As the play's polluting object, its inscription of abomination in the "natural symbol" that is his body, Richard has the possibility of appropriating this aleatory power that "floats between [the] segments," the unstable *predesignation* that can turn a polluting object into a source of revulsion *or* of reverence, depending upon how it is manipulated. Within certain kinds of ritual frames in specific cultures, an "abomination [may be] . . . handled as a source of tremendous power" because the "frame ensures that the categories which the normal avoidances sustain are not threatened or affected in any way."[49]

The ritual frame in Shakespeare's culture is theatrical; and the challenge for Shakespeare's Richard is to produce *in performance* something that will counter the cumulative textual weight of legend, something that will generate new "objective" conditions in which the figure may maneuver and be perceived without triggering fears that "normal avoidances" are being threatened. The play offers the following fantasy: that if through his performance Richard can foster a cooperative performance in others, perhaps the two performances really will objectively reconstitute the social; and perhaps Richard really will have a "loving" public, one that supports his kingship because it is knit into a fabric of public "consent" that has been *histrionically* realized. In this fantasy, social performance would operate as a kind of early modern British "prayer wheel," making Richard's "person" and its repugnant materiality entirely beside the point.

Caveat Emptor

However the fantasy above lays down its tracks, the obvious point to make now is that Richard's "person" can never be beside the point because it *is* the point. Positioning himself *with* others vis-à-vis the relationship of the subject to the fetish (whether of royal charisma or of portentousness), Richard fails to apprehend—until Act 5, scene 3, when he begins to feel its effects—that he is himself the *play's* fetish. That is to say, he is at once "beside himself" insofar as his notorious identity operates on its own, quite apart from the exertions of his will (detachable to the degree that the value of the commodity is always not the same as, or unidentical with, the particular object that it invests); and is indefeasibly attached to his figure. Richard's value as political fetish is anchored *in* his body; and however he might wish to separate the two bodies—the body human (or the thing) and the king's body (or the value of the commodity)—the play re-fuses him. He is the Lacanian *point de capiton*, the "nodal point" at which all the play's ideological elements are fixed, and where the competing elements of text and performance are "quilted" to the play's totalizing ideological structure.[50] For the play's ideology is self-ironically *structural:* while the structure does underwrite moral "design," it does so precisely by laying bare the coercive textual mechanisms that secure that form of historical mystification known as "providentialism."

Looking at the play retroactively, when Richard says at 1.1.30 that he is "determined to prove a villain," we know this to be true. But not because Richard wills it. In Richard's fantasy, to become England's king is not only to replace monstrous difference with royal difference; it is to rule others—those who have "rul'd" a deformed Richard (Nature, his mother, and by extension all women, all previous writers of Richard, and ultimately his coauthor, Shakespeare), and those who have ratified that ruling by reading his body as the expression of political disaster. Of course the play's ultimate structural irony is that Richard's declaration of "determination" leads him into actions that confirm his predetermination, his imprisonment in a body that is the spatial representation of already inscribed political and moral "perversion." With brilliant proleptic legerdemain, the play's ending sets up the play's beginning, repeating compulsively within its own parameters a history of Tudor writing about Richard Plantagenet that increasingly reifies him into a monster. Richard's determination of himself as villain is the literal realization of (and unwitting collusion in) the play's determination of Richard.

In his final soliloquy in 5.3.178–206, he faces the confusion, and final collapse, of the illusory distinction between the play's "two Richards," a distinction that achieving the King's Two Bodies will no longer sustain:

> What do I fear? Myself? There's none else by;
> Richard loves Richard, that is, I am I.
> Is there a murderer here? No. Yes, I am!
> Then fly. What, from myself? Great reason why,
> Lest I revenge? What, myself upon myself?
> Alack, I love myself. Wherefore? For any good
> That I myself have done unto myself?
> O no, alas, I rather hate myself

For hateful deeds committed by myself.
I am a villain—yet I lie, I am not!

Even the textual variations of the play contribute to the confusion regarding the doubling, and fusion, of the two Richards: the Quarto version of line 179 reads "Richard loves Richard, that is, I *and* I." I and I versus I am I: this is the conflict his notorious identity produces. In Richard's soliloquy we hear the confounding of "I"s and his disruptive confusion and doubt about his agency and status—no longer in relation to others, but in relation to himself. Richard is an agent. He knows this. But what emerges in these disturbing lines is Richard's confrontation with the creature of Tudor legend he has simultaneously been delivering and disowning. Is the agency behind his actions his own? The play's answer is a structural one, and it is no. Richard has already revenged himself upon himself and has been doing it throughout the play. When he says "I am a villain—yet I lie, I am not!" he isn't denying his "hateful deeds." Rather, the statement is a last-ditch effort to retain the illusion of textual autonomy. In his disclaimer we see the realization break upon him that he has *been determined* to "prove a villain"; and that consequently, he has no "I" at all. Indeed, if "every tale condemns [him] for a villain" (5.3.195), he has determined nothing for himself.

At this crucial moment before the battle at Bosworth, Richard confronts the fact that he has lost what has always been the real battle—the battle against his own overdetermined textuality. The Richard of Tudor legend proves too weighty an opponent against which to sustain an alternative subjectivity.[51] By abortively invoking and then collapsing in these lines the distinction between "the same" and "the same as," Shakespeare's treatment of the Richard legend materializes at this moment a subject forced finally *to confront and to be identical to* his notorious identity; and furthermore, one that realizes it precisely by resisting it. Richard the actor confronts Richard the text; and in this, his only moment of genuine lucidity—the moment in which he confronts the real conditions of his intertextual existence—we see his subjectivity emerge as an effect of losing his battle with the books. The effect of this retroactive reconstruction of meaning is a kind of deconstruction of the play as a whole. By the end we must rethink, if not refute, our entire experience—for it has not been what it has seemed.

Throughout the play (or at least until Richard acquires the crown) the audience believes, with Richard, that it is watching him chart his own self-proclaimed course. We witness his fantasy of oppositional "self-fashioning" unfold, and we believe (in the sense I've outlined above, in which histrionic identification generates a belief effect, whether we "will" it or not), along with Richard, that he has managed to "see through" the play's didactic and prophetic elements. But by the time we reach the dream-vision sequence before Bosworth, we realize that the play has slowly been coopting "Richard's Richard," using his "revised" version of himself to *demonstrate* temporally and spatially the "authorized," accretive, and legendary text that the figure of Richard has, by the time Shakespeare takes him up, become. In this way, the play stages the question of what it is like to be cheated not by Nature but by textual history: what it is like for the subject who is barred from being anything other than a monster because his conception, gestation, birth, and body bear the mark of a villainy not only always-already accomplished but already written about repeatedly. Canceling the audience's *experience* of Richard as autonomous subject with its relentlessly "providential" logic, the play's structure subverts its content by insisting at the end that its content has always been (if one only goes back to the beginning again) its structure.

The extent to which Shakespeare supports Tudor myth means that we must see Richard as a monster. But the extent to which the play reveals legend as an apparatus that justifies particular regimes and versions of history means that we must also see everyone else in the play as a kind of monster. In the context of the relations mapped by the early history plays, Richard is in fact not the exception everyone in the play (and many audiences and critics) would like to believe.[52] Rather, as the designated embodiment of the violent ambition shared by so many, he is a site of likeness—the vessel in which the less obvious monstrousness of others is bodied forth. In order for Richard to be an effective "sacrifice" to or scapegoat for Tudor politics, he must be the same before he can be rendered "different." As René Girard has said about the psychosocial function of sacrifice: "The proper functioning of the sacrificial process requires not only the complete separation of the sacrificed victim from those beings for whom the victim is a substitute, but also a similarity between both parties. This dual requirement can be fulfilled only through a delicately balanced mechanism of associations."[53] Richard's "separation from those beings for whom [he] is a substitute" is present from the outset in his physical deformity and his relation to it, what Freud calls his "exceptionality"; but his similarity is also present in his blood ties to others—the power lust he shares with his "second self," Buckingham, not to mention Clarence, Edward,

Elizabeth's male relatives, and a host of other Yorkists and Lancas-
trians.

In fact, Richard's success in manipulating others arises out of his ability to be "familiar" or like them in crucial ways, overt and covert. But
this similitude must circuit through misrecognition in order to generate
a socially usable sacrifice: "Sacrificial substitution implies a degree of
misunderstanding. Its vitality as an institution depends on its ability to
conceal the displacement upon which the rite is based. It must never
lose sight entirely, however, of the original object, or cease to be aware
of the act of transference from that object to the surrogate victim; without that awareness no substitution can take place and the sacrifice loses
all efficacy" (Girard, *Violence*, p. 5). Shakespeare provides that "delicately balanced mechanism of associations" between Richard and others in the play to make his version of Richard acceptable to a Tudor
monarch. And the play does conceal, in its structure, the displacement.
Nevertheless, as monstrous as Richard is made, the audience is not allowed to "lose sight" of the transference, of the "original object." Even
while the play encodes that "degree of misunderstanding," it provides
an ironic commentary on reading "rightly," revealing the multiplicitous meanings and uses of reading even while finally insisting on one
"right" reading. What we (and ultimately Richard "himself") must read
is Richard's body as the "legend" or tablet on which his notorious identity is written. Anticipating Kafka's "Harrow," Shakespeare has produced a figure whose own moment of "enlightenment" occurs simultaneously with his final subsumption under the terms of his "sentence."

Richard's ascent to the throne and fulfillment of his notorious identity
culminate in a "providential" defeat. But not before revealing something crucial about the relationship between the monster and the social
body. For Richard is an object of horrible fascination, the focal point of
all affective reactions in the play. We might think about this fascination
in the terms Bataille uses about the peculiar power of modern fascist
figures: "Considered not with regard to its external action but with regard to its source, the force of a leader is analogous to that exerted in
hypnosis. The affective flow that unites him with his followers . . . is a
function of the common consciousness of the increasingly violent and
excessive energies and powers that accumulate in the person of the
leader and through him become widely available" (*Visions of Excess*,
p. 143). Richard may be the play's resident (and Tudor historiography's
requisite) monster fascist, but he is at least given the perks that go with
the job. He exerts the "hypnotic force" that produces "followers"; and

Henry's wounds, along with all the other bodies that have sustained violence in the long and bloody civil struggle for royal power, channel the "affective flow" that unites Richard, however temporarily, with Anne, Buckingham, and others who have allowed powers to concentrate in his person. Richard's "monstrosity," his foulness, deformity, bloodlust, contempt for self and others, hypostatizes the tetralogy's *political* waste, congeals it on the surface of his body where it can be regarded in all its repulsive visibility. The synecdoche of the "increasingly violent and excessive energies" that accumulated during a century of civil warfare in England and that build throughout the first tetralogy, Richard is in fact the play's most historically *authentic* representation—in a grim sense its most "marvellous proper man."

For Shakespeare's Richard materializes what Žižek calls "the hard kernel of the Real," and in this way exerts the kind of attraction for an audience that only arises from a fundamental *recognition.* Shakespeare's Richard does "disrupt the smooth circulation of the symbolic mechanism"; he is "a grain of sand preventing its smooth functioning."[54] Despite the play's pretense of representing Richard as the "perverse," we can see—even through that painful route of misrecognition—that Richard's desire is *identificatory:* to be like others who are allowed "legitimate" social desires, whether for love or affiliation or power. As Mikkel Borch-Jacobsen has said in his critique-revision of Freud, "Desire, in other words, does not aim essentially at acquiring, possessing, or enjoying an object; it aims (if it aims at anything at all) at a subjective identity. Its basic verb is 'to be' (to be like), not 'to have' (to enjoy)."[55] Extending the Girardian model of desire, Borch-Jacobsen posits the object of desire as a kind of MacGuffin—as that thing which is not important in and of itself but rather for what it sets in motion around it:[56] "What we should expect to find, inexhaustibly, at the root of fantasies, dreams, and symptoms is not sexuality but something quite different: jealousy, for example, or envy, or rivalry, or ambition, all of which are passions aroused by the mimesis of another whom one wishes to equal, replace, to be" (*The Freudian Subject,* p. 28). Jettisoning the specifically sexual from the center of the desire drive, this deeply anti-"therapeutic" model implicitly rejects the assumption that there are such things as proper and improper objects of desire, and indeed, defetishizes the "object" altogether. Desire here is about repositioning the self in a system of social relations. It is about "replacing" another whom one also wishes "to be." It reveals, therefore, what is always culturally productive about desire, and never more so than when it seems to arise from heterogeneous "unproductive expenditure," whether mystified in the politi-cal/theological or reviled in the sexually or socially "perverse." The perverse, Jonathan Dollimore has recently argued, "is inextricably rooted in the true and authentic, while being, in spite of (not because of) that connection, also the utter contradiction to it."[57] The "mysterious inherence" Dollimore traces between perversion and authenticity is, I would argue, the homology between "waste" and "superior transcen-dent value"; it is where the Real threatens to efface the boundaries be-tween included and excluded, monstrous and beautiful, marvelous de-formed and marvelous proper, waste and superior transcendent value.

Richard III is the first tetralogy's eruption of the real, which opens its "congeal'd mouth" to speak on behalf of Richard's more fundamental authenticity—to enunciate the way he repeats in fractal miniature the play's (and Tudor historiography's) violent seduction of its audience. Richard is that seductively deformed "dark body," that "secret curva-ture" of historiographical desire which can only reach its peak through the "elsewhere" his body provides. As such, he is the agent of a certain kind of libidinal pleasure, one that exceeds social coding and particular objects of desire insofar as it consists of the peculiar pleasure afforded by watching a figure who is at once horribly impacted and has horrible impact on others. In watching Richard's progress we see *hysteria con-dense into character:* hysteria partly as Lacan defines it—as the subject's fantasy representation of the desire *of* the Other; and partly as Cixous defines it—as an intervention, something that attempts to "break up continuities, produces gaps and creates horror—refusing conformity with *what is* . . . a response to what is unacceptable and intolerable in life."[58] Richard may attempt to refuse conformity with what is, or rather, *what must be;* but in doing so he also *secures* it as the desire of the Other by reproducing the most socially powerful desires in this play, all of which are effected through political violence and all of which ulti-mately achieve their "affective flow" through apertures made by males in other male bodies. Shakespeare's representation of Richard fore-grounds the pleasurable *pulsion* in the repulsive—its irresistible move-ment toward power, identification, annihilation. This is what is most compelling about any eruption of the real. At once exceeding but al-ways "caught"—enseamed—in the social body, its pleasures can be "owned" only by being disowned, by being attributed to *particular* bod-ies. The fascination of Richard's "presence" in the play, then, is that of the "extimate" object—a figure both intimate and external—both inside and outside the social, which is inside and outside him.[59] The libidinal

pleasure he affords can be realized only within the safety of the historical knowledge that England will be "rescued" by Richmond and returned to the misrecognitions of legitimate historiography. In this play
the ultimate truth of the social demands the production, and then the
"cure," of Richard the pathological individual.

Shakespeare's play produces Richard's subjectivity effect by tricking
the audience into identifying with the symptom, urging us to see Richard as an "individual" singled out by his difference, rather than as a
historical product that permits an authorized cultural text to close ranks
around its exclusion.[60] In this way Richard does double duty, both as
Vice *and* as Psychological Individual, allowing an experience of voyeuristic pleasure and identification in which the audience may strive to be
interess'd and still preserve the deniability factor. Shakespeare's first
"psychologically complex" representation is ultimately deeply anti-
humanist insofar as it gives the lie to the very fantasy of subjective autonomy and inwardness it stages. By representing Richard as a "character" in—rather than as a figure for—the hysterical symptomology of the
first tetralogy, the play produces "character" as a necessary function of
social misrecognition.

But so long as Richard has the stage, he demands our ocular communion with his mortified body, and our recognition of its relation to our
own. For in Richard's person we see the crushing, distorting, and ultimately monstrous effect of identity politics grown fascistic: identity that
permits *no difference* between what it mandates and the subject who is
forced to bear its imprimatur. Richard III, then, is Shakespeare's first
notorious subject; and no matter how engaged the play may be with the
ideological uses to which Richard's legend can be put, it is even more
engaged with what it would feel like to be subjected by and to that legend, with what it would be like to have to *be* Richard III, surrounded by
the language and signification of a hundred years of writings about
oneself.

The reflection Richard sees and hears in the eyes and words of others
is that of a monster. To escape this constituting reflection, Richard attempts to achieve the camouflage of royal authority and see reflected
back at himself the king's divine body. But seeking the King's Two Bodies cannot prevent the fusion of the play's two Richards. Richard is unable to "communicate his [new] parts to others" because his parts have
already been communicated by Rous, Morton, More, Holinshed, and
other "historians" whose authority cannot and must not, in the reign of
Elizabeth, be denied because the playwright himself is subject to the

immediate political constraints of his material. Positing a doomed alterity for a figure that must at every stage labor toward its own cooptation, Shakespeare was bound by the characterological requirements of the Tudor "party line." But if Richard ultimately fails to make something "new" of himself, Shakespeare does not. Shakespeare's Richard is "monstrous" because he demonstrates something true about the relationship between subjects and the hegemonic social texts that provide the materials of identity. In "acting out" his authorized text, Richard produces in theatrical performance something which cannot be fully reigned back into the legendary text. Richard is not permitted to "keep" the surplus his performance produces. But the playwright can; and he will push his exploration of intertextual identity even further in *Troilus and Cressida* and *Antony and Cleopatra,* plays in which the major figures are "farther off" insofar as they exist as literary legends rather than nearly contemporary historical figures; and consequently, plays that afford Shakespeare more imaginative leeway in terms of what he makes of his notorious figures and what they can make of themselves.

2

"So Unsecret to Ourselves"
Notorious Identity and the Material Subject in *Troilus and Cressida*

I have a mortal fear of being taken to be other than I am by those who come to know my name . . . Praise a hunchback for his handsome figure, and he is bound to take it as an insult. If you are a coward and people honor you as a valiant man, is it you they are talking about? They take you for another.
Montaigne, "On Some Verses of Virgil," trans. Donald Frame

This is, and is not, Cressid.
Troilus and Cressida, 5.2.14

Troilus' bitter remark as he watches Cressida in the Greek camp may reveal his stupefaction, his inability to comprehend what he sees, his "splitting" of Cressida into "his" Cressida and "Diomed's Cressida." But if we remember that Cressida herself has already warned him that "I have a kind of self resides with you; / But an unkind self, that itself will leave / To be another's fool" (3.2.14–51),[1] we can also consider Troilus' remark to be the first lucid assessment he has made of her in the play thus far. This moment marks Troilus' recognition that he has, in fact, made the mistake Montaigne fears: he has taken Cressida for another. And we can well understand Montaigne's fear. To be "taken for another" is not to be taken at all. Rather, it is to be left behind, "exchanged" as it were for this mysterious "other" for whom one is mistaken. But what happens when it is one's "self" who is the "other" for whom one is mistaken? Or when the "self" for whom one is taken is only a "kind of self," a self that is really beside itself? These questions are central to Shakespeare's *Troilus and Cressida,* as characters throughout the play mis-take each other, and are in turn mis-taken. Paradoxically, the figures who inhabit this play are notoriously "known." And yet, it is precisely these legendary figures who are at great pains to secure their own and each other's identities as they try to lay to rest a haunting sense that they are, and are not, "themselves." Troilus' exclamation in the face of Cressida's "betrayal" is paradigmatic not merely of this moment but of the play as a whole. "This is and is not" is a phenomenon that haunts *Troilus and Cressida,* endlessly repeating and forming the knot to which the play again and again returns.

I

If the meaning of a poetic work can be exhausted through the application of a theory of neurosis, then it was nothing but a pathological product in the first place, to which I would never concede the dignity of a work of art. Today, it is true, our taste has become so uncertain that often we no longer know whether a thing is art or a disease.
C. G. Jung, "Is There a Freudian Type of Poetry?"[2]

If any Shakespeare play seems to invite exhaustion through the application of a theory of neurosis, it is *Troilus and Cressida.* Arguably the most "neurotic" of the plays in terms of the skewed relations among and between characters, the play's generic inconsistencies, its resistance to a "rehearsible" narrative, and its own self-proclaimed "diseased" matter, it is not by any means merely a "pathological product." And yet, I would hesitate to concede it "dignity" as a "work of art," or at least, art or dignity as Jung presumably means them. Those critics who would concede dignity to the play as "art" take it, to borrow Montaigne's terms, for another: if they praise the play at all, they attempt, unconvincingly, to praise a hunchback for his handsome figure. What I propose to do in this chapter is to praise the hunchback for his hump. For it is precisely its deformity that gives the play its power. And I intend to address its "art" in its artifice; that is, the way in which the play calls attention to itself at every level as a construct, a made thing, a deliberately badly made thing, in fact a monstrosity—something that both demonstrates and admonishes. The question to be asked is not whether a thing is art or a disease, but, rather: what is it that is *artful about* disease? As Althusser has said, "What art makes us *see,* and therefore gives to us in the form of *'seeing,' 'perceiving'* and *'feeling'* (which is not the form of *knowing*), is the *ideology* from which it is born, in which it bathes, from which it detaches itself as art, and to which it *alludes.*"[3] *Troilus and Cressida* posits symptomology as art because it is only the neurotic symptomology in the play that detaches itself and alludes to the ideology from which it is born. What I concede to the play as a work of art is its extraordinary capacity for treachery—its *trompe l'oeil* effect, which invites theories of neurosis only to anticipate their claims and, finally, to deconstruct their conclusions.

The famous figures who inhabit this play act out, in perverted and self-deceptive forms, a rebellion against a coercion and oppression of subjectivity that cannot and must not be directly confronted or openly challenged. As epic figures, they are deeply inscribed vehicles of ideology; but as dramatic characters, they don't quite fit their inscriptions. Unable to construct alternatives, they are forced to be and not be "themselves." The play, I shall argue, represents neurosis in the form of subjectivity crippled by cultural inscription. To say, however, that something is *only* a pathological product, "merely" neurotic, would be to deny the subversive signifying power of pathology—the ways in which, although categorized as monstrous and therefore as marginal, it still manages to interrogate the "normal." Neurosis is never "merely" anything: it is, rather, always some kind of political expression, since it is constructed either as opposition to or as perversion from norms of thought, feeling, or conduct. But reading neurosis as a political act does not mean valorizing it or asserting that it is the best or most effective form of rebellion. Quite the contrary. A neurosis may posit resistance to oppression, but its symptomology is largely apotropaic—designed to avert rather than openly to challenge. Neurotic symptomology by its nature helps reinforce and hold in place the original structures of oppression against which it reacts. This is, finally, what makes it neurosis—it is a politics of rebellion turned back upon the self.

It has been argued that in *Troilus and Cressida* Shakespeare represents a longing for a heroism that is irrecuperable, a nostalgia for a time when terms such as "honor" and "glory" were still attachable to the heroes whose actions and attitudes defined the terms; that the play encodes a nostalgia for the origins of epic heroism—for the titular epic forefathers whose names its characters carry around their necks like placards. But this argument reproduces the very myth of origins that the play so relentlessly attacks. Even in the so-called "originals"—Homer's *Iliad* and Virgil's *Aeneid*—there is ironic nostalgia for a lost age of heroism.[4] Far from lamenting lost heroic ideals, Shakespeare's play betrays the awareness that all notions of heroism, of "true" honor and glory, are in their very moments of conception always located in the past, always "originally" conceived of as irretrievably lost. Consequently, the pursuit of a retrievable, reproducible heroism is itself a neurotic symptom, insofar as it rewrites originary absence as loss. How are Shakespeare's famous figures to "be themselves" when their names convey an absolute "identity" that is itself based upon a myth of loss? If, even as the "original" heroes of the "original" epics, they always already encode nostalgia? Achilles may not want to fight in Shakespeare's play; but even as the "hero" of Homer's epic he didn't want to participate in the war. What does it mean that the most famous warrior in Western literature has never wanted to fight in this most famous of wars?

The tendency to read and write absence as loss may render the nostalgic impulse suspect; but it doesn't necessarily make it "neurotic." In order for the nostalgic impulse to be "neurotic," it would not only have to deny originary absence, but would have to deny even the sense of loss that is the nostalgic *revision* of absence. Neurotic nostalgia would produce symptoms that at once represent absence as loss and then deny that representation. In *Troilus and Cressida,* the figures exhibit just such symptoms, the etiology of which can be understood in the way their notorious "identities" have been constituted.

> Experience teaches that for most people there is a limit beyond which their constitution cannot comply with the demands of civilization. All who wish to reach a higher standard than their constitution will allow, fall victims to neurosis.
>
> Freud, "Sexual Morality and Modern Nervousness"[5]

The figures in Shakespeare's play have complied with the demands of "civilization" insofar as they have been "constituted" by those demands. But we expect Troilus to be "true" and Cressida to be "false" because their story is a part of what in turn "constitutes" "civilization." No other Shakespearean characters are as "convicted" as those in *Troilus and Cressida.* These figures have been tried and convicted repeatedly in the repetitions of the story of Troy. We need not be persuaded that Troilus is "true" and Cressida is "false"—we are convinced before the play has even begun. As Montaigne says about the story of Troy: "There is nothing so alive in the mouths of men as [Homer's] name and his works; nothing so well-known and accepted as Troy, Helen, and his wars, which perhaps never existed . . . Not only certain private families, but most nations seek their origin in his fictions."[6] To seek origins in "fictions" is, I suggest, the historiographic equivalent of nostalgia. As a strategy of producing national "identity," however, it "constitutes civilization" so as to make it comply with *particular* political demands.

Thus, nostalgia and historiography converge in a cultural mythography: a use of the legendary to replace epistemological uncertainty with a fiction of authoritative origins—a fiction designed to confer upon notions of authorship the "authority" of the "authentic."

The invidious problem of "originality" lies at the heart of Shakespeare's play. By choosing one of the most notorious stories of the Renaissance (through the writings of Chaucer, Lydgate, Caxton, and Henryson, to name the most influential), Shakespeare takes on the task of giving mimetic spontaneity to, and representing viable subjectivity in, characters who are already deeply encoded in their meaning. Troilus and Cressida, along with their Greek and Trojan counterparts, mean and mean intensely in the Renaissance, long before Shakespeare restages them in his play. Their story (which appeared not in Homer but in the versions of the Troy story that were generated in the Middle Ages) had status as a literary construct within a larger legendary context that was itself deployed both as "history" and as literary fiction.

It is, I believe, this curious coupling of the great "authority" that surrounded the legend of Troy with its unstable classificatory status, its strange existence as both legend and history, that led Shakespeare to use the story as a way to investigate the deeply conflicted relationship between absolutist authority and its coercive forms, and a contrary fantasy (and I wish to stress "fantasy"), represented explicitly during this time, of the possibility of a "self-authored" subjectivity. For unlike the meaning and deployment of other "notorious" figures (such as Richard III), Troilus and Cressida's meanings were not overtly linked to political power: their semiotics had not been appropriated by the Tudor royal line to consolidate its own legitimacy. Theirs is primarily (although Shakespeare will alter this) a literary/psychological significance, at least insofar as these are the discourses into which they enter as significant figures. But it is precisely the fact that they are apparently unanchored in the political axis that enables Shakespeare to explore the relationship between "identity" as that which fixes meaning (both personal and political) and "subjectivity"—the unstable heterogeneity that simultaneously constitutes and unfixes even the most "fixed" of names.

In *Troilus and Cressida*, the figures' legendary status threatens to crush their representational viability as "subjects." Subjectivity in this play is posited as the disruptive effect of simultaneous resistance, and subjection, to the determining force of famous names. The characters' names instantly convey the roles they are required to play—by Shakespeare, by the audience, and, as we shall see, by each other. Their very existence is authorized by these roles. Consequently, to attempt to avoid or subvert their "official" functions is to deconstruct their own origins, to somehow "undo" their own conditions of existence and of meaning. It is to engage in a politics of rebellion against a culturally mandated "self." If, as I claim, subjectivity is the experience of one's relationship to one's own identity, then in this play the subjectivity of the characters materializes in and through their "neuroses": through the return, in various forms, of what they attempt to repress.

II

But though she feels as if she's in a play, she is anyway.
Paul McCartney, "Penny Lane"[7]

I'm not an actor. I'm just going to be myself; and I'll continue to play that role.
Richard Nixon, television interview, 1968

Walter Benjamin has suggested that Brechtian actors "show themselves showing themselves."[8] The characters in *Troilus and Cressida*, like the actors who "play" them, also "show" or "play" themselves *within* the world of the play: self-histrionicism or theatricality is built into their texts. At once bearing their infamous names and wandering through the play like displaced persons, Shakespeare's figures here anticipate not only Brecht's "epic" theater, but the theater of the absurd. No other Shakespeare play so explicitly conjures *telos* only to dismantle it. But this dismantling is complicated by the fact that there is built into the core of the play an ineluctable *textual telos:* that is, the action does move toward a preordained end, but this end itself delivers neither a moral nor a providential ethos. It is "merely" textual, insofar as it has been intertextually predetermined, but the ideological corollaries that normally (not, however, "naturally") accompany *telos* have been negated. *Troilus and Cressida* reveals the ideological contingency of a *telos* that is both absolute and utterly devoid of value. What exactly does it mean, that the teleology in the play is entirely retro-textual? That while pointing "forward" it points only backward, to preceding texts? That, while steadily leading us toward the "promised end," the end itself promises absolutely nothing?

No other Shakespeare play gives so strong a sense of being over before it has even begun. We see this adumbrated in the almost immediate reference Pandarus makes to what will, in fact, be the outcome of the play. He and Troilus are arguing about Cressida's beauty in relation to Helen's, when Pandarus, in a disingenuous huff, replies to Troilus' question "Say I she is not fair?" with "I do not care whether you do or no. She's a fool to stay behind her father; let her to the Greeks, and so I'll tell her the next time I see her . . . Pray you speak no more to me; I will leave all as I found it, and there an end" (1.1.80–83,86). The striking sense of stultification which permeates the play is here condensed: to an audience that knows so well that Cressida going to the Greeks will indeed be "the end," these words ironically foreclose on all that will follow. Obviously Pandarus is trying to raise the erotic stakes for Troilus at this moment; but with a doubleness characteristic of much of the play's language, his words, while helping to propagate the "action," undercut the *effects* of action by literally bypassing it—catapulting the audience/reader ahead to what the outcome of the action will inevitably be. Unlike other Shakespeare plays in which the stories may be well known, this play ironically underscores the "always-already-over" nature of its material, creating for the audience the same dilemma it poses for the characters. How is one to believe in what is happening in the present moment when the future moment is already encoded as a past moment?

A sense of enervation underlies this opening palimpsest, as we feel characters to be somehow "going through the motions," and rather ineptly at that. The play seems mimetically to represent the process of reification, a process inevitable in the reinscription of the legendary: it enacts reification as it "hardens," so to speak, the characters and their actions into the "works" that they already, and inescapably, are. "Let her to the Greeks . . . and there an end." In some sense, the play does end here—for all that follows is a drawing out of this moment as Pandarus has articulated it.

The inevitability of the "promised end" is reinforced throughout the play, as references to the future look, Janus-faced, to the past.[9] That the characters are given an awareness of their "previous" existences surfaces occasionally in overt form, such as Hector's anachronistic reference, in 2.2.167, to Aristotle's *Ethics,* a work that won't be written until long after Hector is dead, buried, and converted into legend. But unlike other plays in which historical figures make "unwitting" references to their own historicity (a strategy of irony that privileges the audience's metadramatic position), this play afflicts the characters with a historical "knowledge" that contaminates most, if not all, of their verbal intercourse. We can see this in the strange initial conversation between

Troilus and Cressida. As Troilus expresses to Cressida his "wishes" about their love (3.2.61), she articulates the relationship of "wishes" to expectations, and the relationship of both to "fears": "Blind fear, that seeing reason leads, finds safe footing than blind reason stumbling without fear. To fear the worst oft cures the worse" (68–70). This is and is not a moment of speculation for Cressida (with all its connotations of wishing, hoping, fearing, gambling, and expecting), as she at once tries to envisage ("seeing reason") and to avoid seeing ("blind fear") what the outcome of her behavior will be. When Cressida speaks of fear as a way to "cure the worse," she ostensibly means that fearing the worst leads one to take precautions that will *prevent* the worst. But to "cure" is also to *preserve*. To cure is to effect something, to make good, to bring about. In the Renaissance, a "cure" was also a duty, a charge, a function of office ("Pan hathe cure of sheep," OED). Cressida's surface text speaks her desire to prevent the worst. But the word she uses to speak prevention ("cure") also speaks realization: to "cure" the worst ironically *secures* the worst. She fears the worst because it is what her reason foresees; and in turn, her "seeing reason" ensures that she will indeed secure it. Troilus responds: "O let my lady apprehend no fear: in all Cupid's pageant there is presented no monster" (72–73). Troilus' denial of Cressida's fears takes the rhetorical form of a ritual apostrophe, a "wish" masquerading as a dismissal ("let her not grasp her fears" rather than "there are no fears to grasp"). This denial signals the particular form of Troilus' "neurosis," which is precisely not to "own" what he already knows: not to "apprehend" "monsters." To rename Cressida's fears "monsters" is at once to dismiss them as bogeys and to mark them as revelations, as warnings. His repression of his own "knowledge" of the outcome of this story returns in the form of obsessive, even excessive denial.

If Troilus' "neurosis" is represented by the fact that the very language he uses to deny foreknowledge (here, foreknowledge of loss) encodes it, Cressida's is that she cannot deny what she wishes to deny—that she is "constituted" to be false. For Cressida, fears *are* "monstruosities": predictive shapes of disasters yet to come.[10] Cressida panics after confessing her love to Troilus: "Why have I blabb'd? Who shall be true to us/ When we are so unsecret to ourselves?" (123–124). Cressida's neurosis is her inability to be "secret" to herself—her futile desire to escape what her "identity," compressed into her name, means. Indeed, how can Troilus be "true" to her when they both seem to know that she will be false to him:

> Troilus: What offends you, lady?
> Cressida: Sir, mine own company.
> Troilus: You cannot shun youself.
> Cressida: Let me go and try.
>   I have a kind of self resides with you,
>   But an unkind self, that itself will leave
>   To be another's fool. I would be gone:
>   Where is my wit? I know not what I speak.
> Troilus: Well know they what they speak that speak so wisely.
>   (142–150)

Cressida here articulates what will follow in the betrayal scene, in which she "fools" with Diomed (see 5.2.102). While some critics have read Cressida's confusion at this moment as a sign of her sense of "self-betrayal," I would argue that she wishes to shun herself at this moment precisely because she knows that she will indeed "leave to be another's fool."[11] Cressida here speaks literally (a use of language she frequently insists upon, as we see in her exchanges with Pandarus). If Cressida is divided into two "selves" here, it is because the "kind of self" that resides with Troilus is "Troilus' Cressida," while the "unkind" self (which I read as dissimilar to, unlike, the former self) will be "Diomed's Cressid." When Troilus remarks that she speaks "so wisely," he inadvertently confirms the confession of inevitable betrayal that Cressida has just made. As she says, "to be wise and love / Exceeds man's might" (3.2.154–155). Cressida's "wisdom" is her affliction: How can she simultaneously love Troilus and know that she is "destined," as it were, to betray him?

While both Troilus and Cressida simultaneously speak and repress their proleptic awareness, they demonstrate different forms of neurosis when they recite their vows to each other. To begin with, both refer to themselves in citational terms:

> Troilus: Yet, after all comparisons of truth,
>   As truth's authentic author to be cited,
>   "As true as Troilus" shall crown up the verse
>   And sanctify the numbers. (3.2.178–181)

> Cressida: Yea, let them say, to stick the heart of
>   falsehood, "As false as Cressida." (3.2.193–194)

The language each employs, however, is different. Troilus sees his name as encoding authorship: to be the source of the citation "as true as

Troilus" is to claim the authority of being "truth's authentic author." Cressida, on the other hand, imagines her citationality in terms of the body. To "stick" her name as the "heart of falsehood" is at once to "fix" it and to stab it.

It is not surprising that Troilus' self-reference is "authoritative" whereas Cressida's is "embodied." For this difference in self-conception produces (and reproduces) social forms of gender difference: Troilus becomes the writer, and Cressida the written; Troilus the doer, and Cressida the done; Troilus the artist, and Cressida the artifact. Cressida's neurotic strategy is teleological; her language always speaks the "promised end," anticipating that end in terms that signal her awareness of herself as a made, finished thing: "Things won are done" (1.3.292). Even as she kisses Troilus for the first time she asks herself, "O heavens, what have I done?" Cressida must bear the awareness that every step she takes toward Troilus seals her "fate" as an artifact, and secures her signification as the "heart of falsehood."

Our sense of Cressida's "subjectivity" is produced by the disjunction we perceive in her efforts to inhabit the present through a language that relentlessly thrusts her into the future. But this awareness of the future paradoxically casts every present moment as a past moment. Her life is not only already over, but already written about, and repeatedly at that. Consequently, her "subjectivity" can only be ghostly, insofar as it haunts a life felt to be "done." Her ghostly subjectivity *is* her "neurosis": that which symptomatizes a wish to resist reification while helping to reinforce the conditions that bring it about. This leads Cressida at once to resist (by wishing to slow the play down: "you men will never tarry"), and to abandon any sense of control over, her fate. Of course, on one level this is the only sensible thing to do, since as a "legend" she cannot control the outcome of her story. But on another level such an abandonment is deeply self-defeating, for it constitutes the present moment of love *as* the certain experience of loss. What she feels for Troilus is always contaminated by her knowledge of the future moment of betrayal. Cressida leaves Troilus not because his suspicions of her make her feel "unknown," but for precisely the opposite reason: they make her feel too known—they confirm what she knows must be true (hence false) about herself.

Troilus' neurotic strategy is epistemological: it encodes the denial of future knowledge through a language that looks toward the past, a language obsessed with "origins." Of course, Troilus cannot really be "author of himself" precisely because he is already legendary; and thus his impulse to establish his epistemological priority to his own name is doomed to failure. If Cressida's neurosis projects her into the future, Troilus' projects him into the past. He imagines himself to be prior to those "true swains in love" who are "full of protest, of oath, and big compare" (3.2.171–173), imagines that his "rhymes" and "oaths" are original, not yet "tir'd with iteration" (174). When Troilus discovers that Cressida must go to the Greeks, he doesn't fight to prevent it precisely so as to realize his identity as "truth's authentic author," which, in terms of the play's system of comparative relations, depends upon Cressida's falsehood. Troilus can be "as true as Troilus" only if Cressida is "as false as Cressid." His "denial" of what he knows leads him to hasten the outcome of the story: he hurries away from Cressida after their lovemaking; he immediately accepts the verdict that she must go to the Greeks; he offers no resistance to this verdict. And his resignation is at once pathological and understandable. Like Sophocles' Oedipus, Troilus runs to meet his legendary apotheosis, which *requires* that Cressida be false.

We thus find ourselves moving through a play whose figures constantly remind us of what we already know, figures who seem tired of their own story. This sense of weariness can be accounted for within the "narrative" of the play by the fact that it begins after the Greeks and Trojans have already been at war for seven years. The war goes on and on—and the reasons for war no longer seem convincing or intrinsically important. In fact, they are increasingly incomprehensible. This calls for increasing rationalization on the part of the characters, who must find ways to keep "making sense" of their own activities.

And yet, if the play were "merely" a representation of reinscription, it would be "merely" stultifying, "merely" ennervating. What is so striking about this play is that its sense of ennervation is so striking—so literally affrontive. If the play reveals the naturalizing strategies of ideology, it does so by blatantly laying bare the dead letter already at the heart of the legendary. As conviction wanes, persuasion takes over as the dominant way of evaluating and justifying the activities of war. But persuasion and conviction engage people at different levels. Contingent and perspectival, persuasion depends upon the martialing of visual evidence to confirm rhetorical assertion.[12]

We can see how conviction devolves into persuasion in the play's two major ideological scenes: the dissertation on order in the Greek council (Act 1, scene 3), and that on value in the Trojan council (Act 2, scene 2). But before turning to these scenes, I would like to look at the circumstances that trigger or generate the *need* for them. The metadramatic conditions of debate that permeated Jacobean culture have been elucidated elsewhere: briefly, these consist of a questioning of absolute, essentialist, providential values in Jacobean culture even while such an ideology was being inscribed and administered by James himself—a relativizing, perspectivizing tendency that counterposed the contingent against what was felt to be a myth of the absolute.[13] But within the play, these metadramatic concerns are compressed and embodied in two very specific circumstances. The first, within the Trojan world, is Paris' possession of Helen. The second, within the Greek camp, is Achilles' contemptuous reluctance to fight. In order to unpack the debates from these compressed instances, we should see that both circumstances generate the necessity for debate, and do so in similar ways.

The possession of Helen is the cause of the Trojan debate on "value," as well as its condition and its effect. If the play is full of questions about who stands for what and how one identifies someone, its mode of interrogation is relentlessly comparative. That is, people are known or understood only in relation to what or who they are like or unlike. Value itself can be determined only through traversals of likeness and difference. The kidnapping and holding of Helen is important only insofar as it enables several kinds of "commerce" between Greek and Trojan men. Helen (and Cressida) are the conduits through which these men form crucial political and psychological connections with one another. Through the holding of Helen, difference is established, and with difference (in the language of the play, "distinction") "reputation" is built and confirmed. Insofar as the possession of Helen authorizes "reputation," it confirms the intertextual identity of the men, provides them with a certain sense of citational presence. But citational presence is built on a substructure of absence: a sense of textual identity ("repute") purchased at the expense of a sense of subjectivity.

In Act 1, scene 1, Pandarus and Troilus establish the "this is and is not" motif that will bedevil the issue of identification in the play. Both use the word "comparison" with regard to Cressida. Pandarus claims that "And her hair were not somewhat darker than Helen's—well, go to, there were no more comparison between the women" (40–41). And Troilus, in itemizing Cressida's charms, describes Cressida's hand, "In whose comparison all whites are ink" (55–56). Even earlier, Troilus compares his weakness, tameness, fondness, and lack of skill and practice to the Greeks' strength, skill, fierceness, and valor (1.1.4–11). This language of comparison quickly devolves into a kind of absurd relativizing, as Pandarus says, "let her be as she is: if she be fair, 'tis the better for her; and she be not, she has the mends in her own hands" (66–68), and "Because she's kin to me, therefore she's not so fair as Helen. And she were not kin to me, she would be as fair o' Friday as Helen is o' Sunday. But what care I? I care not and she were a blackamoor, 'tis all one to me" (74–78). Both men are comparing Cressida in different terms, however, as Troilus speaks the language of the pining Petrarchan lover and Pandarus speaks a language of comparison that is rooted in the play's center of political and psychological "value."

For Pandarus, Cressida is most salable when she can be made to appear most like Helen. However, his strategy has a way of undoing what it does. By emphasizing how like Helen Cressida is, he points up the fact that there is nothing special about or particular to Helen that is not finally arbitrary—Cressida is as fair on Friday as Helen on Sunday, Helen's hair is a bit lighter than Cressida's, but what of that, etc. In this way, Helen is used as that touchstone against which value is judged, but also as that which is curiously stripped of any inherent value, of any value that is not itself produced *by the comparison.* Troilus seems to recognize this, as he remarks after Pandarus exits: "Fools on both sides, Helen must needs be fair / When with your blood you daily paint her thus" (90–91). Troilus here understands that Helen's "fairness" functions tropically as a *hysteron proteron:* a proleptic teleology for the war which reconstructs effects as causes.

Even though Troilus recognizes the extent to which Helen's value is constructed by those who wish to "use" her as the enabler for other kinds of commerce (see his oration on value, 2.2.62–96), he still finds himself unable to resist the comparison between the two women. Troilus seems to vacillate between two vantage points: one which idealizes Cressida by metaphorizing, cataloging, and comparing her charms in a language of Petrarchan rhetoric, and one which sees what is rank at the heart of the war, and speaks a language of sardonic realism. But these two "poles" are not as distinct as Troilus would perhaps like to believe. In Act 1, scene 1, after Aeneas tells him of Paris' wounds, Troilus responds: "Let Paris bleed, 'tis but a scar to scorn: / Paris is gor'd with Menelaus' horn." On one level, this comment is meant to express contempt for Menelaus by trivializing his capacity to inflict wounds of any consequence; but it also pulls Paris into its contemptuous indictment. For Paris to be gor'd with Menelaus' horn is for both men to suffer the ignominious consequences of cuckoldry. And Helen disappears entirely here, synecdochized into the horn which "connects" Menelaus and Paris in the bonds of "homosociality."[14] This phrase conjures an image of sexual penetration not between Helen and Paris, but between the two men, with Helen serving merely as the "horn" which both humiliates Menelaus and penetrates Paris. Taking shape in Troilus' language of "heterosexuality" is a fantasy of sadomasochistic homoeroticism, a fantasy (as we shall see later) that haunts all sexuality in this play. We are led to wonder how Troilus can idealize Cressida while denigrating Helen, particularly since Cressida's erotic "value" is simultaneously produced by and with Helen's. The very terms that heighten Cressida's value within this world degrade her. She is and is not idealized.

That Helen serves both as enabler of conflict and as enabler of erotic commerce reveals her central signifying power in the play. But this power is not hers to wield. Rather, it is available to the men in the play to use on a number of different fronts in their own relations to each other. The "transcendent" Helen is, in fact, the arbitrary signifier that confers "degree" or distinction on the possessor.[15] The Trojans and Greeks define and distinguish themselves according to who has possession of Helen. In some sense, Helen is the phallic signifier—the use of which consolidates masculine identity and difference. And yet, as phallic signifier, Helen is curiously inadequate. Even as the men render themselves distinct by taking possession of Helen, they also render themselves similar by virtue of the fact that they "share" her, as it were. That is, insofar as one camp as opposed to the other "has" Helen, the two parties remain distinct. But insofar as both camps have "had" her at different times, the "opposition" between them seems to collapse. The two sides are perilously "like" each other.

The war, as institutionalized, official "difference," is effective only so long as the enabling signifier retains its original value. The problem in the play is that as the war goes on, the differences become increasingly effaced by the likenesses—Helen, as differentiating object, threatens to lose her value as that which confers distinction. Helen is first assigned her value ("what's aught but as 'tis valued?"), so that the attribution can then be "naturalized" and read back as something intrinsic to Helen herself. But in order for the fiction of "degree" to work in the play, the characters must deny their own sense of cognitive dissonance—must continually ward off their knowledge that they are the producers rather than the possessors of Helen's value. Thus, Helen becomes the characterological equivalent of the legendary text: the site at which both authenticity and "authority" are fabricated—where they are alternately made and "found," depending upon the uses to which the text is put by those who "read" it. The more Helen is *produced* as a rhetorical figure of and for "value," the more she is *reduced* as a mimetic figure, as a "presence" on the stage. The extent to which she is deployed as enabling fiction—for war, for comparison, for homo- and heteroeroticism, for identity itself—is equal to the extent to which she is theatrically and mimetically attenuated.

Thus, Helen is paradigmatic of what happens throughout the play, as characters find themselves and one another etiolated by their own citationality, by a prior textual existence that threatens always to turn them from mimetic into rhetorical figures for others to use. This prior textual identity renders them "unsecret" (that is, always already disclosed) to themselves in direct proportion to their availability to others for rhetorical use. No wonder Cressida doesn't recognize Helen at the beginning of Act 1, scene 2. Helen's function in the play is almost entirely tropic: she has no significance apart from or outside of whatever rhetorical strategy she enables for others. Troilus' query, "What's aught but as 'tis valued?" can be read as "Who has any identity that has not been written for them rather than by them"? In short, is there anything "original" or "essential" at the heart of anyone?

In problematic ways, Hamlet attempts to answer this question by claiming to have "that within which passeth show." But if, as Francis Barker has argued, Hamlet "utters a first demand for the modern subject," that demand is *enacted* in *Troilus and Cressida*.[16] We feel in this play a longing for a "modern subject" pushed to a critical degree by the simultaneous reification and emptying out of "identity" that the play both rhetorically and formally enacts. Of course, to represent a longing for something is not to represent the thing itself. There is, however, something about the play that leads even antiessentialist critics to confuse longing with presence. Jonathan Dollimore, for example, while persuasively laying out the ideological problematics of subjectivity in Shakespeare's plays, makes precisely this mistake. Speaking generally about the plays, Dollimore tells us that "in this period the two themes which I have been exploring—the rejection of Christian-stoic accounts of identity and the subversion of providentialist orthodoxy—were inextricably linked: the sense that reality can no longer be adequately explained in terms of an in-forming absolute goes hand in hand with the realisation that subjectivity is not constituted by a fixed, unchanging essence."[17]

This general formulation seems right—but Dollimore then proceeds

to make several startling remarks about the character of Troilus that signal a difficulty in applying theory to text. In considering the crucial
scene in which Troilus witnesses Cressida's crossing over to the Greek
camp and Diomedes, Dollimore remarks that "once Troilus has witnessed what he sees as Cressida's betrayal he cannot again be the same
person. Shattered idealism finds concentrated expression in disjunction
. . . What happens to Troilus is . . . [that] *misfortune* brutalises him" (*Radical Tragedy*, p. 41, italics added). Dollimore speaks of Troilus here as if
prior to this "shattering" moment he were a firmly constituted subject,
suffering in the face of "misfortune" the loss of a previously stable identity. He speaks of Troilus' "shattered idealism" as if this idealism were
itself, *prior* to the destabilizing moment, unproblematic.[18] In reading
Troilus this way, Dollimore replicates the same kind of nostalgia for a
lost "original" subjectivity that the play continually posits and subverts.
Troilus "cannot again be the *same person*"? What does such a statement
mean? Was he ever the "same person," a unified subject, even if only
unified by his own "idealism"?

In implying that Troilus was a unified subject prior to Cressida's
"betrayal," a "sensitive person" (p. 41) who is subsequently "brutalised
by misfortune," Dollimore absolves Troilus of any responsibility for,
complicity in, or authorship of Cressida's betrayal/dilemma. Thus,
Dollimore, when he turns to the text, reproduces the essentialism that,
in his larger theory, he claims the play ironizes. I point this out not to
detract from the considerable power of his theoretical claims, but to il-
lustrate a point I raised in the opening of this chapter: that *Troilus and
Cressida* invites and anticipates certain kinds of theorizing only to short-
circuit them when one attempts to apply them to the characters. What is
it about the play that generates this inadvertent essentializing? Why do
critics who rightly point out the play's antiessentialist bias slip when
they consider the characters themselves?

We may, I think, answer these questions by turning to an analysis of
the characters' efforts to "confirm" their textual identities on the visual
plane—to seek empirical "evidence" that will corroborate and *constitute*
the strangely emptied, "merely" textual knowledge that pervades the
play. The visual is turned to throughout the play as a way to bridge the
gap between what one "knows," through the language of inter- and in-
tratextual "reputation" about self and others, and those elements which
undercut this knowledge. Characters compare what they see with what
they have heard or been told about one another, in an effort to attach a
present, viable meaning, a "signified," to what seems to be a disjointed,

decathected, and emptied set of signifiers. One of the most jarring aspects of the play is the way it represents a world in which reputation, honor, and renown are obsessions, yet seem bizarrely devoid of any power to signify because they cannot be hooked up to any *thing*—they remain decathected from the bodies from which they supposedly derive.

> Beauty itself doth of itself persuade
> The eyes of men without an orator;
> What needeth then apologies be made
> To set forth that which is so singular?
> *The Rape of Lucrece*, 29–32

The conundrum at the heart of *Troilus and Cressida* is that *nothing* doth of itself persuade without an orator, without a concomitant narrative or verbal reconstruction. The search for that "which is so singular" and for an unmediated way to "set [it] forth" seems doomed by the citational identity of these notorious figures, who can be present neither to themselves nor to others without recourse to narrative reference, without referring to their own legendary citationality.

But against this etiolation, the play enacts its own essentialist longing for something self-evident, something apprehendable without the publishing of rhetoric and narrative authority—a sense of presence that can be empirically grounded. This peculiar longing (one that leads critics to slip into positivistic language in spite of themselves) is generated, I would argue, by the physical and visual conditions of the theater itself. "Playing" opens up an aleatory space in which the "then" of narrative can be set against the "now" of drama—a space in which the familiar ("unsecret") can be "estranged." Drama brings together the textual and the visual, the inscribed and the mimetic, the "original text" and the repeatable performance. As a consequence, alterity to textual identity is an inevitable *condition* of theater, since there are always at least "two" of each character—the written character and the figure on the stage, the actor playing the role.

We can see this duplicity in the complex way the play thematizes the relationship between the mimetic and the citational, the specular and the rhetorical. *Troilus and Cressida* enacts the subversive relation of the mimetic to authorized discourse (here represented as legendary identity) in terms of the characters' struggle to construct some kind of alterity to their "authorized" roles. This impulse achieves its paradigmatic expression in Ulysses' description of the mummery in Achilles' tent

(1.3.145–184), not only because it is an explicitly parodic moment, in which characters grotesquely parody other characters, but more insidiously (and effectively) because the characters who are staging this parody are themselves at the center of the official world. The generals, the Greek camp, the entire Greek enterprise, depend upon Achilles for their success. As their trump card, he elicits their dependence upon him; but their dependence upon him elicits his contempt for them. In a perversion of the "theme of honor," Achilles feels loathing for those who have cast him as "hero" in this play.

The mummery enacted by Patroclus in Achilles' tent enrages Ulysses and Agamemnon not merely because it is "disrespectful" of the Greek generals and what they represent, but because its disrespect is mimetic. Patroclus mimics or acts out the roles of Agamemnon and Nestor, and in doing so, transgresses their authorized "texts" by subversively re-creating them in mimetic terms—terms which "translate" them from epic to comic figures. Agamemnon's "great oratory and authoritative presence" become bluster and puffery, swaggering ineffectuality; Nestor's experience and aged wisdom become hoary incompetence. Achilles' tent becomes the site of subversive theater—a space in which legendary texts (in this case, Agamemnon and Nestor) are transgressed by performance and mime.[19] In this space, mimesis takes precisely those most underlined aspects of authorized "identity" and destabilizes them.

When Ulysses begins his diatribe, what irks him most about the "pageantry" in Achilles' tent is that what he would term "slander," Patroclus calls "imitation" (1.3.150). And yet, as Ulysses describes this so-called "slander" he reminds us of the "fusty stuff" (1.3.161) we have in fact already heard from the long-winded Agamemnon earlier in the scene. There is a double irony here, as Ulysses, in renaming Patroclus' "imitation" "slander," speaks in a way that demonstrates precisely the mimetic accuracy of Patroclus' rendition of Agamemnon. The mimetic triumphs, despite Ulysses' attempt to rename it "slander."

When Nestor joins in to indict Ajax and Thersites, he claims, in 1.3.185, that they act "in imitation of these twain" (Achilles and Patroclus). What becomes clear is that the problem isn't "slander" but, rather, the potential metastasis of imitation. Even Ulysses is infected as he mimics Patroclus' mimicry. Mimesis threatens an endless chain of imitation in which "versions" become increasingly distant from their supposed "originals." This is where the language of comparison we noted earlier intersects with the topos of imitation: Cressida is "like"

Helen, Troilus is "like" Paris, Menelaus is "like" Paris, Achilles is "like" Agamemnon (since opinion crowns him with an "imperial voice"). Whereas dramatic mimesis is dangerous because of the difference it inevitably opens up between version and "original," rhetorical comparison is dangerous because it reveals that no "distinction," no "degree," is inherent or "original"—that the language of comparison constitutes rather than reflects differences in ways that, like dramatic mimesis, threaten the very notion of origins. Subversive imitation threatens not only "degree" as Ulysses choreographs it spatially (in his Elizabethan "cosmography") but temporal "distinction" as well.

We see temporal "distinction" emerge as perhaps an even greater concern, as Ulysses continues:

> They tax our policy and call it cowardice,
> Count wisdom as no member of the war,
> Forestall prescience, and esteem no act
> But that of hand. The still and mental parts,
> That do contrive how many hands shall strike
> When fitness calls them on and know by measure
> Of their observant toil the enemy's weight—
> Why, this hath not a finger's dignity.
> They call this bed-work, mapp'ry, closet-war;
> So that the ram that batters down the wall,
> For the great swinge and rudeness of his poise,
> They place before his hand that made the engine,
> Or those that with the fineness of their souls
> By reason guide his execution. (1.3.197–210)

Two issues are foregrounded here. The first is the problem of *priority* (both in its chronological and hierarchical senses), and the second, the problem of authorship. But these two are crucially linked. When Ulysses claims that they "forestall prescience," "esteeming no act but that of hand," he presumably means that they set no store on planning ahead, on imagining possible future scenarios and strategizing accordingly; rather, they value the "execution," the actual performance of the actions. But Degree is shak'd here also because Achilles not only fails to value the "still and mental parts" that "contrive how many hands shall strike," but fails to recognize the literal, temporal *priority* of that "contrivance"—that the "writing" of it came first and thus, for Ulysses, is more "real," more important.

In forestalling (obstructing, hindering) prescience or foreknowledge,

Achilles denies the textual (represented here by the "mental parts" that "author" action) both its epistemological *and* teleological priority. To "place before his hand that made the engine" the "engine" is spatially and temporally to displace *authorship* itself. And if authorship is threatened, so is its work—the maps, plans, texts, and figures that encode and represent the strategies of war. Thus, in denying the causal force of "prescience," Achilles is denying the validity of textual determination. Ulysses' anxiety is that for Achilles, playing, and not the play, is the thing.

For Ulysses, if "reason" doesn't "guide the execution," it cannot so easily claim what is *produced* by the execution. Without such "guidance" or "contrivance," "acts of hand" deny any notion of origin that derives from someone other than the actor himself: acts of hand deny priority. Consequently, whatever they produce cannot be "legitimately" appropriated by the "hand that made the engine." Throughout Ulysses' diatribe, authorial power is linked to phallic power; and both are linked to patriarchal power as the play registers the fear that such potency, such power to generate, and its products or consequences, will escape patrimonial control—in this instance, will produce new performances (and hence, competing ideologies) unforeseen by Ulysses' authorial and authoritative "prescience." For to make the engine and to guide its execution is to lay claim to its effects. As the Greek camp's CEO (Agamemnon is, after all, merely a corporate figurehead), Ulysses will not relinquish to his chief laborers the credit for their labors.

Ulysses speaks like a disgruntled author (and father) whose "characters" (sons) forget, in Unamuno-esque fashion, whence they derive their existence. We might even say that Ulysses speaks like a disgruntled Homer, whose "fineness of soul" is unappreciated. Ulysses refers repeatedly to hands and fingers, complaining that the soldiers "esteem no act / But that of hand." Hands are here lined up with actions, with performance. But hands and fingers are also used for writing—the "hand that made the engine." What disturbs Ulysses here is the displacement, the appropriation, of the writing "hand"—the "author's" hand—by the acting hand, the performing hand. Mimetic disrespect turns the writer into the written, or the figure who represents into yet another represented figure. Depriving authority of its myth of self-authorship (and, by extension, its "legitimate" claim of authorship of others), mimetic disrespect consequently deprives it of interpretive hegemony as well—denies it exclusive "rights" over the uses of texts.

Patroclus "mimes" Agamemnon and Nestor: Achilles "Cries 'Excellent! 'Tis Agamemnon right!'" (164), "'Tis Nestor right!" (170). Ulysses claims it is not Agamemnon or Nestor "right," that it is "ridiculous slander." But we see for ourselves that it is exceedingly close to Agamemnon "himself." This is and is not Agamemnon; this is and is not Nestor. And then, pat Aeneas comes, to stand directly in front of "Agamemnon right," to look upon "his kingly eyes," his "imperial looks," and fail to "know them from eyes of other mortals" (see 1.3.215–252 passim). The subversion of authority enacted through Patroclus' "imitation" and the displacement of "authorship" effected by putting the "engine" before its designer are mimetically reinforced by Aeneas' inability to discern "which is that god in office, guiding men? / Which is the high and mighty Agamemnon?" (1.3.230–231).

This inability, following Ulysses' description of and response to the "slanderous" Patroclan theater, illustrates the way in which the play both posits and deconstructs an essentialist "reading" of the characters. In order for Ulysses to construct Patroclus' "imitations" as "slanders," he must assume that there is a "real" Agamemnon, a "true" Nestor— entities "fixed" and stable in their characterological properties, which these imitations misrepresent. We see, however, that Agamemnon is not necessarily a "god in office," not the entity Ulysses describes earlier in the scene as the "great commander, nerves and bone of Greece" (1.3.55). Like so much of Ulysses' language in this scene, the words he uses at once speak his ideology and its opposition. His description of Agamemnon's "topless deputation," in its ideological deployment, speaks the language of absolute hierarchy, of proper "degree"; but on its oppositional axis, it beheads Agamemnon by suggesting his ineffectiveness as a commander, his failure to serve as a guiding force for his troops. Ulysses, in the very process of rhetorically addressing Agamemnon as the occupant of the highest "authentic place" among them inadvertently reveals that the place is empty.

But if Agamemnon doesn't fit Ulysses' rhetorical construction of him, and if he doesn't occupy the "place" that such a construction is designed to "authenticate," we still cannot say that Agamemnon doesn't fit anywhere at all, that we see nothing "stable" about him whatsoever. The problem is the location of this "stability": in whose representational "camp"—Ulysses' (textual) or Patroclus' (mimetic)—we find it. That we hear Agamemnon speak a fusty language of hyperbole inclines us toward Patroclus' representation. But this inclination becomes a certainty when we see Aeneas fail to recognize that he is speaking *with* Agamemnon. Aeneas enters the Greek camp equipped with the same ideological language Ulysses and Nestor use when they address Agamemnon. Of course, there is more than a hint of sarcasm in Aeneas' tone; but he asks to speak to the great, godlike Agamemnon, whose visage *should* show differently from other men's—and he asks Agamemnon himself how he will recognize this great man. When, some thirty lines into their exchange, Aeneas (still apparently unaware) addresses Agamemnon in the generic "Greek" (1.3.245), he demonstrates the absolute difference between the rhetorical, ideological construction of Agamemnon—the "topless," peerless, *inimitable* "god in office"—and the figure in front of him, who is indistinguishable from those who surround him, and is, as Patroclus proves, most "imitable." This discrepancy reveals the vacancy of the office, the arbitrariness of the signifiers, the contingency of "degree," and the failure of "reputation" to anchor, secure, and—more important—to render visible an authorized identity.

III

I want people to be able to recognize me by just looking at a caricature of me that has no name on it. You see, I want to be great, and you can recognize great people like Muhammed Ali and Bob Hope by just looking at a nameless caricature. When everybody can look at my caricature and say, "That's him, that's Richard Pryor!" then I'll be great.
Richard Pryor, *Washington Post*, 15 April 1976[20]

Obviously, Richard Pryor can say this because he lives in a world in which the dominant mode of "publishing" identity is visual. Entertainers today become famous because we see their faces before us on television, in magazines and newspapers, and in films. I'd like to suggest, however, that a similar fantasy about the visual runs throughout *Troilus and Cressida*. For if the fame of the characters is the result of their intertextual citationality, if their notorious deeds and lives can only be conjured by their names, then built into the very heart of their fame is the eclipse of their faces, the gratuitousness of their physical presence. To be famous by name only is already to be relegated to the past: to be, paradoxically, *absent*. What the visual would secure for Pryor—to have his unique facial features etched into the public eye—is longed for by these famous figures. A famous name, a reputation, is "imitable," but a face is not.

To be instantly recognizable without the need for one's name, or, rather, to have the public instantly able to conjure one's name by seeing one's face, is a fantasy deployed to counteract the void of rhetorical citationality, a fantasy that figures a desire to replace an identity that is only *referred to* with one that is *mirrored*. To have one's face recognized prior to the announcement of one's name (for Pryor, prior to "Pryor") is to have one's present, physical existence confirmed—to be, in the language of object-relations theory, mirrored. It is also, in the language of Lacanian psychoanalysis, to fantasize a return from the realm of the symbolic to the immediacy of that of the imaginary—from the triadic relationship determined by the phallic (signifying) presence of the father to the diadic relationship determined by the apprehension of one's reflection in the eyes of the mother, and of one's image in the mirror. If one is "merely" a reference between two others, one is "identified," but displaced in the process—or, rather, replaced—by one's symbolic "value." But to be mirrored is to be returned, as it were, to a diadic relationship: one's physical presence is required.

Laura Mulvey, in her well-known analysis of the scopophilia built into modern film, describes this process in terms useful here: "This mirror-moment . . . constitutes the matrix of the imaginary, of recognition/misrecognition and identification, and hence of the first articulation of the "I", of subjectivity. This is a moment when an older fascination with looking (at the mother's face, for an obvious example) collides with the initial inklings of self-awareness."[21] The play's "this is and is not" paradigm reveals precisely the "collision" Mulvey describes: it forms the play's matrix of recognition/misrecognition and identification. But this relationship between the self-awareness produced by the mother's gaze and the "congealing" of identity produced by the mirror image is itself problematized, and transformed within the play into a conflict between the need to exist in the eyes of an other and the need to control the gender of that other. For if the Lacanian "imaginary" posits a pre-Oedipal state of reflection and fascination existing between mother and child, in this play it is the female who "intrudes on the imaginary satisfaction of dual fascination."[22] The male fantasy in this play is to move freely between the symbolic (the realm of "honor," renown, reputation) and the imaginary (the realm of the confirming, immediate gaze), without any of the threats posed by the "intrusion" of women.

But such movement cannot occur without the use of women. As Eve Sedgwick has said about the set of relations between men that she terms "the homosocial," "My point is not . . . that we are here in the presence of homosexuality . . . but rather that we are in the presence of male heterosexual desire, in the form of a desire to consolidate partnership with authoritative males in and through the bodies of women" (*Between Men*, p. 38). And the purpose of consolidating this "partnership" is precisely to *escape* the need for confirmation from the eyes of women. René Girard, while arguing rightly that "Helen is at the center of the Trojan war, its object or rather its pretext," is wrong in claiming that "thousands of rival desires converge upon Helen."[23] Helen is "at the center"—but as a fulcrum rather than as a core. Helen is, as Troilus says, "a theme of honor and renown,/ A spur to valiant and magnanimous deeds" (2.2.200–201): she provides the material for the construction of this male world of mutual fascination and obsession. By using women as "themes and spurs of honor," the male characters can confirm their identities in the realm of the symbolic: they can become their "names." And by appropriating the diadic, imaginary relationship to the realm of the homosocial, by seeking reflection in the eyes of other men, the male characters can conflate the gaze of a differently gendered "other" with the gaze at the self in the mirror, thus eliding the female from the realm of the imaginary. But why is it necessary to eliminate women from this circuit? What exactly is the threat of the female in this play?

If the use of Helen (and, in general, a "traffic" in women) is necessary to confirm masculine identity, actual sexual engagement with women can dissolve it.[24] Ulysses' complaint in Act 1, scene 3, about Achilles' tent "theater" clearly displays his anxiety about maintaining control over the production and use of texts; but it is also shot through with sexual anxiety. What really inflames him is that his policy is called "bed-work," a term which implies sexual activity in the domestic realm. An opposition is set up throughout the play between "bed-work" and "ram-work." When Achilles and Patroclus call Ulysses' policy bed-work, they transpose the general's arena from battlefield to bedchamber, placing him in a "closet-war."

But Achilles' raillery goes further than merely relocating Ulysses. It renders him ineffective even in this new location. Ulysses is put in the closet and emasculated. To "count wisdom as no member of the war" is to generate a split between thought and action, and to characterize that division in terms of effeminacy versus phallic aggression. Ulysses' "part," his "member" as it were, is "still and mental," granted not even "a finger's dignity." Ulysses' wisdom is here rewritten as a kind of impotence, against which the "large Achilles" is figured as the phallic ram that batters down the wall, whose "rudeness of poise" (blatant, forceful weight or bulk) has "great swinge"—massive, potentially unruly violence—without "reason guiding the execution." In this play, any member that is not used for war is without dignity—literally unerect—and especially members used for actual "bed-work." What keeps the Greek phallus erect is precisely the fact that Helen is in Paris' bed, and not Menelaus'. The possession of Helen, as the excuse for the war, provides a metaphorics of sexual aggression that is paradoxically rendered impotent when applied to sexual activity. To have sex in the play is to be quite dis-armed.

But Ulysses has his revenge on Achilles in Act 3, scene 3, by suggesting that Achilles is also engaged in a "closet-war," that the "commerce [he] has had with Troy" (204) is sexual:

> Ulysses: The cry went once on thee,
>   And still it might, and yet it may again
>   If thou wouldst not entomb thyself alive
>   And case thy reputation in thy tent . . .
> Achilles: Of this my privacy
>   I have strong reasons.
> Ulysses: But 'gainst your privacy
>   The reasons are more potent and heroical:
>   'Tis known, Achilles, that you are in love
>   With one of Priam's daughters. (184–195)

To be "entombed alive," "cased" in a "tent," is, Ulysses implies, to be in a closet, a bedchamber; and when Achilles claims these as privileges of his "privacy," Ulysses equates his "privacy" with impotence. The suggestion here is that Achilles' supposed "love" for Polyxena renders him less "potent and heroical." According to Ulysses, "better it would fit Achilles much / To throw down Hector than Polyxena" (206–207). "Throwing down" takes on the double meaning of bedding and fighting, as bed-work becomes a poor substitute (ill-fitting) for ram-work. If heterosexual activity is spoken of in terms of war, war is spoken of in terms of homoeroticized sex.

This homoeroticizing of warfare permeates the play, as we see earlier, in Act 1, scene 3, when Aeneas brings Hector's challenge to the Greek camp, asking "if there be one among the fair'st of Greece" (264) who dares avow love for his mistress "in other arms than hers" (271). Aeneas' explicitly sexualized language of warfare here equates sexual valor with "avowals" made in martial arms. The "fair'st of Greece" are, in his terms, the men.[25] The possession of Helen, the "sign" of public "desire," provides the conditions necessary for war; while war provides the conditions necessary for what I would argue is the production of a "myth" of heterosexual desire. In other words, sexual desire in this play, constructed around the possession of Helen, is itself a profoundly ideological category, one that reproduces the conditions that authorize war. But the war in turn only reproduces the conditions that enable desire; and so the play, in Althusser's terms, actually "produces" nothing but its own conditions of reproduction.[26] We might posit the circuit thus: possession of Helen generates desire for war, desire for war generates desire for Helen, desire for Helen generates mimetic desire, mimetic desire generates competitive identification between Greek and Trojan men, competitive identification generates homoerotic aggression, homoerotic aggression generates desire for more war, and, finally, desire for more war reproduces desire for Helen.

Situating itself in conditions of enervation, repetition, and exhaustion, the play openly poses the problem of how to convince its legendary characters to keep fighting. An ideology must be constructed that will enable the war (and consequently the retelling of this story) to continue, for only its continuance will enable these figures to "become" their own legends. The desire for Helen *is* this enabling ideology: one that simultaneously constitutes and is constituted by conditions which derive their coercive power from their ability to conflate public and private forms of desire while maintaining a myth of the difference between them. The purpose of this myth is to disguise intertextual compulsion (the fact that these figures are literally predetermined to act in a particular way) as personal agency, as "voluntary" activity. While the characters profess to be deeply disillusioned about the fight waged over a "cuckold and a whore," the "production value" of Helen's beauty underwrites the actions that enable the male heroes to "recognize" one another, to generate reputations and renown among themselves. Helen and the war she enables provide these male characters with the necessary means for realizing their notorious identities, as well as for experiencing a kind of displaced sexuality that will not threaten them with loss of "distinction" in their joys.

But controlling the use of Helen's beauty is crucial, since the accompanying fear is that female beauty not appropriated by male agency and turned toward male ends carries with it the threat of the Medusa: that which turns men to stone (rendering them at once rigidly "erect" and incapable of the *use* of that erection). In this play however, castration anxiety is not the ultimate threat. As Nancy Vickers has said about the Medusa's head, "that threat is also a threat of forgetting."[27] And being forgotten would mean losing "distinction," losing even the desire for "reputation." Female beauty may be, as Mulvey puts it, "an indispensable element of spectacle . . . yet [the beautiful woman's] visual presence tends to work against the development of a story line, to freeze the flow of action in moments of erotic contemplation" ("Visual Pleasure," p. 11). Anything that works against the story line, that freezes the flow of action, threatens to turn these heroes to stone. And if they cease moving, fighting, acting out their roles, they cannot make "legends" of themselves. Paradoxically, any "autonomy" in this play is represented as the male ability to turn the self to stone. But in turning themselves into legends, the male characters can at least avoid the terror of being consigned to oblivion, of ceasing to exist in the eyes of the world.

For to be consigned to oblivion is the opposite of being signed into legend. But literature is filled with male heroes who must renounce their "privacy" in order to achieve renown. This is the choice Aeneas is forced to make in the *Aeneid*. As Leo Braudy puts it, "Fame is a crucial question for Virgil, because it is the place where personal desire confronts historic destiny."[28] Fame is a crucial question for other authors as well; but the confrontation it forces between "personal desire" and "historic destiny" does not always necessitate a choice between the two.

In *Troilus and Cressida*, "personal" or private desire is a myth, one built out of the same structures that constitute public desire; and public desire is precisely what confirms the "historic destiny" of these legendary figures. That is to say, Troilus' love for Cressida exists in his mind as his own "private realm"—his world apart from the battlefield, apart from the fight to keep Helen. And yet, the fact that he and Pandarus "produce" Cressida's desirability by comparing her relentlessly to Helen, whose desirability is itself always destined for public commerce and consumption, reveals the artificial "distinction" between public and "private" forms of desire, a distinction necessary for Troilus' fiction of himself as "idealistic" lover. Thus, far from providing Troilus with "private" experience, a refuge from the crass world of public "commerce," the desire he produces for Cressida is inevitably contaminated by its metonymic connection to its paradigmatic source.

Consequently, to say that the play forces a "choice" between "privacy" and honor, "personal desire" and "historic destiny," "closet war" and Trojan war, would be to imbricate ourselves in the characters' web of bad faith. For these legendary male figures can conceive of themselves as heroes only by maintaining a fiction of "private existence," something that they can then "renounce" for the onerous but "inevitable" burdens of historic destiny. In short, realizing a myth of heroism in this play depends upon renouncing a myth of "personal desire." *Troilus and Cressida,* however, demonstrates that the two are mutually constituting, and inextricable from each other, just as identity and subjectivity are inextricable. The translation, then, of "heterosexual desire" into homoerotic warfare is a function of the play's ideological legerdemain: the way it attempts to package "historic destiny" *as* personal desire.

In *Anti-Oedipus: Capitalism and Schizophrenia,* Gilles Deleuze and Félix Guattari have asserted that "there is only desire, and social production, and nothing else."[29] As provocative as this claim is, it essentializes desire by putting it in a compound, rather than reciprocal, relation with social production. However, if we slightly revise this claim, we can see that Shakespeare's play performs its own kind of *materialist* psychoanalysis by demonstrating that there is only desire *as* social production, and nothing else. After all, everyone in this play realizes that the holding of Helen is not the point. The point, rather, is: how do we get these epic figures to act out yet again their designated roles, once more, with feeling? How do we get Hector and Achilles to keep being Hector and Achilles? These figures must trick themselves into believing that the war is worth fighting, because without such conviction, the narrative stops, the story ends, legendary identity cannot be reproduced, marketed, and staged.

When Ulysses says to Achilles in Act 3, scene 3, that no man "feels what he owes, but by reflection" (99), Achilles confirms the observation:

> eye to eye oppos'd
> Salutes each other with each other's form;
> For speculation turns not to itself
> Till it hath travell'd and is mirror'd there
> Where it may see itself. (107–111)

We now have the myth of "private" motivation for this public war between Greek and Trojan men; and it tells us that the aim of the "speculation," the hazarding all upon the "market value" of Helen, is to become visible, present to oneself, to experience as viable subjectivity an identity that has been emptied by its own intertextual redundancy. But according to Ulysses, Achilles' mirroring is not enough:

> I do not strain at the position—
> It is familiar—but at the author's drift,
> Who in his circumstance expressly proves
> That no man is the lord of anything,
> Though in and of him there be much consisting,
> Till he communicate his parts to others;
> Nor doth he of himself know them for aught,
> Till he behold them form'd in the applause
> Where th'are extended . . . (3.3.112–120)

For Ulysses, ever concerned with "authorship," seeing and being seen are merely prologue. Until one is "communicated," turned into reproducible matter, one doesn't know oneself "for aught." Shot through with imaginary representations, the play nevertheless reveals these figures' relationships to their "real conditions of existence"—or, to put it more plainly, although they feel as if they're in a play, they are anyway.

Despite the longing these male figures feel to "live and die" in each others' eyes, the nature of their "matter" guarantees that even this confirmation is finally only a strategy of the legendary machine, a way of insuring that they will meet their own notorious apotheoses. This exchange between Ulysses and Achilles underscores the tension in the play between a desire for presence that can be secured through vision, a sense of immediacy provided only by a mutual salute of "eye to eye"; and an *ideology* of presence (the "author's drift"), which is generated not by two bodies face to face but, rather, by the translation of bodies into texts to be circulated, commodities for consumption by an audience that knows the outcome of this story and expects to get what it pays for. But this translation is, as we have also seen, not entirely without rewards. Through "reputation"—that paradigmatic intercourse between social production and desire—masculine gender identity is consolidated. As a "man's parts" are "form'd" and "extended" in the "applause" of others, he is erected as legend; and as legend, he remains erect.

IV

Non sum qualis eram. (I am not what I was).
Horace, *Odes*

Elizabeth Freund has argued that "nowhere does [Shakespeare] strip *both* his sources *and* his own text of their 'original' substance with such spirited iconoclasm" ("Rhetoric of Citation," p. 35). And for Freund, the play remains merely stripped: Shakespeare has not bothered to "replace" the "original substance" with anything else. Consequently, she calls the play Shakespeare's "noblest failure." But Freund simply carries the play's own deconstructive tendencies to their ultimate extreme, finishing off in her Derridean argument what the play fights so subversively to leave behind. The Derridean argument here produces a critic who cannot see ghosts. There seems to be a temptation to "solve" the problems raised by the play by making the play *itself* the problem. But as we have also seen, the extent to which the play's disjunctions and fissures *produce* subjectivity means that we cannot "cure" the play by reading it as an angry or embittered indictment of the loss of stable "original" values. *Troilus and Cressida* may deconstruct every ideological strategy which consolidates "identity" in its characters; but the intrinsically "double" nature of the play as both text and script produces something that cannot be deconstructed.

Far from arguing that Troilus' subjectivity is dismantled by witnessing Cressida's "betrayal," I would say that in this moment just before his precognitions are visibly confirmed, Troilus is most fully constituted as a subject. Like Richard III before Bosworth, it is the moment of greatest confusion for Troilus, when he becomes aware of contradictory ontologies in which identity is both "the same" and "the same as" (both metaphor and simile), the moment that provides the enabling condition for a subjectivity in which there is something "secret." This is the only time in the play that Troilus is genuinely confused, and therefore the only moment that for him *escapes* prior encoding. We might even say that this uncertainty exists *between* encodings, in a moment in which what he thinks and feels is undecided, affording him an opportunity in which to experience subjectivity rather than identity.

Consequently, subjectivity in this play depends upon those moments of "lost" identity. Hovering in the space between *fort* and *da*, subjectivity appears in the interim during which identity is lost and found, in which it "is, and is not" (this is why nostalgia is always an expression of subjectivity, since it results from a similar perception of the difference between then and now). The release from the safety and the constriction of absolute signification is both resisted and desired; and in this interplay between resistance and yearning, between the self-consolidating compulsion to be "identifiable" and a need for mobility, are the conditions for subjectivity. For it is precisely those moments that "unfix" us that render us present to ourselves *as* subjects: by becoming aware of our divisions, we again become "secret" to ourselves.

Of course, what makes this play more of a "tragedy" than anything else is the ironic fact that the very moment that should provide Troilus with the possibility of knowing himself anew is the moment he has "expected" all along. Unlike Cressida, who throughout the play is haunted by a sense of her own division (her two "kinds of selves") and therefore is more fully a subject in the sense I am arguing for here, Troilus' moments of subjectivity are always, finally, reappropriated by his legendary identity.[30] Because, as Barbara Everett has aptly put it, Troilus "exists to distrust"; his moment of subjectivity returns him to the same old story.[31] The point at which he fully "recognizes" (with its sense of seeing "again" what one has seen before) himself as betrayed thrusts him out of subjectivity and locks him into his notorious identity. This is the moment that literally *realizes* their earlier encodings of "true Troilus" and "false Cressid." Troilus "hardens" into the bitterly betrayed lover his name always already represents. In dramatic terms, the "identity" of the characters is confirmed precisely at the moment that their actions *become* their names.

Of course, the outcome is also determined by the presence of others, the collective force of the complicity of the audience and reader, who know so well what is going to happen. The scene of multiple voyeurism in Act 5, scene 2 (in which the audience watches Thersites watching Ulysses and Troilus watching Diomed and Cressida) is the *playing out*— the visual equivalent—of intertextual citationality. That there are so many sets of eyes "watching," "marking," and "noting" Cressida's "crossing" symptomatizes in spatial terms the chronological inevitability of that conveyance. What is for Troilus a "betrayal" is for the audience not betrayal at all but rather the meeting of a textual obligation, the paying of a legendary *debt*. The multiplication of the "original" scene in the repetitions of the story here intersects with the multiplication of eyes watching this scene, in what becomes an ingenious staging of the *theatrical equivalent* of intertextual identity.

The play, then, not only indicts the totalizing force of notorious identity by demonstrating the reification inherent in legendary narrative, but also indicts the specular, calling into question the ocular politics of an audience that has come to watch these figures suffer yet again their preordained ends. If, as Laura Mulvey has argued about modern film, "the mass of mainstream film, and the conventions within which it has consciously evolved, portray a hermetically sealed world which unwinds magically, indifferent to the presence of the audience, producing for them a sense of separation and play on their voyeuristic phantasy"

("Visual Pleasure," p. 9), Shakespeare's play portrays no such magical indifference to its audience, permits no safety in a "hermetically sealed world." It does, however, play upon our "voyeuristic phantasies." But not without revealing our investment in such fantasies. When Pandarus enacts his specular frenzy in Act 1, scene 2, his commands to "look there," "mark him," "note him," "see him" resonate out to the audience, as we, too, are inscribed in the kind of voyeuristic referentiality that Shakespearean drama at once exploits and challenges. The play constitutes the audience as a part of the coercive visual "frame" that locks these characters into their textual places. The physical conditions of the theater make it impossible for the audience to forget the structures of voyeurism that are built into the staging of plays. We watch characters watching. Thus, the play reproduces within itself the audience's relationship to spectacle, and foregrounds that relationship. Thersites, as the play's "representative" audience member thus becomes the site of identification, as he watches and provides jaded commentary on what he sees. His scopophilic activity contaminates the audience, threatening its own capacity to remain "distinct" from the events being staged, and making the audience itself a part of the coercive machinery of the play.

And it knows what it has come to see. On the one hand, what would Shakespeare's audience have thought of a Troilus who fights to keep Cressida as strenuously as he fights to keep Helen? Or of a Cressida who kills herself rather than submit to Greek embraces? But on the other hand, why would the playwright assay a story as citational as this if he could not produce something new in the staging of it? The brilliance of this play resides in the way it at once pays its legendary "debt" and prods us to anticipate that this time, maybe, Troilus will "stand up" for Cressida and that she will "hold out" for him. And it takes up the audience's double expectation—at once of seeing what it expects to see and seeing something "different"—and builds it into the experience of the figures within the world of the play. So that the process of going to the theater to see this famous story reenacted produces the same affective disjunction in the audience that it imposes on the characters, who are subjected yet again to their notorious "fates."

To say that the play demonstrates the ultimate triumph of notorious identity over subjectivity is not to say that the play fails. On the contrary. The victory of "identity" in this play is clearly pyrrhic. For if the only subjectivity possible in the play is ghostly—one of prodigious belatedness—it haunts an identity that has been emptied of any essential meaning. The play shows us that legendary "things" are dead things. In this way, Shakespeare's play demonstrates that drama has the power to challenge the most "unquestionable" forms of cultural authority by subjecting them to different standards of "evidence," evidence that will always be provisional, perspectival, and open to restaging and therefore to recontextualization and reinterpretation. By deconstructing the "legend" of Troilus and Cressida, Shakespeare reconstructs theater and drama as a new site not for representing "identity" but for staging "kinds of selves." In *Troilus and Cressida,* Shakespeare proves that the "face that launched a thousand ships" is really a thousand faces launching a thousand ships a thousand times. Thus, drama—as that which stages infamous events and figures and represents "inimitable" Gods in office—authorizes infinite replications of the "inimitable," each one representing "the original," and each one wearing a different face.

3

Spies and Whispers
Exceeding Reputation in
Antony and Cleopatra

One of the things we want to do with our coverage all week long is to differentiate between the essence of the reality and the agreed-upon appearance of things.
Dan Rather, reporting on the 1984 Democratic National Convention in San Francisco

Bringing you the world.
ABC News

> and every hour
> Most noble Caesar, shalt thou have report
> How 'tis abroad.
> Messenger, *Antony and Cleopatra*

Dan Rather's remark is significant in two ways that will be crucial to this chapter. The first is its tone of "common sense," and the second is its labyrinthine ideological complexity. Making the claim to "differentiate" that we've come to expect from the reporter/commentator, Rather's pose is investigative—that of uncovering for his less sagacious viewers a difference between "the essence of reality and the agreed-upon appearance of things."[1] The implicit claim being made is that behind what is in fact a complex performative situation there is an "essential" reality, and that this reality derives its authority or "authenticity" precisely by being the antithesis of the "agreed-upon." In short, if we want to apprehend the "reality" of this Convention we must not be fooled by the "conventional." Wedging himself between the actors (politicians) and the audience (the viewing public), Rather disguises the real aims and effects of his interventions: the fact that he constructs many of the distinctions he claims to discover, and that his "differentiation" produces not the "essential" reality of difference, but the politically productive category of the difference-between.

103

For Rather (as for all reporters), it is not possible simply to tell what happens. All "messengers" narrate within that negotiable space between actor and audience, and consequently take an active part in constituting the "reality" (realized only in the reception) of any performance. Occupying the neutral territory that is the ideological *sine qua non* of news media, Rather lays claim to the "real," helping to generate conditions in which the actors must play to and through him rather than directly to an audience. The actors must craft a performance that will satisfy the reporter's notion of the "essence of reality" if they are to have any influence on what filters through to a larger audience. To be credible and therefore to fabricate (in the sense both of creating and dissembling) the power they wish to exercise, actors-politicians must take pains to perform in such a way that the reporter can either perceive or produce a minimum of "difference" between an "agreed-upon appearance of things" and the "essence of the reality."

Of course, we must acknowledge the fact that Rather works in the medium of television, in which whatever narrative he constructs will be buttressed by appropriate visual images. The actors play to the audience through the visual medium of television, and the audience—like that at a theatrical performance—watches the actors perform "before their eyes." However, unlike a theater audience, the televiewer is given only selected bits of the "original" performance, segments cobbled together by Rather and his editors, reframed by his commentary in ways that make the reporter's "devising" an inextricable aspect of the overall "performance." Rather becomes both intermediary and substitute for the viewer, an expert "eyewitness" who conveys to his audience the "upshot" of his *audience*. The performance the televiewer consumes, then, derives not from the "original" site (the Democratic Convention), but from the "site" of its mediating apparatus (the news media). We learn little about what "really" happens at such events. What we do see, however, is how representational mediation positions itself as the authoritative origin of "reality": the degree to which reporting is a constitutive, rather than merely conductive, performance all its own; and how complex a trajectory "original" performances must chart if they are to achieve any of their "intended" effects.

Dan Rather helped create a version of the Democratic Convention in which an exoticized San Francisco (aligned with liberal Democrats and "radicals") was juxtaposed against the sober, "official" world of Washington, D.C., the symbolic center of state (Reaganite Republican) power. By focusing his reports on a circus-like atmosphere and showing footage of the city's colorful street life (and its vocal groups demonstrating for various social and sexual causes), Rather synecdochized the Democratic platform with these spectacular and "exotic" elements, producing for the televiewer a set of oppositions in which everything "official" about the convention—its issues, its seriousness, its stakes, and even its candidates—was transgressed by intercourse with San Francisco "itself."[2] Much like the division of the worlds of Rome and Egypt in Shakespeare's *Antony and Cleopatra*, Rather's "coverage" demonstrated that the "agreed-upon appearance of things" in one exoticized location can be appropriated and repackaged as the "essence of the reality" through its transmission to, and reception in, another. San Francisco became the site of a multiplicitous and heterogeneous "theater"—the fragmented locus of competing identity-politics. Against what it constructed as a cross-dressed "rainbow coalition" of gypsies, Washington—imperial domain of the "great communicator"—pitched its rhetoric of "manifest destiny": its hymn to "Morning in America."

Through the metastatic technologies of the media coverage of the last decade (most obvious recently in the hegemony of the Cable News Network or CNN), Washington now stands revealed as its own site of exotic and transgressive activity. (The earlier scandal of Watergate notwithstanding, the city was not, before the Reagan-Bush reign, regarded in the same way it is now.) Whether learning about "arms for hostages" deals, the sale of weapons to Iraq before the war in the Persian Gulf, the BCCI conspiracy, check-kiting in the House, the endless sexual powermongering of those who hold authoritative offices, the Clarence Thomas–Anita Hill debacle and (lateral yet relevant) the William Kennedy Smith trial, to name only a few such events, we've seen again and again how the strategies of power—patriarchal, military, sexual, racial, nationalist, and economic—contaminate themselves from within by their efforts to displace onto other persons and into other places the symptoms of their relentless self-consolidation.

For all efforts to establish the difference between the legitimate and the illegitimate require displacement and a place for it. Not surprisingly, then, colonialist and imperialist claims to new and/or occupied territories are always underwritten by claims of difference (and implicitly, of superiority) to native inhabitants. In every historical struggle for power, it is the constitutive "distinctions" that provide the ideological justification which only retroactively consolidates a particular version of history. If constructing "providentialism" in *Richard III* and "heroism" in *Troilus and Cressida* depends upon constructing their notorious figures as "one of a kind," in *Antony and Cleopatra* it is not notorious identity per se that is being interrogated (this is already, within the play, an acknowledged given for its titular figures) but the representational mode of its reinscription.

No other Shakespeare play is as filled with reporters and messengers as *Antony and Cleopatra*. Unlike other plays in which the action is also divided among several locations, this play is scored with the ceaseless circulation of messages, "reports," and "news." The word "report" occurs more frequently in this play than in any other; and messengers appear so often that they substantially constitute the mise-en-scène for the performances of the main figures, both within the play and for the audience. By "reporters," I mean not just the play's ubiquitous anonymous messengers but also major figures—such as Octavius, Enobarbus, Antony, and Cleopatra—all of whom deliver discursive re-creations of other characters' performances. Just as Dan Rather rendered the principal figures in the Democratic Convention actors to his audience, in Shakespeare's play, as Janet Adelman has pointed out, "major characters become in effect actors and the minor characters their interpretive audience." Report is "the pattern of framing [which] suggests that we see the central figures as actors in a play within the play."[3] But while all the "actors" in this play are obsessed with playing to reviewers near and far, they are not equally in control of the effects of their performances. In *Antony and Cleopatra*, the accretive weight of report is pitted against the destabilizing histrionicism of acting in a contest over appropriable, and expropriable, forms of notorious identity. How the figures play to, and against, competing representational apparatuses determines the degree to which they become the successful subjects or entrapped objects of spies and whispers.

II

We seek other conditions because we do not understand the use of our own.
Montaigne, *Complete Essays,* trans. Donald Frame

Other regions give us back what our culture has excluded from its discourse . . .
We travel abroad to discover in distant lands something whose presence at home has become unrecognizable.
Michel de Certeau, *The Practice of Everyday Life,* trans. Steven Rendall

In talking about Shakespeare's Rome and Egypt as milieus as well as locations, many critics have characterized Rome as representing the "workaday" world of politics, civic duty, public existence, official posterity, and masculinity; whereas Egypt represents the pleasures of "private" existence, eroticism, feasting, excess, physical pleasures, sensuality, preoccupation with the present, and femininity.[4] Though I will return to challenge several of these oppositions later, I wish now to foreground an opposition that I shall argue frames all the others: a division between the compulsion to narrate—what might be called the narrative "imperative"—and the resistance of mimetic improvisation, or mimetic subversion. Mimetic subversion is not, however, to be understood as antidiscursive per se. Rather, it filches from and poaches on existing discourses. It is to be understood as resistance to a full and final articulation *as* narrative, antipathy toward the "identifiable," linear tropes of "inevitability" that always subtend narrative, and therefore resistance to the political, territorial, and ultimately subjective appropriation that is always the hidden (and not so hidden) aim of narrative forms of reproduction.[5]

In early modern England, drama is the most powerful and visible site of the diacritical operations of discursive and nondiscursive forms of cultural production. And Shakespearean drama, perhaps more than that of any other playwright, demonstrates the ways in which absolutist ideologies can find themselves undermined in their deployment by the visual, spatial, and gestural choreography of their own performance. Without the ceaseless reporting in *Antony and Cleopatra,* there would be no "audience" within it for the performances produced in Rome and Egypt. But while the figures in the play are always aware of the importance of narrative—of how they are spoken about—the play is also one of Shakespeare's "stagiest" insofar as figures are obsessively concerned with how they "appear" to others (and with how others appear—for example, Cleopatra's curiosity about Octavia's looks), what "visible shapes" they will hold (or not hold).[6] While these two representational modes—the discursive and the visual—chafe against each other, they also jointly inflect the experience and reproduction of notorious identity.

Rome is, as many critics have noted, the play's "original" center of the narrative imperative, of the incitement to discourse that drives imperialist historiography. Again and again, figures in the play refer to the way their histories and "characters" are constructed in Roman report. At the opening of the play, Philo tells Demetrius to "take but good note" (1.1.11); and the first "news" that comes in the play comes from Rome.[7] Later, Caesar demonstrates this kind of narration in 1.4.55–70,

as he tells of Antony's sojourns for the empire ("On the Alps / It is reported thou didst eat strange flesh"). When Antony tells Octavia to
"read not [his] blemishes in the world's report" (Act 2, scene 3), it is
clear that the "world" he refers to is the Roman empire, the source of the
only "report" that Octavia would be likely to receive and that he would
feel accountable to. Whatever happens in this play is always reassembled back in Rome in the "square" (2.3.6.) of narrative; and it is no accident that the play filled with references to "reporting" is also the play
which represents the ultimate triumph of Octavius, who will later
sculpt himself into the Augustus of Virgil, Horace, and Ovid. This
leader (under whom three of the writers who were to be most influential in the Renaissance produced texts that would serve as Shakespeare's sources) had a monumental machinery of language at his disposal. As Augustus Caesar, Octavius was to become chief executive of
a massive discursive empire, the productions of which would be referred to again and again, from Dante to Pope, as models of literary,
moral, and historical "authority."[8] More crucially, this "authority," as
Leo Braudy has claimed, involved a privileging of one mode of transmission over another:

> The "vulgar fame," or fame of the masses, that appears when Dido
> and Aeneas go into the cave or when Aeneas sees the scenes on the
> wall, Virgil associates primarily with visual representation. His
> distinction between true and false fame thus also emphasizes the
> moral ascendancy of one mode of communication over another.
> The basic precept, which becomes a central part of the idea of fame
> in Christianity, is the superiority of the ear to the eye, its receptivity
> to words rather than images.[9]

This "basic precept" may have been reemphasized in Reformation political theology; but it was apparently unstable enough in the theater-
going population of Shakespeare's England to keep certain Puritan elements railing against the pernicious influence of the images shown on
stage (see Stubbes, *Anatomie of Abuses*, 1583: "Playes are no images of
thinges"). In fact, efforts to establish and police the "moral ascendency"
of the ear over the eye can be regarded as a drive to counteract the extraordinary suasive force of the visual. It is much more obvious today,
in the visual media age, that the perceptions of the eye can easily over-
whelm, and even abrogate, those of the ear.

By figuring virtually all of its power relations in terms of the subjection, and resistance, to the narrative imperative, the play advances its

plot as a relationship between *strategies* and *tactics*. Michel de Certeau, whose meanings of the terms I adopt here, defines "strategy" as

> the calculation (or manipulation) of power relationships that becomes possible as soon as a subject with will and power (a business, an army, a city, a scientific institution) can be isolated. It postulates a *place* that can be delimited as its *own* and serve as the base from which relations with an *exteriority* composed of targets or threats can be managed. As in management, every "strategic" rationalization seeks first of all to distinguish its "own" place, that is, the place of its own power and will, from an "environment" . . . The "proper" is a triumph of place over time. It allows one to capitalize acquired advantages, to prepare future expansions, and thus to give oneself a certain independence with respect to the variability of circumstances. It is a mastery of time through the foundation of an autonomous place.

Strategies, then, are deeply dependent on the notion of place (and, by extension, of property). According to Certeau, strategies are "institutional" modes of action that have a space in relation to events that occur over time. They are *propre*, proper to the strategist, and their results or products are therefore appropriable or "keepable." Tactics, on the other hand, are defined as

> a calculated action determined by the absence of a proper locus. No delimitation of an exteriority, then, provides it with the condition necessary for autonomy. The space of a tactic is the space of the other. Thus it must play on and with a terrain imposed on it and organized by the law of a foreign power. It does not have the means to *keep to itself*, at a distance, in a position of withdrawal, foresight, and self-collection . . . It operates in isolated actions, blow by blow. It takes advantage of "opportunities" and depends on them, being without any base where it could stockpile its winnings, build up its own position, and plan raids. What it wins it cannot keep.[10]

Tactics can be regarded as flexible but unauthoritative "seizures," with no space or place outside of time (one is reminded here of Lacan's argument that Hamlet exists in the "hour of the Other").[11] In Certeau's terms, a tactic depends on what time and opportunity present, and consequently its gains are momentary and cannot be kept, cannot be "appropriated."

In other words, tactical gains are defined as unkeepable because they are not accretive. Without a locus to store momentary gains, without a way to convert them into "property," they are soon lost; entirely aleatory, they are replaced by other gains that may or may not add to or reinforce earlier gains. Like guerrilla warfare (the tactics of the disenfranchised), tactics are most effective at destabilizing the strategies of others, and not at constituting a strategy of their own. In this way, tactics arc "unidentifiable" because they cannot necessarily be rendered the same as, or identical to, earlier tactics. As disruptive "interventions" into the established discourses of others, they are themselves finally nondiscursive.

In *Antony and Cleopatra,* then, we can see that Cleopatra and Octavius—both of whom are representatives of "proper" places—engage in a war of competing strategies; while Antony, the "displaced" or uprooted agent who moves between the locations (and different habitus) of Rome and Egypt, is forced from a strategic into a tactical mode—a literal displacement which finally does him in.[12] To say that Cleopatra and Octavius are engaged in strategic battle is not, however, to say that their strategies are identical. In fact, we might say that Octavius' strategy is literally "identical" whereas Cleopatra's is "anti-identical." In other words, Rome's "proper place" is aligned with the authoritative (and authoritarian) representational institution of epic and narrative history. Octavius' strategy from and within this place *is* the narrative imperative, the development of a unified, self-consistent temporal story line that involves the binding up and appropriation of ever-expanding territories, a narrative whose reproduction depends upon an ever-increasing acquisition of property, an ever-widening *place.* Rome's geographical imperialism is the spatial equivalent (and strategic requirement) of its ever-more-authoritative narrative imperialism: its efforts to triumph over time through the colonization of space. It is, in short, the project of establishing its own absolute identity, in relation to which others will either conform or be rendered "alienable."

In contrast, Cleopatra depends upon a *strategic use* of tactics which can be appropriated by her because they are launched from a space that is "proper" to her. Cleopatra's proper place is aligned with the less "authoritative" (but increasingly powerful in early modern England) representational institution of the theater. Her strategy consists of a use of tactics that have accretive strategic potential: her campaign seizes the momentary opportunities presented over time by the strategies of others and transforms them into "capital"—something she can both keep and exchange. Every momentary gain becomes another element in the constitution of her "identity" as Egypt, which consists precisely of being "unidentifiable" in the discursive terms of Roman narration. For Cleopatra, tactics are "proper," insofar as what they achieve is stored in the space that has been marked off as "Egypt," the space that is itself composed of contradictions and nonidentities, the place that is always synecdochized with the figure of Cleopatra "herself." Cleopatra's tactics may resemble the "arts of the weak"—they do involve trickery, deception, "wit," legerdemain (she is, after all, "other" to Rome on three fronts: gender, race, and nationality).[13] But the fact that they are given a domain to which they clearly belong and which they help reproduce means that they can be used by Cleopatra (and, as we shall see, by the playwright), to constitute herself in ways not available to Antony.

In Act 1, scene 1, messengers come to Cleopatra's court with news for Antony from Rome. Before even hearing the news, Cleopatra uses the appearance of the messenger as a way to increase her erotic hold on Antony by emphasizing the extent to which he has been entrapped by the "mandates" of Rome:

> Nay, hear them, Antony:
> Fulvia perchance angry; or who knows
> If the scarce-bearded Caesar have not sent
> His powerful mandate to you, "Do this, or this;
> Take in that kingdom, and enfranchise that;
> Perform't, or else we damn thee." (1.1.19–23)

Cleopatra understands that the powerful attraction she holds for Antony depends on the extent to which their life together disrupts the role he is required to play in the imperious Roman master narrative. For Antony, whose identity is already constituted as one of the "triple pillars of the world," Cleopatra and Egypt effect his "transformation"—in Roman eyes into "a strumpet's fool" (1.1.12), but in Antony's eyes (at least in the eyes through which he wishes to see) into someone whose every minute of life is endowed with some pleasure (1.1.46). Pleasure for Antony is here figured as nondiscursive and antinarrational, existing outside the teleological constraints of time. Caught between competing versions of his "transformation," Antony is positioned at the intersection of conflicting structural modes and the subjectivities produced by different systems of representation.

So long as Cleopatra can reinforce the pleasures of their life in Egypt, she can disrupt Octavius' efforts to reclaim Antony for Roman imperialism. And her goading of Antony in the play's opening scenes represents her tactical subversion of the very discourses which Rome spins out to net him back.[14] Ridiculing any sense of duty Antony might feel toward Octavius or Fulvia, Cleopatra derides Antony's attachment to Rome itself. Her aim here is to revise or even supplant the "original" reason for Antony's presence in Eygpt, which was precisely as an operative for Roman expansion and annexation. "Preposterously" revising the reasons for Antony's sojourn in Egypt, Cleopatra subrogates cause with effect. Her strategy reveals her awareness of the overdetermining force of discourses of "original causes" (particularly when they are inextricable from constructions of masculine identity).[15]

The real battle in this play, then—that between Caesar and Cleopatra—is staked out across the terrain of Antony's "identity": the set of representations, images, and narratives he needs to recognize himself as "Antony." Both Octavius and Cleopatra understand how susceptible Antony is to attacks on his "manhood." And their respective strategies for claiming his "membership" have all the force of their embeddedness in their proper places. From Rome, Octavius works to undermine the "subject position" of the Antony of Egypt by characterizing him as "a strumpet's fool," an emasculated identity unworthy of the great Roman named Antony. From Egypt, Cleopatra works to undermine the "subject position" of the Antony of Rome—"Caesar's Antony"—who in this version is also emasculated because subservient to the mandates of the "scarce-bearded Caesar" (1.1.22).

In Act 1, scene 1, Cleopatra goads Antony out of his allegiance to the place and narrative of Rome and Romanness. She is successful, and he responds cooperatively:

> Let Rome in Tiber melt, and the wide arch
> Of the rang'd empire fall! Here is my space,
> Kingdoms are clay: our dungy earth alike
> Feeds beast as man; the nobleness of life
> Is to do thus: when such a mutual pair,
> And such a twain can do't, in which I bind
> On pain of punishment, the world to weet
> We stand up peerless. (33–39)

The Roman Antony attempts to re-place himself with an Egyptian Antony ("here is my space"), one who no longer recognizes the monumentality and endurance of the Roman vision of empire but, rather, wants only to see the futility of such narratives—that all kingdoms are clay, that all rang'd empires fall, and that men are not gods who master the earth but creatures who are fed by it. This is a space in which things are continually changing, "wrangling," where Cleopatra herself "becomes every thing" and consequently no *one* thing.

The problem, however, is that Antony doesn't have the means to "re-place" himself. For while he may claim that he and Cleopatra "stand up peerless" (without equal), his language also signals his will to misrecognize his conditions, his desire to believe that he can reconstruct himself as a legend outside the Roman machine. If this fantasy is encouraged by Cleopatra, she also exacerbates its symptoms; for although her strategy aims at keeping him for herself, it works only by virtue of the fact that they *do* belong in different places. Cleopatra's hold on Antony depends on the tactical opportunities provided by the difference between a Roman Antony and an Egyptian one; it depends on being able to offer in herself and Egypt a pleasurable alternative to the Roman ties that bind. Consquently, while Cleopatra tries to "shame" Antony out of his bonds of allegiance to Rome, she must nevertheless keep him in Egypt as a Roman. Hence he is at once re-placed and dis-placed. He cannot properly be Egyptian, nor can he continue to meet the requirements of being properly "Roman" in all of its implications.

Antony comes to realize that he is occupying an untenable position as a kind of "sojourner" in his own life—one who exists between places, unembedded, without the firmness of identity provided by unwavering allegiance to a particular place. The more Antony sojourns emotionally, imaginatively, and literally between Rome and Egypt (and the two subject positions they offer and mutually critique), the more unconstituted his identity becomes. It is this experience of "infirm" boundaries, of being unidentical to himself and what he has been in the past, that becomes intolerable to him (see, for example, 4.14.1–15: "yet [I] cannot hold this visible shape"). Whatever pleasures, freedoms, spontaneity, and surprises Cleopatra's Egypt offers him, they cannot overpower the imperative to narrative production that *is* Rome, his own narrative past, and the origin of his notorious identity as Antony. In this position of territorial insecurity, Antony becomes like the land Roman imperialism seeks to conquer: vulnerable to continual remappings and reappropriations of his own subjective terrain.

Not surprisingly, it is the Roman messengers and their intrusion onto the stage of his life in Egypt who "recall" Antony to himself. "These strong Egyptian fetters I must break, / Or lose myself in dotage" (1.2.112). Here Antony fantasizes that breaking Egyptian fetters will mean a return to "autonomy" and self-determination. But in fact, there is only one alternative: a return to the role that has already been scripted for him by Caesar and the Roman empire, a reentry into the continued reproduction of himself as part of Roman history. This Antony does upon returning to Rome, his own "proper place."

When Antony and Caesar meet in Act 2, scene 2, Caesar accuses him of breaking his oath "to lend [him] arms and aid when [he] requir'd them" (87–88). Antony replies that he has "Neglected, rather; / And then when poisoned hours had bound me up / From mine own knowledge" (2.2.90–91). It is not an accident that he speaks to Caesar of "poisoned hours"; for whatever its spatial requirements are, the narrative imperative ultimately thinks itself chronologically. Earlier, in Egypt, Antony had said, "Let Rome in Tiber melt," "Here is my space." Ironically, Antony's return to Rome doesn't embed him in his proper place but rather reinserts him into narrative time; and his stay in Egypt is reconceived not as an occupation of pleasurable space but as wasted time. Of course, that has been precisely the appeal of Egypt—the way it seems to supplant purposeful time with pleasurable space and all the seductions of the "imaginary." Egypt puts time itself out of joint in the way that everything fascinating functions: by replacing awareness of the passage of time with the sense of a plenitude of presence, of "being *for* itself" rather than for some purpose or goal. To replace a sense (however imaginary) of full presence with the infinitely deferrable gratifications of historical *telos* is to move from Egypt and Cleopatra back to Rome and Octavius. No wonder that Antony tells Octavius to be a "child o'the time" (2.7.98): that is precisely what Octavius is—the "boy" who will grow up to be, in the "ripeness" of Roman time, the mighty emperor Augustus.

Unfortunately for Antony, this return to the identity of chronological narrative is not *for* himself: he cannot "own" what the strategy of proper place produces because, thanks to Cleopatra, he is no longer fully Roman, no longer fully "himself"—or, to put it another way, no longer fully *one* self. She has split him from "himself," given him two sets of coordinates, two places which now claim different Antonys. He can no longer occupy the unified, integral identity that Rome provided for him (and, more crucially, through which he provided for Rome). But we can't lay this all at Cleopatra's feet, since Antony's identity as Roman was never his to "own" anyway, being a function of Octavius' larger strategy in the intertextual history that always already precedes him. That is to say, Antony's identity as "Antony" belongs properly to the larger body of historiography that is the story of Rome. This is why he remains throughout the play so susceptible to Roman shaming, "lest [his] remembrance suffer ill report" (2.2.156). Rome in this play stands for the process of interpellation itself. Antony's "intercourse" between Rome and Egypt has disrupted the fit of the "hailing": he now experiences as subjection what, prior to Cleopatra, he had experienced as his own "place" in the story—a "proper" kind of embeddedness. For Antony, contact with Cleopatra has changed the meaning of being a subject.[16]

Antony tries to bind himself back to Rome—he marries Octavius' sister (and name-double) as a gesture of good faith. The messenger who delivers the news to Cleopatra describes Antony's condition as a kind of slavery: "Free, madam, no; I made no such report, / He's bound unto Octavia" (2.5.57). Bound to Rome, to Octavius Caesar, to Octavia, to Octavia's bed—this is the "autonomy" Antony achieves by breaking his strong Egyptian fetters. By marriage to Octavia, as Menas puts it to Enobarbus, Antony and Caesar are "for ever knit together" (2.6.112). In terms of the "traffic in women," the breach between Antony and Octavius was effected by the interference of Cleopatra, by her insertion of herself between the Roman and his Roman purpose (by her seizing, in other words, of the Lacanian Phallus). Consequently, Caesar and Antony can be "knitted with an unslipping knot" (2.2.127) only through the use of another woman. In the apotropaic logic of this exchange, what one woman has put asunder let another woman join together.

But for Antony, perhaps Shakespeare's most literal representation of a split subject, there can be no knitting together of component parts, no eradication of the difference that has been opened up in himself by displacement. Antony's subjective choreography now matches the map that splits this play and its two competing realms. Belonging fully in neither, yet being pulled by both, he becomes incapable of rooting himself in a position that would enable him to launch an effective strategy of his own.[17] This is what makes Shakespeare's Antony different from, say, Virgil's pious Aeneas, who in spite of his sojourn with Dido manages to suture himself successfully enough to return to his narrative "destiny" as founder of Rome.

For narrative destiny is precisely what is at stake in this play. When Antony prepares to levy war against Caesar in Act 3, scene 6, Octavia attempts to act as intermediary for peace between them. Caesar counsels his sister:

> Be you not troubled with the time, which drives
> O'er your content these strong necessities,
> But let determin'd things to destiny
> Hold unbewail'd their way. Welcome to Rome . . . (81–85)

Welcome to Rome indeed. Ever the "child o'the time," Octavius speaks of the strong and "determin'd" necessities that drive the destiny of Rome; and for Shakespeare's audience, these "necessities" are those of legend, of the fact that the outcome of this story has already been irreversibly inscribed by the scribes of Augustus Caesar himself. When Antony travels abroad, he discovers (*pace* Certeau and Montaigne) something he had been incapable of recognizing at home: his own entrapment in and subjection to the conditions of legendary reproduction.[18]

The more Antony tries to establish a place of his own, the more drastically he undoes himself. Belonging neither in Rome nor in Egypt, it is no accident that he decides finally to take on Caesar's forces by sea. "Let Rome in Tiber melt," says Antony. "Sink Rome," says Cleopatra. There is in this language a shared fantasy in which Rome might be dissolved: a fantasy of moving beyond the "solid ground" of Roman discourse onto a sea that will somehow support them differently. Ill prepared for battle by sea, Antony nevertheless insists on it. Why? Because Octavius has "dared him to't" (3.7.29). Warned against such a plan by Enobarbus, Antony says, "By sea, by sea" (40). To which Enobarbus replies:

> Most worthy sir, you therein throw away
> The absolute soldiership you have by land,
> Distract your army, which doth most consist
> Of war-mark'd footmen, leave unexecuted
> Your own renowned knowledge, quite forgo
> The way which promises assurance, and
> Give yourself merely to chance and hazard,
> From firm security. (41–47)

Once again, Antony answers: "I'll fight at sea." In this response, we can read Antony's yearning to escape the overdetermined way which "promises assurance," his desire to give himself over to something other than the "firm security" of his own Roman past. An effort to mount a strategy from a place of his own (the sea) and to recast his "absolute soldiership" in terms of his own, Antony's decision is pathetic precisely because the terms of the strategy are not his own—they have been set by Caesar's "dare." Literally disdaining the ground on which his "renowned knowledge" and "absolute soldiership" have been built in the past, Antony here makes an effort to constitute himself anew on a "ground" that is neither Caesar's nor Cleopatra's.

But this attempt is, as Enobarbus points out, merely a set of tactics—tactics because dependent upon the exigencies of "chance and hazard" rather than on the certainties of place. Even Antony's footsoldiers understand what is at stake for them in this battle:

> O noble emperor, do not fight by sea,
> Trust not to rotten planks: do you misdoubt
> This sword, and these my wounds? Let the Egyptians
> And the Phoenicians go a-ducking: we
> Have us'd to conquer standing on the earth,
> And fighting foot to foot. (3.7.60–65)

Of course, the notion of the sea being hazard's territory is a mercantile commonplace in Shakespeare's plays (most notably in *Merchant of Venice* and in the "romances") and in seventeenth century Europe generally. But it is so precisely because the sea can swallow up what has been acquired, can make the accretion of properties—whether of wealth or of military power or of identity (the "sea change")—disappear. The sea is a site of traversal, engulfment, or dissolution; but it is not one of domain. It is, rather, that territory between domains; and everyone who is "at sea" is perforce a sojourner. Antony's reckless insistence on fighting at sea literalizes the symptomology of his own displacement: a "seizure," it is a hysterical attempt to constitute an identity from the midst of "nowhere." "Hailed" from both directions—by Egypt and Rome, Cleopatra and Octavius—Antony can only wander between the shifting embankments of two identities, neither of which offers him a solid place to stand.

III

The coercive force of report produces an Antony who is not in control of the narratives for which he provides material. If Antony is the one major figure in this play who seems least able to appropriate for his own ends the discursive structures which knit him in, it is because he is the one figure most invested in a need for "integrity": a stable image by which he may know himself and be known by others. However much he may desire the multiplicity Egypt represents, Antony is simply not constituted to occupy the position, to borrow Pico's phrase, of "this, our chameleon." Antony does not understand that it is precisely the weight he gives to how he is narrated by others that secures his subjection to the narrative imperative.

Similarly, his earnest investment in his own narratives renders him at once sympathetic to the audience and a source of potential embarrassment—both for himself and for other male figures whose own status depends upon Antony's maintenance of a "proper" masculine persona. As operative for Rome, Antony is expected to enact what Erving Goffman has characterized as "distantiation": a requirement for successful social interaction and performance. This process requires that:

> Actors enact intellectual or emotional involvement.
> They have to guard against getting carried away.
> They have to master their script.
> They master their script.
> They are alert.
> If need be, a well-trained actor can indicate why a role need not
>   be taken seriously.
> They possess self-control and can suppress emotional reactions.
> They can be serious when seriousness is required.
> They can move from informal privacy to the public sphere
>   without becoming confused.
> They control their facial expression and voice.

Failure to "mobilize these competences" results in unease not just for the subject but for those who witness it as well.[19] In Goffman's view, embarrassment is "contagious" because

> members in a social setting play a supporting role and feel responsible for one another. Generally they all work together to remove embarrassment. A terminal stage of embarrassment is reached, however, when someone loses composure completely . . . At this point, the interaction as a whole is then threatened and here the social regulation of affective standards comes into its own. The moment of crisis is socially determined: the individual's breaking point is that of the group to whose affective standards he adheres.[20]

Threatening the "affective standards" of the Roman group to which he is, and is not, struggling to "adhere," Antony threatens the way the other Roman men construct themselves.

At this point the social regulation of affective standards kicks in, as others attempt to "remove embarrassment." Antony has forgotten the "proper" place of women in the process of enacting misogynist Roman historiography. Unlike other male figures in the play, when Antony describes Cleopatra he cannot regard his narratives merely as social performances, because his movement between "informal privacy" and "the public sphere" has become confused. Although his Roman counterparts expect him to retain control over his particular "investment" in this Egyptian queen, Antony is unable to regard Cleopatra simply as matter for use in his own narrative self-construction.

But others in the play do regard Cleopatra in just such terms, and Antony is faced repeatedly with the way others account for her. Simultaneously denigrated and exoticized, she provides commodifiable material for male figures who compete with one another in terms of an *imaginative* imperialism that renegotiates their own social and political status. Cleopatra's self-staging may always be calculated to assure her mobility within a set of power relations; but she is not necessarily capable of determining what the effects will be or how she will be "reviewed" by others. For between the delivery and the reception of her performance is the aleatory space of the "reviewer." In this space, the audience/reporter acquires symbolic capital by how he narrates what he has seen, by what he demonstrates about himself and his position in the marketplace of commodity identity—literally, by what kind of "consumer" he proves himself to be.

In this respect, Enobarbus is the most notable of Cleopatra's "reporters," and he adopts a variety of interpretive stances depending on the nature of his audience and the particular social effects he hopes to achieve. In Act 1, scene 2, Antony decries his susceptibility to "this enchanting queen" and "her ten thousand charms" (125), enacting precisely the kind of loss of composure that puts the social regulation of affect at risk. Enobarbus (with palpable embarrassment) attempts to operate as a foil to Antony's subjection, ostensibly to restore proper masculine decorum to what is a threatening situation on several fronts. Using a language of deliberately ironic mystification, Enobarbus works to demystify the effects of Cleopatra's "charms" on his general. As Antony laments his vulnerability to what he experiences as Cleopatra's "essential" power (her "charisma"), Enobarbus recasts this power in histrionic terms as the effect—not the cause—of a performance:

Enobarbus: What's your pleasure, sir?
Antony: I must with haste from hence.

> Enobarbus: Why, then, we kill all our women. We see how mortal
> an unkindness is to them; if they suffer our departure, death's the
> word.
>
> Antony: I must be gone.
>
> Enobarbus: Under a compelling occasion let women die: it were
> pity to cast them away for nothing, though between them and a
> great cause, they should be esteemed nothing. Cleopatra catching
> but the least noise of this dies instantly. I have seen her die twenty
> times upon far poorer moment: I do think there is mettle in death,
> which commits some loving act upon her, she hath such celerity
> in dying. (129–142)

Enobarbus here provides ironic, if chummy, commentary on Cleopatra's
strategic use of melodrama as manipulative device. But in blatantly
pointing out his own ability to see through Cleopatra's "celerity in
dying," he also demonstrates something about his relation to Antony.
These lines exhibit the effort (frequent among Shakespeare's male
figures) to efface or eclipse class and rank differences between men—
in this case between Enobarbus and his general—by consolidating
likenesses based on a shared misogyny.[21] While these lines apparently
bespeak camaraderie, they do more than create a momentary parity between the two men. Enobarbus' ability to play openly at this moment
with the sexual connotations of "dying" at once signals his awareness
of Antony's "dotage"—which he assumes to be "merely" sexual—and
demonstrates his own freedom from such manipulation. The cheeky
banter he levels at Antony points to the ignominy of allowing oneself to
be subject to such "transparent" histrionics.

A subtle power struggle builds between the two men, as Antony
again asserts his sense of the reality of Cleopatra's power:

> Antony: She is cunning past man's thought.
>
> Enobarbus: Alack, sir, no, her passions are made of nothing but the
> finest part of pure love. We cannot call her winds and waters
> sighs and tears; they are greater storms and tempests than alma-
> nacs can report. This cannot be cunning in her; if it be, she makes
> a shower of rain as well as Jove.
>
> Antony: Would I had never seen her!
>
> Enobarbus: O, sir, you had then left unseen a wonderful piece of
> work, which not to have been blest withal, would have discred-
> ited your travel. (143–153)

Breaching decorum by misreading the depth of Antony's affective distress, Enobarbus' efforts are mistimed and misplaced: the version of Cleopatra he produces (a tourist attraction) is not right for this audience at this moment. Whereas we are aware that Antony's abjection is fueled by the news of Fulvia's death, Enobarbus does not yet know. However, even when Antony bluntly tells him that "Fulvia is dead," Enobarbus fails to correct his rhetorical trajectory. Antony tries to recover dignity and reestablish his class superiority by shifting the conversation away from sexual innuendo and onto the more "important" matter of the damage Fulvia has done to the state:

> Antony: The business she hath broached in the state
> Cannot endure my absence.
> Enobarbus: And the business you have broach'd here
> cannot be without you,
> Especially that of Cleopatra's,
> which wholly depends on your abode. (169–173)

Antony's attempts to deflect attention from his "emasculating" sexual subjection to Cleopatra by turning it toward his role as one of the "triple pillars of the world" remains unsuccessful with Enobarbus, who, by reading Cleopatra's "cunning" and trivializing their "business" as sexual, reinforces rather than ameliorates Antony's shame concerning his "strong Egyptian fetters."

Though on one level Enobarbus aims at crafting a social performance that will elevate his own status, he here misrecognizes the nature, limits, and conditions of the license a servant is given to speak plainly with his master—he seems ignorant of the fact that such license operates between social unequals only so long as the "superior" doesn't feel himself to be the object of excessive scrutiny. But this is precisely what Enobarbus reveals to Antony: that not only has he been the object of scrutiny, but scrutiny of a particularly public kind. Antony's response should be understood, in Bourdieu's terms, as

> the embarassment of someone who is uneasy in his body and his language and who, instead of being "as one body with them," observes them from outside, through other people's eyes, watching, checking, correcting himself, and who, by his desperate attempts to reappropriate an alienated being-for-others, exposes himself to appropriation, giving himself away as much by hypercorrection as by clumsiness. The timidity which, despite itself, realizes the ob-

jectified body, which lets itself be trapped in the destiny proposed by collective perception and statement . . . is betrayed by a body that is subject to the representation of others even in its passive, unconcious reactions.[22]

Although Bourdieu describes this disempowering form of self-consciousness as being characteristic of (although not exclusively limited to) the modern petit-bourgeoisie, the distinctions he makes are not solely functions of the habitus of advanced capitalism. Built into Antony's experience of himself is precisely this kind of commodifying self-regard. For to be legendary is to be equated both with the exchange and the surplus values of one's name: to be aware of oneself as a profitable social and political product. We have already seen the extent to which Antony suffers in the world's "report"—the extent to which he feels "unqualitied with very shame" (3.11.44). When he says that he has "offended reputation" (3.11.48), we see the degree to which he lets himself be trapped "in the destiny proposed by collective perception and statement." Under the pressures of such collective perception (reinforced by the visibility of his sexual thralldom), and the reproduction of such collective statement ("reputation"), Antony begins to watch, check, "correct" himself in what will be, as the play continues, his own "desperate attempt to reappropriate an alienated being-for-others."

At this point in his exchange with Enobarbus, Antony has no recourse but openly to pull rank: "No more light answers" (1.2.174). Returning to the elevated speech of the commander, Antony deploys the royal first person: "Let our officers / Have notice what we purpose" (174–175). Enobarbus' exchange with Antony has served not only to allow Enobarbus a social performance in which he can safely "one-up" his commander by demonstrating his immunity to the feminine wiles that are "unmanning" Antony, but also to facilitate Antony's return to a "superior" position precisely because Enobarbus is his social subordinate. The importance of this scene lies not in the extent to which it supposedly reveals to Antony the truth of his emotional subjection to Cleopatra, but in the fact that it reveals something even more threatening: the perception of his sexual subjection by his social inferiors.

Of course, Enobarbus' discursive strategy shifts drastically when he "reports" to Agrippa and Maecenas, in Act 2, scene 2, on Cleopatra's personal splendors. After his "light answers" to Antony earlier and his demonstration of his ability to see through Cleopatra's "act," these words to Agrippa and Maecenas constitute an entirely different kind of social performance, again having less to do with Cleopatra's "infinite variety" than with Enobarbus' apparently infinite capacity to vary his reports of her. If, with Antony, Enobarbus' narrative is meant to demonstrate his own sagacity in the face of her "winds and waters"—his ability to remain undeceived by her theatrics—in this scene, Enobarbus appropriates Antony's perceptions of Cleopatra, building into his new narrative the very terms of "enchantment" that he waxed upon so ironically in Act 1, scene 2. In this new context it is more to Enobarbus' credit to serve a general who has had the extraordinary and enviable pleasure of consorting with an "enchanting queen" who can "make defect perfection" (232) than it is for him to report that between Cleopatra and "a great cause" she should have been esteemed nothing and wasn't. Ever concerned with "earning a place in the story" (3.13.46), Enobarbus here reconstructs Cleopatra precisely as the "great cause," thus redeeming in the telling not only his general's position but his own.

Enobarbus pretends to have in his possession a kind of magical knowledge generated by having seen this queen. And of course, in contrast, Maecenas and Agrippa do not. Thus, Enobarbus' words don't beggar description; rather, they beggar his audience (and Shakespeare's as well), positioning them as supplicants who will never get more than verbal scraps of the visual feast Enobarbus has consumed:

> Maecenas: Eight wild-boars roasted whole at a breakfast, and but twelve persons there; is this true?
> Enobarbus: This was but as a fly by an eagle: we had much more monstrous matter of feast, which worthily deserved noting.
> Maecenas: She's a most triumphant lady, if report be square to her.
> Enobarbus: When she first met Mark Antony, she purs'd up his heart upon the river of Cydnus.
> Agrippa: There she appear'd indeed; or my reporter devis'd well for her.
> Enobarbus: I will tell you. (2.2.179–190)

Determined to outdo any reports that Maecenas and Agrippa have already received, Enobarbus here equates himself not only with Agrippa's reporter ("I will tell you"), but with Antony as he claims to have consumed some of the "feast" (Cleopatra) that belongs, properly speaking, to Antony. Like his general, Enobarbus has also eaten with his eyes—although, unlike Antony, he has not paid his heart "for what his eyes eat only" (225).

Banking now on the symbolic capital of "mystery," Enobarbus enacts the upwardly mobile courtier's strategy of claiming special knowledge that is at once "unfathomable" and yet can somehow be adumbrated (in veiled form) to others. What Castiglione calls "a certain *sprezzatura*" also promotes "glamour," which in Kenneth Burke's definition is

> a charm affecting the eye, making objects appear different from what they are; witchcraft, magic, a spell; a kind of haze in the air, causing things to appear different from what they really are; any artificial interest in, or association with, an object, through which it appears delusively magnified or glorified.[23]

Enobarbus' words, precisely by not focusing on Cleopatra "herself," do make her appear "different" from what she "is," and his language itself generates a kind of haze in the air as he "describes" this mysterious commodity:

> Enobarbus: . . . For her own person,
> It beggared all description: she did lie
> In her pavilion—cloth of gold, of tissue—
> O'erpicturing that Venus where we see
> The fancy outwork nature. On each side her
> Stood pretty dimpled boys, like smiling Cupids,
> With divers-coloured fans, whose wind did seem
> To glow the delicate cheeks which they did cool,
> And what they undid, did.
> Agrippa: O rare for Antony! (2.2.207–215)

It would be more to the point, perhaps, to say "O rare for Enobarbus!" whose abstracted language encodes what Frank Whigham has described as a "phenomenological notion of glamour [that] links mystery and value."[24] Far be it from Agrippa not to "comprehend" glamour, as he responds further to Enobarbus' tale with interjections such as "Rare Egyptian!" (228), and "Royal Wench!" (236). Of course, far be it also for him to let Enobarbus successfully one-up him (as Enobarbus did earlier to Antony): he simultaneously demonstrates his "competence" at apprehending Cleopatra's glamour and reduces its symbolic value by rooting it in her sexual and (by patriarchal extension) reproductive value only: "She made great Caesar lay his sword to bed; / He ploughed her, and she cropped." Enobarbus counters, again in ways like Antony's earlier, by emphasizing the *force* of Cleopatra's "indescribable" charms, the way she makes "defect perfection":

Age cannot wither her, nor custom stale
Her infinite variety: other women cloy
The appetites they feed, but she makes hungry,
Where most she satisfies. For vilest things
Become themselves in her, that the holy priests
Bless her, when she is riggish. (235–240).

Deploying the "hierarchic motive that affects the very nature of perception," Enobarbus generates Cleopatra's glamour by setting up a chain
of oxymoronic images that ingeniously "beggar description" by canceling it out.[25]

The material Cleopatra provides, then, enables others to constitute
themselves through reporting as social performance. This kind of performance has well-established roots in the historical and rhetorical tradition, as biographers or "eyewitnesses" relate to others the deeds and
lives of famous figures. By doing so, they accumulate for themselves the
prestige attributed to someone who has witnessed extraordinary or li-
minal events or persons: someone who has "been there," or "seen it
with his own eyes." In this way, witnessing partakes of the power of the
fetish: one becomes oneself an object of fascination by virtue of having
"rubbed elbows" with the surplus value always attributed to celebrity.
By appropriation, one partakes of the very charisma one invents: that
particular kind of essentialism produced when persons are attributed
with unique, magical, "original" qualities. Such charisma is only en-
hanced when the rhetorical stance of the narrator is *vatic:* conveying the
fact that he has been transported with the wonder of what he has seen
and the inner knowledge he now has. The narrator cashes in on what
Benjamin calls the "aura of the original," an experience that cannot be
duplicated but can only be approximated.[26] "*I* will tell you," Enobarbus
says authoritatively (sounding not unlike Dan Rather at this moment).
His "I" materializes in this complex social and political situation as a
function of his discursive representation of Cleopatra. If he earns a
place in the story it is because it doesn't exist apart from his role in the
telling of it.

IV

Cleopatra may provide "monstrous matter of feast" for others, but she
also actively performs "herself." In a play in which a male author represents a textually citational female figure who is literally "feigned" by

a boy actor, and when this figure's operations within the play "as a woman" depend precisely on her own ability to feign "herself," it is not surprising that Cleopatra is attributed with "infinite variety." Permitting no stand-in to "boy her greatness" in any theater that is not under Egyptian control, Cleopatra insists on establishing herself as both the playwright and actor of all performances of herself. For Cleopatra, the key to power is to lay claim to everything produced on her property (and out of her properties): to be sole beneficiary of whatever profits are produced in and by her Egyptian theater.

And this theater is, not surprisingly, posited as exterior to the Roman habitus, located beyond the bounds of Roman discursivity but linked to it by its appropriation and use of Roman discourses as occasions for histrionic improvisation. As Steven Mullaney has said about the physical marginality of Elizabethan playhouses to central, "official" London:

> Popular drama in Renaissance England was born of the contradiction between a Court that in limited but significant ways licensed and maintained it and a city that sought its prohibition; it emerged as a cultural institution only by materially embodying that contradiction, dislocating itself from the confines of the existing social order and taking up a place on the margins of society. Erected outside the walls of early modern London in the "licentious Liberties" of the city, the popular playhouses of Elizabethan England occupied a domain that had traditionally been reserved for cultural phenomena that could not be contained within the strict or proper bounds of the community.[27]

The figure of Cleopatra embodies precisely those material contradictions. Occupying a domain reserved for cultural phenomena that cannot be contained within the strict or proper bounds of the Roman narrative imperative, Cleopatra's Egypt—like the English space of festivals, bear-baitings, and plays—becomes a site for the pleasures of the moment. Elizabethan London, too, had its space where impulse and improvisations were indulged, where, according to city officials and Puritan zealots, people wasted their time and money on the "poison'd hours" of plays, and where the delayed gratifications of status and power promised by mercantilism and an increasingly capitalist society (the work ethic that also fuels the legendary machine) were upstaged by the delights of the present.

And if Egypt represents the "place of the stage" in the play, the figure of Cleopatra represents its subject.[28] When Enobarbus delivers his "blazon" of her in Act 2, scene 2, we can understand why it is impossible to determine the appearance of Cleopatra herself. Regardless of whatever "image management" Enobarbus is engaged in, his language evinces a problem around Cleopatra's "own person." In fact, descriptions of Cleopatra in this play are never more than descriptions of the effect she has on the onlooker. Cleopatra's "identity," as others perceive it, is a function of the reception of whatever performance of herself she happens to be staging. There is only one figure in the play who says anything about her physical person at all, and that is Cleopatra herself— who says she is "with Phoebus' amorous pinches black / And wrinkled deep in time" (1.5.28,29). She is the only figure to whom Shakespeare has given the authority to refer directly to her own person.

This is a very different standard from that granted to Antony. To say that Cleopatra is contingent, mutable, local, variational, histrionic, and produced for final constitution in and by the audience is not, however, to say that she has no identity. As Annette Kuhn has argued,

> Understood in its everyday sense, performance is allied with acting, and acting is regarded as an activity that involves pretense, dissimulation, an intent to seem to be something or someone one is, in reality, not. An actor's role is assumed like a mask, the mask concealing the performer's "true self." The disguise is a cover, and in many schools of acting the more the audience is taken in by the performance, the better that performance is judged to be. In effecting a distance between assumed persona and real self, the practice of performance constructs a subject which is both fixed in the distinction between role and self and at the same time, paradoxically, called into question in the very act of performance. For over against the "real self," a performance poses the possibility of a mutable self, of a fluidity of subjectivity.[29]

Shakespeare's Cleopatra does have a kind of "stability"—but it is the paradoxical stability of a *histrionic* constitution. Cleopatra's conditions of existence are always already theatrical, always already mediated by a performative "identity" located not in particular performances but in the place from which these performances are launched. In other words, Shakespeare's Cleopatra represents not (as some critics have argued) some "fluid principle" that stands for whatever is "unrepresentable" about the figure of woman, but, rather, what is necessarily theatrical in all successful forms of subjectivity.[30] Cleopatra may be predictably histrionic, but she is never "identical" with any one performance of herself.

Cleopatra's "identity," then, is conjured not by a sequence of linkable performances which form a continuous and self-consistent narrative (the material of official historiography), but by the appropriateness of her performances to the theatrical space that Egypt represents in this play. Her identity can be comfortably inhabited as subjectivity because she is invested with all the property that goes with the playhouse—the costumes, the cross-dressing, the right to borrow from a stockpile of culturally defined gender attributes, both "masculine" and "feminine," the "special effects" (her barge burning on the water). Enobarbus' "portrait" of Cleopatra demonstrates the way she operates as theatrical effect rather than as narrative product. The "portrait" is in fact never more than a frame: a description not of Cleopatra but of everyone and everything that surrounds her. He "conjures" Cleopatra by articulating a mise-en-scène in which any number of Cleopatras can appear.

Cleopatra's "fame" in this play is largely the result of the way she stages herself as spectacle. Cultivating that more "vulgar" sort of fame (because, in the spirit of its Latin etymology, it is more popularly accessible than the "literary," which requires literacy), Cleopatra manages to sidestep the overdeterminations of legendary narrative by locating herself in the *machinery* of theatrical production rather than in any of its representational products.[31] In Cleopatra's theatrical habitus, "infinite variety" constitutes identity as a source of flexible strength; while in Antony's narrative habitus, such variety can only represent the infirmity of being unable to hold one's visible "shape." This is because (and it may seem paradoxical at first) under the narrative imperative, to be watched is to be the subject of voyeurism; while within the representational space of the playhouse, to be watched is to be the subject of spectacle.

Watching and being watched mean different things under different circumstances, and the stakes and effects of voyeurism differ from those of spectatorship. A spectacle is a visual event openly staged. The activities of watching and being watched are mutually acknowledged (openly or tacitly) by both actor and audience; and the actor is aware of acting *for* the audience, of deliberately putting on a show. Voyeurism, on the contrary, situates looking in ways inseparable from a desire to control, since the voyeur at once objectifies and (at least in fantasy) controls his object by refusing either to disclose himself watching or to subject himself to the scrutiny of a returned gaze. From his privileged position, the voyeur watches unwatched. Conducting itself as a kind of covert "anatomizing," a skulking "investigation of mysteries" (Kuhn,

Power of the Image, p. 52), voyeurism aims at disclosure and the literal discovery of its object's presumed "mysteries." The first principle of voyeurism in terms of the power relations it inscribes is that the observed be caught unawares. Here we note a crucial distinction between voyeurism and spectacle, since the "performance" that the voyeur witnesses is not (supposed to be) an "act." The power—real or imagined—that the voyeur feels derives from the experience of having witnessed something taken to be "private," and therefore, by extension, presumed to be "authentic."[32] In other words, voyeurism seeks to investigate "the essence of the reality," while spectacle offers the literally conventional, "the agreed-upon appearance of things."

However, as "conventional" as spectacle may seem, it is complicated by its very obviousness: it presents the opaque surface that paradoxically results from total *appearance* ("there she appear'd indeed; or my reporter devis'd well for her"). As Baudrillard has evocatively argued, "There is something secret in appearances, precisely because they do not readily lend themselves to interpretation. They remain insoluble, indecipherable."[33] This is why the spectacle of histrionicism among Renaissance courtiers, as well as the privileging of the theater as a cultural forum, generated such anxiety in the Puritan sensibility. Not only did it foreground surfaces; it simultaneously fostered the sense that something "true" was being masked or dissembled "beneath" or behind the performative. "Ocular proof," as Iago knows, can be the most unreliable kind of "evidence" (Hamlet anticipates this: a man can "smile and smile and be a villain"). For Cleopatra, spectacle serves to increase rather than to dispel mystery in ways that disclose nothing so much as a *refusal* to disclose. She appropriates to herself, both in terms of social performance and self-image, what Robert Weimann has described as "the intrinsic indeterminacy opened up by the interaction between text and stage."[34]

If we are accustomed to thinking of women as the objects of the pornographic gaze (and its structural imperialism), in this play Cleopatra manages to take a reconnaissance activity that leaves Rome as voyeurism and translate it into something that returns to Rome only the strangely void "information" of spectacle. Antony however, is not so successful. In this play it is Antony who experiences himself as the subject of the voyeuristic gaze—and not surprisingly, since, as Octavius tells his sister, "I have eyes upon him, / And his affairs come to me on the wind" (3.6.62). It is Antony who feels "his corrigible neck, his face subdued / To penetrative shame" (4.14.75). And this shame is *obscene* because "obscenity begins when there is no more spectacle, no more stage, no more theatre, no more illusion, when every-thing becomes immediately transparent, visible, exposed in the raw and inexorable light of information and communication" (Baudrillard, *Ecstasy of Communication*, p. 21). Antony's sense of shame is the result of an experience of himself as obscene, as completely open to the appropriating eyes of others without any of the *distance* between actor and audience that the theatrical habitus provides. He is entirely "exposed in the raw and inexorable light of information and communication"—laid bare in the world's "report." Unable to "objectify that objectification," to "appropriate that appropriation," to "impose the norms of apperception of [his] own body" (Bourdieu, *Distinction*, p. 208), Antony is unmanned by a shame that is penetrative precisely because it inscribes him in a subject-position almost always historically reserved for women, for the female "captives" of the voyeuristic, pornographic imagination (the word "pornography" etymologically means to "enslave a female harlot in writing").

Cleopatra avoids this kind of inscriptive entrapment, partly by determining what she will and will not "internalize," and partly by anticipating how other figures are likely to talk about her. The difficulty of identifying "one" Cleopatra is reinforced throughout the play. When Antony, in 1.1.48, calls her a "wrangling queen, whom everything becomes," he is saying not only that every posture or passion suits her but also that she becomes everything—a blueprint of transmutability.[35] Cleopatra's histrionic capacity, like that of all good actors, derives from her ability to "note the qualities of people." As canny an observer of other people's theatrical strategies as a manipulator of her own, Cleopatra appropriates representational systems "proper" to both genders, loading them into her own strategic repertoire.

Antony, asked by Lepidus "what manner o'thing is your crocodile," replies:

> Antony: It is shap'd, sir, like itself, and it is as broad as it hath breadth: it is just so high as it is, and moves with it own organs. It lives by that which nourisheth it, and the elements once out of it, it transmigrates.
> Lepidus: What colour is it of?
> Antony: Of it own colour too. (2.7.41–47)

While we can read in these lines Antony's refusal to "reveal" Cleopatra in any specific way, they are also, paradoxically, a description of the process of identification, insofar as the term is self-corroborating. The creature Antony describes is identical only to itself, and cannot be rendered *the same as* anything other than itself. But what is evoked here in the speech act as uniqueness can also be considered the perfect playtext description, insofar as it permits any actor to play the role by providing no "identifying" physical characteristics of Cleopatra at all. These lines offer a blueprint for disidentification. Anything could be this "crocodile"; any actor could play Cleopatra. Antony's text of Cleopatra—as nonpareil—is here conflated with the playwright's text of Cleopatra—the infinitely inhabitable theatrical role for any number of actors. It is this combination of "inimitable uniqueness" and theatrical indeterminacy that renders Cleopatra's representational mode so subversive to Octavius' imperialist project; for it makes it difficult to strategize how to appropriate her as a manageable "text."

After Antony's death, the struggle between Cleopatra and Octavius turns toward where and how the triumph of Caesar will be staged. Cleopatra clearly is politically defeated at this point; but the fifth act of the play is concerned almost exclusively with the *representational* politics of this defeat. The final scenes are permeated with references to the theater, as Octavius' project becomes how to stage Cleopatra's defeat as a performance back in Rome. Cleopatra is aware that her capture will be the occasion of a grand theatrical event, a recasting of her "identity" in terms of the male-dominated, exotic gypsy-queen, brought "home" to Rome. The exoticizing of Cleopatra has helped set this moment up, since her "capture" and appropriation by Rome will foreground all the more the political distinction of Augustus Caesar, emperor of Roman "stability."

When his guards seize and disarm her, Proculeius says:

> . . . Cleopatra,
> Do not abuse my master's bounty, by
> The undoing of yourself; let the world see
> His nobleness well acted, which your death
> Will never let come forth. (42–46)

Explicitly referred to as material for Caesar's "nobleness well acted," the stakes of this conflict are now clear to Cleopatra. Caesar understands that in order to appropriate Cleopatra's power, he will have to defeat her in her own representational mode. And Cleopatra' understands that she will be made a show *of,* forced to perform in a play in which she is not the playwright, in a "theater" that is not her own. She laments to Iras, "Shall they hoist me up, / And show me to the shouting varletry / Of censuring Rome?" (5.2.54–56). The censure she repudiates is less the contempt she is sure to receive: we have already seen how little she esteems Roman "opinion." But censure has another set of meanings that pose a greater threat. To "censure" (according to the OED) is to subject something or someone to official judgment; but it is also, more literally, a correction—a revision or recension, especially of a literary work. In other words, to censure is to enclose in a formal sentence, to set firm grammatical limits—in short, to censure is to *identify:* to determine in an "authoritative" way what someone or something *is.* It is here that the narrative imperative, with its censuring apparatus, reveals the reifying investigative impulse it shares with voyeurism. Both processes fix the object in view with the aim of deciphering and delimiting its meaning. Octavius may need Cleopatra to show his greatness "well-acted"; but his use of political theater is only a stage—chronological more than spatial—along the way to narrative inscription: a factory in which Cleopatra's histrionic evasiveness can be reassembled into something appropriable by Rome.

Cleopatra fears that if deprived of the power to choreograph herself, a Roman "character" of "Cleopatra" will be produced: a *pornograph* in which she will be corrected, revised, entrapped "I'the posture of a whore." She would rather "undo herself" than let Caesar redo her in his own terms. She warns Iras that

> Thou, an Egyptian puppet shall be shown
> In Rome as well as I: mechanic slaves
> With greasy aprons, rules, and hammers shall
> Uplift us to the view. In their thick breaths,
> Rank of gross diet, shall we be enclouded,
> And forc'd to drink their vapour.
> Iras: The gods forbid!
> Cleopatra: Nay, 'tis most certain, Iras: saucy lictors
> Will catch at us like strumpets, and scald rhymers
> Ballad us out o'tune. The quick comedians
> Extemporally will stage us, and present
> Our Alexandrian revels: Antony
> Shall be brought drunken forth, and I shall see
> Some squeaking Cleopatra boy my greatness
> I'the posture of a whore. (5.2.208–221)

For Cleopatra, theatrical presentation is fine so long as she is playing "herself." The issue is not whether one is to be a spectacle, but, rather, who is producing it and to what ends. As John Fiske has said about another charismatic performer attributed with "infinite variety," "[Madonna] turns herself into a spectacle, and thus denies the spectator the empowered position of the voyeur."[36] Fiske argues that "spectacle involves an exaggeration of the pleasure of looking . . . It exaggerates the visible, magnifies and foregrounds surface appearance and refuses meaning or depth" (p. 243). If this is so, then controlling the conditions of the production of spectacle also means controlling the uses of the pleasure it affords. It means, to some extent at least, controlling the spectator. By presenting surface only, an experience of pleasure that does not permit penetration (and, consequently, no "penetrative shame"), spectacle also denies voyeurism, which depends on controlling not only the image of the object but its meanings as well. Cleopatra as self-staged spectacle denies the voyeur his power—he can narrate the spectacle, but not determine with any confidence its "character."

But a Cleopatra staged for and by others would be reduced in the censure of Rome to the squeaking boy whose postures "mean" one thing: whoredom, the condition of prostitution, defined as the use of a person, by someone else, to unworthy or debasing purpose. All this is complicated, of course, by the fact that the actor in Shakespeare's theater was already "boying" Cleopatra's greatness. What does it mean to have a boy (or young male) actor speak a line decrying what boy actors do?

Annette Kuhn, in her discussion of sexual disguise and cinema, has said that

> In its performance aspect, clothing sets up a play between visible outward appearance—in this case, gender as signified by dress—and an essence which may not be visible but is nonetheless held to be appearance and essence is a fundamentalism of the body, an appeal to bodily attributes as final arbiter of a basic truth . . . Dress constantly poses the possibility of distance between body and clothing, between "true" self, the fixed gender of ideology, and assumed persona. Crossdressing as a realisation of such a potential turns this distance to account, constructing sexual disguise as a play upon the fixity and the fluidity of gender identity. (*The Power of the Image*, p. 54)

The conditions of Shakespearean drama are such that investigations of gender difference are structurally built into theatrical performance. Gender difference as dissemblance is quite literally performed each time a female character is played on the stage by a male actor. If what

Peter Stallybrass has recently called "the body beneath"[37] is always assumed to be an unspoken "truth," the ideological touchstone of an essentialized gender, then the audience at a Renaissance theatrical performance was always being asked to willingly suspend its belief in such difference—to function imaginatively as if such differences were in fact merely "put on."[38] By calling attention to this theatrical convention at this point in the play, Cleopatra claims something "essential" about herself by speaking as if she were a "real female person" who is to be "enacted" by boys in a debased and debasing Roman theatrical production. Referring to the real metadramatic conditions of her staging in Shakespeare's play, Cleopatra can at once deploy and disown them: deploy them to deflect the penetrating gaze of the voyeur from the body of her character (a gaze which would in fact uncover the "essential truth" of the boy) and disown them by implying that such conditions may obtain in vulgar Roman theater, but not in her elite Egyptian theater. No verisimilitude here. Cleopatra constructs Roman theater as ersatz or kitsch, while Egyptian theater can claim to present the incomparable and original "thing itself." In making Cleopatra call explicit attention to her own constructedness in her disdain of vulgar imitations, Shakespeare ingeniously induces the authenticity effect through the *obscenity*—in Baudrillard's sense—of her metaleptic disclosure.[39]

Like Shakespeare's Richard III, Cleopatra understands the necessity of getting others to "abdicate their generic power of objectification and delegate it to the person who should be its object" (Bourdieu, *Distinction*). But unlike Richard, Cleopatra has a place separate from the official center in which to succeed in the enterprise. Unable to impose her own self-image in Rome under conditions of Roman defeat, Cleopatra is nevertheless unwilling to give up being her own "absolute subject." And her unwillingness to submit to the voyeuristic and objectifying spies and whispers of Rome can also be understood as a resistance to the *sadism* of narrative. As Laura Mulvey has argued about the relationship between narrative and voyeuristic cruelty,

> voyeurism . . . has associations with sadism: pleasure lies in ascertaining guilt (immediately associated with castration), asserting control and subjecting the guilty person through punishment or forgiveness. This sadistic side fits in well with narrative. Sadism demands a story, depends on making something happen, forcing a change in another person, a battle of will and strength, victory/de-

feat, all occurring in a linear time with a beginning and an end. Fetishistic scopophilia, on the other hand, can exist outside linear time as the erotic instinct is focused on the look alone.[40]

Western historiography always demands a story. And no place has demanded it more than Rome. Octavius *is* trying to force changes in other people, he is launching a battle of will and strength, victory and defeat, against Cleopatra and Antony, and in the linear time that is the representational and ideological mode of imperialism. And whereas Antony has suffered from "shame" and "guilt" and, alternately, sought the forgiveness and suffered the punishment of Rome's sadistic insistence on its narrative, Cleopatra has fostered the "fetishistic scopophilia" of her own self-staging, refusing the punitive voyeurism of Roman report, and confounding its schedule of linear time.

Significantly, Cleopatra's refusal takes the form of an unwillingness to emigrate, to leave the space that authorizes her own "relative agency."[41] This is, of course, where she demonstrates her greatest difference from Antony. In Egypt, her "proper" theater, Cleopatra can be for the group what she is for herself. In Rome, she cannot. Cleopatra, the subject of theater, will alter "texts" to fit her performances of self. Antony, the subject of narrative, will alter his performances to fit the mandates of the text. Antony is defeated in the play's "symbolic struggle" because he cannot finally avoid the domination of being for himself what he is in the opinion of others. And this is because built into the production of notorious identity are conditions which demand and construct subjects who will "fall in" to the reproductive apparatus (in this play, "the world's report") and secure its structures by internalizing them. It will relentlessly survey and shame those subjects, as it does Antony, beggaring anyone who does not go along with its reckoning.

V

There's beggary in the love that can be reckoned.
Antony (1.1.14–15)

What's love got to do, got to do with it?
Tina Turner, "What's Love Got to Do with It?"

As important as it is to see how the representational technologies of Egypt and Rome produce structurally dissimilar subjects, the notorious identities of Antony and Cleopatra are ultimately secured by another less obvious but perhaps more powerful apparatus.[42] For centuries this play has been regarded, by readers, audiences, and critics, as a legendary *love story*. But before turning to what love has to do and to do with it in Shakespeare's play, I want to consider what makes a question such as Tina Turner's intelligible in the first place. As a speech act, this song is a critical "intervention": a disruptive response to a narrative that precedes and exceeds it. Exactly what the question challenges is unimportant—for its rhetorical effectiveness depends not on the particular discourse it targets but, rather, on our recognition of the strategic use of the word "love" with regard to it. In other words, what matters is not the matter, but the form imposed on it "in the name of love."

That we understand instantly what the question does betrays our awareness of the use of the concept of love as an authoritative and sacralizing epistemology. The "love story" has been one of the most pervasive and effective of all ideological apparatuses: one of the most effective smokescreens available in the politics of cultural production. One need only think of the historical popularity of crime stories purveyed as "love stories": from the Trojan War—that paradigmatic "linkage" of love and genocide—to Bonnie and Clyde, from the subcultural Sid and Nancy to the hyperreal Ron and Nancy, we see the degree to which the concept of love is used as a "humanizing" factor, a way of appropriating figures whom we have no other defensible reason to want to identify with.[43] It is also a way of containing whatever political or social threat such figures may pose within the more palatable and manipulable (because simultaneously fetishized as universal and individual) motivations of love and sexual desire. Throughout the play, all political narratives are articulated against the love of Antony and Cleopatra. But while on one level the play posits love as a different realm from politics, on another it reveals the love story as yet another representational strategy, with its own investments in politically useful fabrications.

It is (both for the protagonists and for most critics) the "love story" element that renders this historical narrative "mythic." As Hayden White has pointed out about interpretations of history, their comprehensibility tends to depend on their "figuration as a *story of a particular kind*." Drawing analogies between fictional and historical narratives, White claims that "there are at least two levels of interpretation of every historical work: one in which the historian constitutes a story out of a chronicle of events and another in which, by a more fundamental narrative technique, he progressively identifies the *kind* of *story* he is telling—comedy, tragedy, romance, epic, or satire, as the case might be. It would be on the second level of interpretation that the mythic consciousness would operate most clearly."[44] Shakespeare's *Antony and Cleopatra* tropes on each genre White lists above. But unlike Shakespeare's history plays or the other tragedies, its "comprehensibility," finally, seems always to boil down to this more "fundamental narrative"—the "love story," a narrative that frequently disguises itself (*qua* narrative) or is taken as "natural" as opposed to the contrivances of other generic forms.

In a recent essay significantly entitled "The Personal Shakespeare: Three Clues," William Kerrigan claims that it is the "worth" of Antony and Cleopatra's love, and their fidelity to it, that "inspires" their legend. Arguing that "as [Shakespeare] allied his dramatic art with the mythological greatness of his lovers, [he] struck against the designs of history," Kerrigan's reading exemplifies precisely the kind of excision I have mentioned above, one in which "love" is universalized, naturalized, and, more important, essentialized in its separation from the discourses that construct "other" kinds of cultural experience.[45] But the "love story" in this play produces what White calls our "mythic consciousness" because it is a narrative that *pretends* to stand apart from other narratives. The legend effect that Kerrigan attributes to the love story "against the designs of history" I wish to attribute to the love story *within* the designs of history. To situate a love story in a play that examines the ideological implications of different forms of representation is to posit love "itself" as a crucial stratagem of ideological production. The central issue, then, must be regarded not as what the love story *is* apart from the play's other discourses but, rather, what it *does* in relation to them.

Despite centuries of being celebrated as a tragic yet transcendent love story (especially in the last two centuries), there is little evidence that Shakespeare's *Antony and Cleopatra* was popular in his own day, and much that it was not. There were few critical statements about the play for several centuries after its first production in 1606–1607; and as Michael Steppat points out, "though Chaucer about 1385 in his *Legend of Good Women* had spoken about Cleopatra's 'passioun' and her 'trouth in love' . . . most Elizabethan discussions focused on what were seen as her moral and political crimes. The Elizabethan writer Richard Reynoldes asserted that a 'harlotte' like Cleopatra, who had committed 'horrible murthers,' [was] [in]capable of dying for love."[46] In general, there doesn't seem to have been much critical interest at all in

Shakespeare's version of the story until, as Steppat says, "the early nine-teenth century, when the Romantics showed an interest in *Antony* as a play to be read in the study."[47]

The increasing historical popularity of the play has been inseparable from a critical revisionism that has transformed it from what it was in Shakespeare's time—a notorious story about politics on every level—to what it is now: a "legendary" love story about Great Individuals in Love. And this transformation owes more to a misrecognition of what love's got to do with it than with what love actually *does* in the play. In order to understand how the play's reception has revised it as a tale of epic, paradigmatic, and "transcendent" love, we must look at what is culturally productive about this kind of reconstruction. The play's crit-ical reception has by and large (with exceptions along the way) tended to mantle love as a carapace under which the play's political conflicts are subsumed and rendered secondary. But against this reconstruction (which begins most portentously with Dryden's *All for Love*), the play itself demonstrates how the production of legendary love can be one of the most effective ways to deflect, defuse, and contain perceptions of irreconcilable political differences.[48] This transformation is effected in the play through the figure of Octavius Caesar, who in his closing lines inaugurates centuries of critical reception by taking an unruly general he has been trying to reclaim, and a doubly unruly woman he has alter-nately regarded as a whore and a major political threat, and translating them into "Antony and Cleopatra": legendary lovers.

Behind Octavius' strategy (and, one suspects, that of many critics) is an effort to come up with a definition of love that will stand safely apart from politics; one in which love is defined precisely as other than the political. Regarded as transcendent "in the end," the love of Antony and Cleopatra is reckoned "above" the politics in which the play's other power relations are mired.[49] But rather than regard the love of Antony and Cleopatra in such "bracketed" terms (which would be to consent to Octavius' "clipping"), I would like to consider it precisely in terms of all the play's other power relations, specifically its investigation of compet-ing representational strategies. To understand why Octavius so quickly turns to "legendary love" in the play's closing lines, we should look at the extent to which its structures are already in place, and the complic-ity of Antony and Cleopatra themselves in manipulating a "love" that is always to double business bound.

In this play, the politics of desire that motivate imperialist ambition are perfectly congruent with those that operate "privately" in the realm of love; and whatever Antony and Cleopatra feel for each other is comprised of the same materials that constitute the rest of their world. "Naturally" Antony loves Cleopatra—she is exotic, mysterious, capricious, charismatic, sensuous, challenging, charming, earthy—the characterological equivalent, in other words, of the imagined terrain of Egypt, with which she is always synecdochized. "Naturally" Cleopatra loves Antony—he is magnanimous (in the Aristotelian sense), expansive, aggressive, powerful, manly, famous like the imperial Roman terrain he both extends and is an extension of. "Naturally" they are drawn to each other; they are both so much "larger than life." But to think of their love in these terms is to consent to Antony and Cleopatra's self-representations without paying adequate attention to Shakespeare's representations. It is to fall into what Bourdieu calls "the interactionist fallacy," or to assign to them "personally" the qualities that are in fact the metonymic extensions of their paradigmatic source: the "internalized" functions of their respective habitus. In a play that is simultaneously about legendary Roman expansionism and legendary lovers, it is not surprising that the play records (and produces) a confusion (and fusion) of persons with places. For the shared ideologies that construct Egyptianness and Romanness reproduce in subjects (as aspects of self) the structures that structure, and therefore make sense of, their worlds.

Whatever love text these figures weave is repeatedly ruptured by political exigency. This is especially true of Antony, who can justify himself in his own eyes only by mystifying "this wrangling queen, whom every thing becomes." But even the erotic rhetoric Antony uses is abandoned in those moments when he fears political betrayal, as he demonstrates in Act 3, scene 8, when he calls Cleopatra "a morsel, cold upon/ Dead Caesar's trencher" (116), a "boggler," a "fragment." That Antony can lapse so quickly into the debasing terms his fellow Romans use against Cleopatra (note Enobarbus' reference to her in 2.7.123 as an "Egyptian dish") reveals the extent to which his own construction of her as love object cannot be kept uncontaminated by that of his countrymen. Such terms are ever-present in his mind, ready to be mobilized under the appropriate political conditions.

Antony's rhetoric of transcendence is apotropaic—a way of warding off an intolerable awareness of Rome's view of him as "a strumpet's fool" (1.1.13) who has "offended reputation" (3.11.48). In a play in which the political is set up as the "real," Love becomes Antony's representation of his own "imaginary relationship to his real conditions of existence," a way of shoring up an identity grown blemished "in the world's report." Unable to objectify the objectifications of himself produced in Rome, Antony feels "unqualitied with very shame" (3.11.44). Unable to escape his own constitution as a Roman (in the history of Augustus Caesar as Shakespeare's own sources wrote it), his heightened rhetoric of love for Cleopatra is his "attempt to reappropriate an alienated being for others," to counter the "penetrative shame" that, I have argued, underlies every aspect of his character in this play. Using "love" to produce "distinction," Antony and Cleopatra themselves posit a transcendent rhetorical realm in which they can underwrite endangered reputations with the symbolic capital to which transcendent love always lays claim.

This is not to say that this is not love. But it can and must be regarded as inextricable from sociopolitical purpose. To put it plainly, Antony and Cleopatra talk about their love in ways that contradict what they actually *do* with it. In 1.1.14–18, we hear what amounts to a theory about love:

> Cleopatra: If it be love indeed, tell me how much.
> Antony: There's beggary in the love that can be reckon'd.
> Cleopatra: I'll set a bourn how far to be belov'd.
> Antony: Then must thou needs find out new heaven, new earth.
> (1.1.14–18)

This language posits a love that cannot be "reckoned," that exceeds the supposed baseness of thinking in quantitative terms. But for these two figures, thinking in any terms other than those of an acquisitive expansionism seems to be impossible, as even their "alternative" terms of measurement rely on colonialist images of new territories: finding out a new heaven, a new earth. The "expansiveness" frequently attributed to Antony's love for Cleopatra (in a term that, like "misrecognition," refracts the truth of what it misspeaks) can be understood as part of the play's lexicon of imperialism. This expansiveness is in fact expansionist. Here is not a love that cannot be reckon'd but, rather, a love that requires even *more* territory—more even than that which Octavius covets. Antony's claim of unwillingness to perform what Aristotle calls "exact bookkeeping" is itself a kind of social performance, one that generates symbolic capital by observing in the realm of love what Castiglione describes as a "certain *sprezzatura*," a way of treating artfully acquired and politically usable skills (in this instance, a style of loving) as if they were intrinsic or "natural."[50]

This love story, then, far from providing a refuge from Rome's impe-

rial project, a "distinction" from the world of Octavius Caesar, conceives imaginative space for itself in language that partakes of similar
narratives, in similar terms. What has frequently been taken as the "alternative" world of Egypt and Cleopatra turns out to be not so different
after all. While on one level the play seduces us with the allure of "difference" and its hold over Antony, on another it reveals that while
Egypt and Rome may be the sites of different representational strategies, the stakes of their conflict are finally the same. And these are the
ability to lay claim to authoritative space in which the acquired can be
appropriated (in senses both personal and political) and kept as *property*. However much the play engages us imaginatively with Antony
and Cleopatra as two lovers who playfully enjoy each other, who feast
and drink and wander the streets ignoring their political responsibilities, it never lets us forget that they are always simultaneously advancing their own political campaign.

The connections, then, between the "epic" narrative of empire and
the "timeless, mythic" narrative of love are imbricated, as Octavius' political defeat of Antony is figured in language similar to Cleopatra's sexual "conquest" of Antony: both are represented as strategic, and in military terms. In Act 4, scene 14, just before Mardian tells him, falsely, of
Cleopatra's death, Antony informs Eros,

> I made these wars for Egypt, and the queen,
> Whose heart I thought I had, for she had mine:
> Which whilst it was mine, had annex'd unto't
> A million moe, now lost . . . (15–18)

Antony, here convinced that Cleopatra has betrayed him to "pack
cards" with Caesar, explicitly reveals the connections between his love
and his soldiership, passion and militarism, the conquest of one heart
and the annexation of "a million moe." Antony and Cleopatra's mutual
"having of hearts" gives them the ground and impetus for their own
"imperial project": theirs is, literally, a "consuming" passion insofar as
the power it gives them is the power to consume new territory. When
Antony believes Cleopatra no longer loves him, what he says is "She
has robb'd me of my sword." Falsely informed of her death by Mardian
a few lines later, Antony makes it clear that without Cleopatra, all that
is left to do is "unarm, the long day's task is done" (35). If Antony is "No
more a soldier" (42) it is because he is now no more a lover. Unlike
Troilus, who renounces his role as lover in order to play the soldier,
Antony cannot be the one without being the other. Although the play

encourages us to misrecognize Antony's love for Cleopatra as an alternative to the identity and project he bears for Rome, we see that in his role as *Cleopatra's* Antony he is put to similar use. Except that now, in and from Egypt, he is misplaced in a representational habitus alien to his "original" constitution as "Antony," a constitution which requires the submission of self to the demands of legendary posterity.

This achieves its paradigmatic expression in Antony's death scene, where he reverts to "type," his dying words most concerned with how he will be narratively re-membered. Ever obsessed with "report," Antony narrates his own memorial, calling himself "the greatest prince o'the world," "a Roman valiantly vanquished" (4.15.57–58). After bungling his fall on his sword, this rhetoric exemplifies the split between what these figures do and how they characterize what they're doing—a disjunction reinforced by Cleopatra, who is less concerned with the time Antony has left than with remaining in a secure position on her monument. Denying Antony's request that she descend to kiss him in his last moments, Cleopatra answers,

> I dare not, dear,
> Dear my lord, pardon: I dare not,
> Lest I be taken: not the imperious show
> Of the full-fortun'd Caesar ever shall
> Be brooch'd with me, if knife, drugs, serpents, have
> Edge, sting, or operation. I am safe:
> Your wife Octavia, with her modest eyes,
> And still conclusion, shall acquire no honour
> Demuring upon me: but come, come, Antony,—
> Help me, my women,—we must draw thee up:
> Assist, good friends. (22–30)

Ever obsessed with how she is staged, Cleopatra is more anxious not to be a "brooch" in Caesar's imperious (empire-building) show than to grant her dying lover's last request. Her foremost thoughts at this moment are on how to keep Caesar and Octavia from "acquiring honor" from her capture; and her references to suicide are prompted here, at least syntactically, not by Antony's impending death but by the prospect of being made Caesar's spectacle. For both Antony and Cleopatra, love—even at this most critical of moments—cannot transcend the particular textual material it operates in.[51]

The fact that Cleopatra is successful in stage-managing her own suicide while Antony cannot properly manage his (Eros won't run him through, nor will the guards) reinforces the degree to which the gestures attributed to love are only legible within the particular structures of a representational habitus. Antony's wish in Act 4, scene 14, is to be "conqueror of himself" (60), as he imagines Cleopatra has been. And of course he imagines this death in the "high Roman fashion," for noble Romans commit suicide rather than suffer capture and execution. But Antony's agency is continually thwarted (Shakespeare has him fall ineptly on his sword rather than stab himself) because he is on a stage that is not his own. However much he would like to play the Roman, in this Egyptian theater he can neither properly handle this Roman "prop" (his sword) nor choreograph this Roman moment. To persist in calling himself, even after all this, "a Roman, by a Roman valiantly vanquished" (4.15.57) is to fictionalize to the bitter end the nature of his position, doggedly asserting an autonomy that the play repeatedly denies him.

After Antony's death Cleopatra eulogizes him in terms that at once echo his self-mythologizing and reveal, however indirectly, her awareness of the impossibility of his position. Cleopatra's rapturous language is moving, and it is easy to get caught up in her sense of loss at this moment; but the metaphors she mixes compose a picture too awkward to pass unexamined. Claiming that "his legs bestrid the ocean" *and* that "his delights were dolphin-like," she perhaps does not realize what a strenuous posture this has been to maintain. To stand as a monument with legs "bestriding" the ocean (joining, as it were, the coasts of Egypt and Rome) is logically (not to mention physically) incompatible with swimming in that ocean. Cleopatra's rhetoric about her lover encodes an awareness of the incongruity of these postures, figuring even while celebrating the morphological inconsistency that robbed Antony of his "visible shape." Cleopatra's panegyric—at once contradictory and true—represents a figure split from himself (self-bestridden, we might say), one foot encased in an imperialist monument while the other is immersed in a sea of mimetic (dolphin-like) pleasure. It is no wonder that when the time came for him to do so, Antony could not position himself to fall properly on his Roman sword.

For many critics the play affectively "ends" here, in Act 4, scene 15, with the death of Antony, and Cleopatra's poetic eulogy to him. Her language contrives the emotional "sense of an ending" that the play at once invites and refuses. For Cleopatra says she will commit suicide as a tribute to Antony, that she will "do it after the high Roman fashion" (4.15.87) and seek "the briefest end." The problem, however, is that she doesn't—and still has the entire fifth act of the play to get through. We watch her efforts to secure resources, her heightened language of theatricality ("show me, my women, like a queen: go fetch / My best attires"—5.2.225), her efforts to maneuver a way out of her predicament, all to no avail. Does she at last commit suicide *for* Antony or because she cannot tolerate watching "some squeaking Cleopatra boy [her] greatness / I'the posture of a whore"?

Of course, none of this is meant to indict Cleopatra for not loving "truly" or even well enough. Quite the reverse. The play posits two versions of love: love as poetic construct or usable material for fiction, and love as realpolitik; love that is "to die for," and love that is to die for if nothing else can be worked out. In control of the choreography even as the political situation spins out of her control, Cleopatra takes charge of herself in a way that Antony has never been able to do. And when she does dispatch herself, her method is anything but Roman: it is as Egyptian as it is theatrical. Invoking the actor's ideal sympathetic audience by imagining that Antony will "rouse himself / To praise [her] noble act" (5.2.284), Cleopatra stages her death scene as exotic, erotic Egyptian, a mother nursing a strange baby at her breast rather than a stalwart "marble-constant" Roman.

Appropriating the discourse of autonomy that accompanies the "Roman fashion" of suicide, Cleopatra revises its terms in theatrical and self-mythologizing language that, on this stage and in this performance, does not ring hollow. Like Antony, Cleopatra is engaged in weaving a representation of her own imaginary relationship to her real conditions of existence. But unlike Antony, she can *own* the representation because she understands the crucial connection between the structures of the habitus and those of identity: between where one is and *what* one is. Shakespeare's Cleopatra understands that the former will authorize, enable, and support the successful inhabitation of the latter only if they are structurally congruent. This is why Cleopatra must die in her own place and on her own stage. By doing so, she exerts final control over herself as a subject. Cleopatra's suicide will eliminate the possibility of staging her defeat in Rome; and this thought clearly permits her to "own" herself as she undertakes her death. If Antony dies the absolute object of others' regard, Cleopatra dies the absolute subject of her own.

Upon learning of Cleopatra's suicide, Octavius understands immediately the political uses to which he can put a mythologized "Antony and Cleopatra." For like Cleopatra, Octavius is capable of seizing an opportunity—of tactically poaching on the strategies of others. He swiftly translates them from rebellious figures who escaped his control and punishment into legendary lovers. Like other figures who are branded as renegades or deviates while exercising agency for their own ends, Antony and Cleopatra can become epic lovers in the world's report only once Octavius has full control of the machinery of reproduction. Only then can they be put to historiographic use. Reversing the rhetoric he deployed at the beginning of the play (that it is shameful and unmanly to neglect one's political responsibilities for love), Octavius now suggests that their love is the sign of their "nobility." By reinscribing love as a form of transcendence, Octavius renders Antony and Cleopatra "safe" for the lessons of "posterity." No longer a direct threat to Roman law and order (which in Shakespeare's play ultimately "stand for" Jacobean England's centralized monarchical and reinforced patriarchal authority, control of overweening aristocratic ambition, and authorized versions of history), they can now be reconstructed as figures who bravely hazarded "all for love." Providing Dryden and centuries of critics and audiences with the terms (and structures of feeling) by which to interpret this play, Octavius takes Cleopatra's suicide—"the dreaded *act* which [he] / So sought'st to hinder" (5.2.325)— and turns it into "their *story*":

> She shall be buried by her Antony.
> No grave upon the earth shall clip in it
> A pair so famous. High events as these
> Strike those that make them; and their story is
> No less in pity than his glory which
> Brought them to be lamented. Our army shall
> In solemn show attend this funeral,
> And then to Rome. Come, Dolabella, see
> High order in this great solemnity. (5.2.352–360)

While many critics have observed that Octavius' historiography "officially" wins in the end, most tend to assume that Antony and Cleopatra have triumphed on "other" grounds that are not, finally, Caesar's. But such an assumption occludes the fact that it is Octavius *himself* who legitimates, and hypostatizes into frozen monumentality, this ground. In order to eliminate any lingering threat Antony and Cleopatra may still pose as exemplars of political rebellion, Octavius' closing lines encase them in the frame of a tragic "story," which is then excised from the political arena and relocated in the realm of the transcendent Aesthetic. In the turn to "high order" and "great solemnity" (the *edification*—in all of its meanings—that high tragedy aims to impose), Antony can finally be acknowledged as "her Antony" because Cleopatra is now Octavius' Cleopatra. Both can be "clipped" into that famous pair in the grave now that they are appropriable as a tragic (which ultimately implies *inevitable*) story that Caesar can inflate into legend precisely because it is "no less in pity than his glory which / Brought them to be lamented." In the logic of his own terms, Octavius cannot elevate them enough, since whatever symbolic capital he produces by generating "pity" for their story is commutable into the surplus value of his own glory.[52] As the self-proclaimed maker of "high events as these," Octavius—who earlier assured Cleopatra that he was "no merchant, to make prize with you / Of things that merchants sold" (5.2.182)—in fact will return to Rome in his new role as the venture capitalist of notorious identity: the Merchant of Legend. Thus, Shakespeare's play ends where the history of its reception as a great tragedy begins: with the construction and marketing of a legendary love story.

No matter what position it has come to occupy in the Western canon of tragic love stories, Shakespeare's play posits an Antony and Cleopatra who are defeated not just by the political reality of Roman history as Shakespeare inherited it from his sources, but by the coercive force of representational politics. The play demonstrates that in a world structured by the linear, totalizing, and paradigmatic functions of narrative history, displacement becomes deviation—a source of pathology. But in a world structured by synchronic spectacle, histrionicism, and improvisational performances, multiplicity becomes the condition of political and psychological possibility—the ability to put aside one form to take on for a while the enabling dimensions of another. If, for Cleopatra, theatrical indeterminacy offers a way to remain "other" to any unifying inscription, for Antony the space of Egypt is one in which he can exist only as an alien creature. After all, what's good for the goose can be good for the gander only if in fact they are members of the same species. But the play gives us an Antony and Cleopatra who belong to different generic species. Behind the play's foregrounding of all other differences—whether of gender, race, or culture—is its attention to the constitutive power of representation: its capacity to determine, through the modes and technologies by which they are produced, reproduced, authorized, and disseminated, structures of subjectivity as well as versions of "history."

Shakespeare uses the figure of Antony to represent a fantasy of *defection* from textual and authoritative overdetermination, a fantasy of being able to change the element one lives in, to pack up and leave for a new place where scripts and stories are ever new and can be continually revised. But Antony also represents the truth of what every emigrant knows: that identity is always a function of proper place, that the construction of meaning is inextricably embedded in whatever particular system authorizes one's actions and agency. That, in short, you can't *not* take it with you when you go. Antony is forced to conform to the representational technology that has made him a narrative product before he even begins his "traffic" with this queen.

Cleopatra, on the other hand, remains a *practice* rather than a product; and as such, her "infirmity" of identity is the source of her strength. Shakespeare uses the figure of Cleopatra and her multiplicitous and marginal domain as representatives of the place and players of the Renaissance stage: the habitus of those continually changing persons who performed "wrangling" playtexts outside the margins of London and exercised a fascination over the city that uneasily tolerated and kept watch over—through its own spies and whispers—their operations.

Finally, the play enacts what one imagines might have been both a tactical and a strategic fantasy for the playwright: how to appropriate for theatrical authorship figures whose meanings had been massively overdetermined by their prior constructions in "legendary" narratives; how to "poach" on the texts of others, and how then to claim as "new" what is produced on the stage out of the most overly "known" of stories. After all, no other form of poaching could be more of a challenge to the powers of a playwright. And what could be more of a boast of the powers of the theater: that representational space in which there is a necessary nonidentity between actors and roles—where "character" is an artificial "thing" put on by those who are "other" to what they enact, and therefore not required to be identical to whatever representation they temporarily and provisionally inhabit. Shakespeare stages his own relationship to his narrative sources and to the theater, as well as his relation to the authorities that were determining what could and could not be performed in the subversively reinscriptive Renaissance playhouse. And by doing so, he counters the "antitheatrical prejudice" with an antinarrational one, whose allure resides in the fact that one doesn't have to be "identical" to oneself in order to materialize as a subject and lay claim to a proper place.

Conclusion

Always leave them wanting less.
Andy Warhol

Andy Warhol's motto should be understood in relation to his other famous dictum, that in the future everyone will have his or her fifteen minutes of fame.[1] Speaking about the reproductive force of media technology, Warhol points to the accelerated matriculation of persons through the fame apparatus: the way that media produces almost "instant" celebrity through its increasingly pervasive and efficient machinery. His ironic prophecy notes the temporal compression not just of the interval between when a person does something "noteworthy" and when he or she becomes famous, but of the duration of the fame as well. In this vision of a radically promiscuous fame, we can also imagine a change in its value as cultural currency, one in which it becomes a kind of monstrous hybrid, a remarkable banality, an impossible thing: a transcendental portmanteau signifier.

The really important implication of Warhol's statement has to do with the way fame becomes its own object/cause of desire, quite apart from the figures to whom it presumably attaches. With an autologous logic that conforms perfectly with that of capital, it takes fame to make fame. To talk, then, about "always leaving them wanting less" is to point to conditions in which there is always already a surplus—an overexposure which one must work to *renege*. One must labor not to produce less but to produce *a desire for* less: a desire which depends precisely on being already saturated with whatever it is one wants less of.

If all this sounds confusing, it is meant to. For how exactly does one leave them wanting less? It is not hard to understand how to leave them wanting more; for the fascination generated through withholding and mystery constitutes the dominant form of desire and eroticism in our culture. The commodity fetish achieves its power by virtue of what it pretends not to disclose about itself—by the projections it invites onto its supposed screen of mystery. The challenge is not to produce a desire

148

based on lack but, rather, to produce a desire—launched from a position of saturation—*for* a lack. Not that such a desire is unheard of: the cliché about "getting back to basics" (or about "less is more") is familiar to a culture whose forms of desire sustain themselves only by remaining unfulfilled. Nevertheless, the injunction to "always leave them wanting less" is literally pre-posterous because it mandates a paradox of reversal that, like missing the last exit off a one-way street, provokes imaginative catalepsy: a situation in which grasp (to paraphrase Browning) always already *exceeds* reach.

It is, I believe, just such a desire that Shakespeare's legend plays provoke through their stagings of notorious stories and subjects. Constructed as the surplus to their fame, these figures generate the kind of identificatory fascination that always results from the recognition—conscious or not—of a shared cultural symptomology. Carrying the weight of Western society's fetishizing of identity, Shakespeare's notorious figures demonstrate what happens when the fantasy of citational consistency, of characterological "oneness," unravels in the process of reproduction. In other words, these plays reveal that a legend is what happens when historical displacement becomes cultural symptom—when that which cannot be fully "refamiliarized" because it no longer "fits" must be made to fit anyway. Legends are history's hysterical symptoms: those figures whose "identities" become the site and sign of cultural overemplotment. To say this is not just to remark the obvious fact that we are dealing here with plays that lent themselves to matters of "history." Rather, it is to say that the plays at once secure and undercut history by revealing legends as the anchoring nodes—the *points de capiton*—of positivist historiography.

The extent to which Shakespeare and his contemporaries believed in legendary history as the guarantor of Providence is arguable. There are innumerable references to the role of Providence in England's chronicle histories and historiographic texts. But it is also clear that in post-Machiavellian England historiographers understood the political constructedness of what they recorded. That these two attitudes coexist isn't necessarily contradictory or even paradoxical. As I have said about the belief effect, one needn't choose between two apparently contradictory views. The case can be made for a "belief" in historical providence as the effect of the deliberate manipulation of political rhetoric. Shakespeare's legend plays mobilize both attitudes toward history extant in his day, generating a "deformed" version of Providence simultaneously as "merely" rhetorical and as absolutely true in its effects. If, as

Peter Sloterdijk has argued, "theology begins with automatic writing," I would argue that "providential" ideology begins (and continues) with automatic performance, a form of structural providentialism that operates on its own quite apart from the beliefs of individuals.[2] The plays demonstrate that one needn't believe in order to enact belief. And enacting it "proves" the truth of such belief and—postsequently—its "manifest destiny."

At once constantly reminding the audience/reader of what he or she already knows and provoking a sense that *this* time things might turn out differently, Shakespeare's notorious figures leave their audience wanting less—less knowledge, less of a sense of narrative destiny, less "history." And in generating this desire for a historical "lack" that might make these figures once again "new," *Richard III, Troilus and Cressida,* and *Antony and Cleopatra* provoke in the audience the same affective symptomology represented in their protagonists: the wish (whether expressed as a desire or as a fear) that this time the "destiny" of "Character" might be avoided. It is the same thing that happens when we go to see a film we have already seen, or one about "famous" figures. We know how the story ends; but the *work* of the representation is to convince us that while we think we know, we don't *really* know, even though, of course, we've been right all along. Proving that the repetition compulsion is alive and well in the cultural consumption of legends, these plays reveal the ways in which legend conflates the ideological "inevitability" of History with the factitiousness of Character: the degree to which the former is secured by the the latter. Belaboring their own obviousness, Shakespeare's notorious figures generate within the plays (and within the audience) the affective dislocation and cognitive dissonance necessary for each new round. The audience or reader, like the figures in the plays, must disown knowledge in order to permit the reinscription that is only afterward consolidated into legend and positioned within the providential "designs of history."

This is the peculiar "spin" Shakespeare puts on the problem of fame in these plays. And while early modern England was experiencing only the nascent forms and relations of capitalism (and was obviously not structured by the reproductive technologies of industrial and electronic mass media), they seem, with uncanny precocity, to anticipate the ways identity and subjectivity are produced in the culture of late capitalism. Shakespeare's notorious figures appear like proleptic holograms of the promised end of a commercially obsessed culture at the moment, loosely speaking, of its historical emergence. And though it may at first glance seem anachronistic to say so, the peculiar power of these plays resides in the way they seem to prefigure in other terms the political and psychological conditions of labor exploitation that will be fully theorized only centuries later, when the operations of industrial capitalism are firmly in place, and when the "alterity" it produces (in the form Marx called "alienation") becomes a constitutive condition of subjectivity. These plays demonstrate that in the age of textual and theatrical reproduction, the profits to be made from notorious identity return not to the famous figures themselves, but to whatever system "produces" their reproduction.

In this way we can see that the making of notorious identity has much in common with the making of "individual" identity. With the anticipatory quality that is always so surprising in Shakespeare, these plays deconstruct the bourgeois Cartesian subject, with its monadic fantasies of autonomy and self-determination, on the very eve (broadly speaking) of its historical inception, demonstrating through the exaggerated conditions of cultural notoriety what is nonetheless true for everyone, no matter how known or unknown: that it is neither possible to be the sole author of oneself, nor possible to control all the uses to which one's identity may be put. These plays suggest that *all* identity is "notorious" insofar as without the cultural inscriptions that code us, no one, to quote Ulysses, "knows himself for aught."

But if the plays suggest the extent to which we all enact—whether we "will" or not—versions of our own prescriptedness, they also posit a powerful desire for autonomy—however fantasmatic—a desire that is itself a by-product of a culture that, for the first time in European history, begins to define the term "individual" as distinctly separate (rather than in the original sense of inseparable) from others. For as much as performance may reiterate the material existence of ideology, it also (as we have seen especially in the figure of Cleopatra) marks the distance and differences between acts and texts, bodies and narratives, visual and discursive representations. Acting out a role can be the realization of a narrative—its literal embodiment in social space. But "acting out" can also, in the current colloquial sense, conjure acts of embodied and gestural resistance to rehearsal, to following authoritative scripts, to staying within the bounds of authoritarian expectation. To "act out" is to misbehave in the eyes of others who have the means—ideological and material—to put and keep one in one's "proper" place.

Shakespearean theater in general and his legend plays in particular are the sites for the acting out of authoritative cultural texts and the forms of "acting out" that they always produce in subjects. To go from *Richard III* to *Troilus and Cressida* to *Antony and Cleopatra* is to move from a figure who embodies in his own "person" the material inevitability of authoritative ideology, to figures who seem to wander bemusedly in search of their own citational predecessors, to two figures who act defiantly against the demands of their own legends, with different degrees of success. If in *Richard III* the hysterical symptom—the "deviant" individual—is also the historical cure, in *Troilus and Cressida* the symptom—the phallic signifier Helen and the empty "motivation" she offers—is preserved at all costs, guaranteeing the continued reproduction of a story that Shakespeare treated as a paradigm of a masculinist culture's repetition compulsion. Shakespeare's Antony, like Richard, is determined to determine himself, and achieves a good deal more than Richard before he reinters himself in the language of Roman "valor." Cleopatra, however, remains in-appropriate to the very end, refusing to permit Rome to "cure" itself of the symptom she represents by bringing her under its censuring Harrow.

With these three plays Shakespeare charts a notorious identity that begins with Richard, the fusion of signifier with signified; then splits the difference between figures and names in Troilus and Cressida, who ultimately purchase their legend with the small change that's left from its exhausted and devalued recirculation; and ends with his most successful contradiction: the notorious autonomy of Cleopatra. We might even consider Cleopatra the playwright's own version of a "new hystericist": a figure whose mimetic disrespect (like that of Patroclus) threatens the integrity of the imperial party line by poaching on its structures while refusing to reside within its boundaries.

That even Cleopatra ultimately ends up as material for Octavius' historicizing machine does not mean that Shakespeare's legend plays fail to destabilize the narratives they reproduce and revise. If, as Walter Benjamin claims, "the authenticity of a thing is the essence of all that is transmissible from its beginning, ranging from its substantive duration to its testimony to the history which it has experienced," then we might expect Shakespeare's versions of these legendary figures to be deeply inauthentic, insofar as each has suffered the "depreciation" of the "quality of [his or her] original presence."[3] But it is just this "depreciation" of a *false* "original presence" that paves the way for a reconsideration of what is meant both by "origins" and originality. In a twist of epistemological fate, the plays reveal that even notorious figures who had "real" historical existence must be textually reproduced before they can be their own "originals": that the notorious subject by definition *never precedes* his or her reputation.

Nevertheless, the translation of legendary narrative figures into dramatic ones does give them a new set of generic, relational, spatial, and temporal conditions within which to negotiate their "identities." This translation may engender (and gender) the "this is and is not" phenomenon; but the extent to which these figures do and do not fit their own "reputations" paradoxically grants them a provisional authenticity. It is, however, an authenticity that directly corresponds to the degree to which they resist their notorious identities: an authenticity produced not as the authoritative pedigree of legend but, rather, as a peculiarly inverted version of the "uncanny"—the mimetic capacity of Shakespearean drama and the theater to embody the ghosts in the machine— the "unknown" that always resides in the "known."

Spanning more than a decade in Shakespeare's career, the legend plays reveal the special claims the playwright makes for what drama can do, for how much it can loosen the seams of even the most tightly knit of narratives, as well as of identities. These are claims not of representational autonomy or freedom from determining structures, but of a mimetic mobility that makes the most of whatever symptoms appear in the fissures of cultural texts. The implications of all this extend beyond the parameters of the Renaissance playhouse, as they do beyond those of early modern England. Which is not for a moment to say that the local forms they take are either "timeless" or "universal." But it is to say that in a culture that has seen patriarchal capitalism reach, if not quite its promised end, then at least the image of that horror, these plays still have something of the "monstrous" about them—something about which they can both warn and admonish. And that is the inevitable pathological effects of a culture that markets ideologies of absolute freedom and endless self-invention to the very subjects it continues to demand properly "identify" themselves.

Epilogue

I do love Shakespeare, Judge, and Shakespeare would love this.
Senator Alan Simpson

I would like to close this book with some reflections on Shakespeare's own notorious identity. For his is among the most notorious of names, and how it has been constructed and deployed reveals much about how both the consumers and the producers of texts re-member histories—their own and those of others. Shakespeare has long been used to reinforce England's "distinction," and more recently has been appropriated for a similar purpose within American culture. For the last decade especially, "Shakespeare" has been unusually visible in the productions—and venues—of American popular culture: in movies, either versions of the plays "themselves," such as Branagh's *Henry V* and Zeffirelli's *Hamlet,* or as dismembered fragments within other movies (the parody of the gravedigger scene from *Hamlet* in Steve Martin's *L.A. Story;* the extensive quotations from *Henry V, Richard III, Hamlet, The Merchant of Venice,* and other plays in *Star Trek VI: The Undiscovered Country;* the *Henry IV* "allegory" in *My Own Private Idaho,* to name just a few); in corporate promotions ("To be or not to be," the motto for Minute Maid's sponsorship of the 1992 Summer Olympics); in ads for car mufflers ("Shakespeare" says "I'm not going to pay a lot for a muffler!"); in advertisements for woman's lingerie ("Now is the winter of our discontent ended"); and many more, too numerous to chronicle here.

This is not the place to go into the details of what these various appropriations mean. But it is clear that no matter how "dismembered" the use of Shakespeare's texts (and Shakespeare *as* text) might be, the widespread and foregrounded visibility of the name has consolidated it into the kind of commodity identity I have been describing throughout this book. Ironically, at the very historical moment that textual scholars have come to understand "Shakespeare" to be a speculative appellation attached, uncertainly, to multiplicitous texts that have fragmented and unstable production histories, American culture has hypostatized

Shakespeare's "identity" into a form of symbolic capital that circulates in the culture like unalloyed gold coin. And it is no accident that at the very moment Shakespeare's plays are, by and large, no longer being read (outside the classroom, that is), Shakespeare "himself" is becoming a mass-cultural icon. Whereas for centuries familiarity with Shakespeare's plays has been used to make distinctions between high and low culture—literally between the "cultured" and the "uncultured" (and especially in Britain)—frequently it is now enough simply to invoke the name.[1]

To notice this is *not* to express nostalgia for a time when people "really read Shakespeare," nor is it to wish to "rescue" Shakespeare from the jaws of philistine masses who don't properly appreciate him. Rather, it is to observe a recent mass "revival" of "Shakespeare" that has more to do with the cultural logic of notorious identity than with the specifics of what attaches to it. Or perhaps it would be more accurate to say that the nature of what has been attached to Shakespeare's name has changed. "Shakespeare"—like "Willie Horton"—has become a general equivalent, a medium of exchange, pure (that is, so saturated with itself as to signify nothing but "itself") ideological value available to authorize whatever "structures of feeling" are being promoted. In this way, "Shakespeare" has come to function in contemporary culture more as vehicle than as author, even while the myth of the sovereign Bard remains crucial to the effectiveness of the purveyance. Shakespeare the playwright is superseded by Shakespeare the paradigm, in a series of performances in which "Shakespeare" plays a role ideologically central yet textually peripheral.

While the categories of the modern and postmodern are still in the process of being defined, the nature of Bardolatry in postmodern culture is different from that of Bardolatry in the last century, having less to do with worshipping at the shrine of editorially reconstructed and "uncorrupt" Shakespearean texts and more to do with the strategic deployment of fragments.[2] Bardolatry now is more widespread and less informed, consisting not of knowledge of the plays but of awareness of their presence in the cultural "background" as universal arbiters: removed but vigilant trustees of Western culture's enduring ideological provenance. Like a collective certificate of deposit, "Shakespeare" continues to accrue interest in the way that protected capital does: by shoring up a sense of the reliable returns of continued long-term investment in white Western patriarchal "values."[3]

While I have no wish to contribute to this kind of Bardolatry, I have never wanted more to assert Shakespeare's authorial "intentions" than when Senator Alan Simpson quoted lines from *Othello* to Clarence Thomas during the Thomas/Hill hearings. Beginning by saying "I do love Shakespeare, Judge, and Shakespeare would love this," Simpson exhorted Thomas to "read *Othello,* Judge, and never forget these lines":

> Who steals my purse steals trash, 'tis something, nothing,
> 'Twas mine, 'tis his, and has been slave to thousands:
> But he that filches from me my good name
> Robs me of that which not enriches him,
> And makes me poor indeed.[4]

Speaking Iago's words as if they were Shakespeare speaking to Thomas from the grave, Simpson appropriated for his own authority the Bard that literary theorists and textual scholars have so assiduously been dismantling. Failing to attribute these lines to their "proper" speaker (of whom he was probably unaware), Simpson unwittingly performed in his act of cynical Bardolatry an act of deconstruction: he exorcised the particularities of voice (and therefore of agency) from the play in an effort to sever the effects of the utterance from its origins. However, in the mise-en-scène of the hearings, a kind of double reappropriation occurred. While Simpson may have been putting Shakespeare to the service of his own conservative agenda, Shakespeare's play was putting Simpson to the service of demonstrating the continuing cultural truth of Iago's agency: that when politically ambitious white men "bond" with the token "other" who does the state some service against the threat of a dangerous "female sexuality"—whether attributed to a Desdemona or to a "scorned" Anita Hill—they are all, to one degree or another, positioned as Iagos to Othellos. During that moment in the Thomas/Hill hearings, it wasn't Simpson who spoke the metatruth of Shakespeare but Shakespeare's play that spoke the metatruth of Alan Simpson and Clarence Thomas.

> If I ever have to cast an acting role, I want the wrong person for the part. I can never visualize the right person in a part. The right person for the right part would be too much. Besides, no person is ever completely right for any part, because a part is a role is never real, so if you can't get someone who's perfectly right, it's more satisfying to get someone who's perfectly wrong. Then you know you've really got something.
>
> Andy Warhol, *The Philosophy of Andy Warhol,* p. 83

In one of the most bizarre, *inadvertently* appropriate moments ever recorded on camera, Simpson became Iago to a Clarence Thomas who was cast as Othello (right down to the young white wife). The point is not that Simpson had probably never read the play (nor apparently had Thomas, who nodded gratefully rather than responding with outrage, since, after all, Othello murders his wife), but that in casting what he took to be Shakespeare "himself" in "the right part" (the spokesman for the enduring value of the "good name"), Simpson in fact cast the wrong "person" in it. Iago *would* have been "perfectly right" for the part; but he was elided from the text. The right person for the right part in this scenario would have been "too much": it would have revealed a multiply exploitive "reality" obscene on too many levels at once.

Nevertheless, in reassigning Iago's words to Shakespeare, Simpson really "had something"—the value of which was commutable the moment it was realigned with the Bard "himself." Simpson banked on rescuing Thomas' "good name" by backing it with a really big good name: Shakespeare's. In a hearing in which the two most prominent "literary" texts invoked were Shakespeare's play and William Peter Blatty's *The Exorcist,* it isn't surprising that what the hearings performed above all was their own kind of exorcism—of anything that disrupted the "confirmation" of a "supreme" male justice. In order for Clarence Thomas to ascend to the highest judicial position in the country, one authorized *for life* on the assumption of the "essential" credentials of "Character," he had to be (like the Bard) refined or purged of any "adulterating" substance, whether sexual licentiousness, a fondness for pornography, crude jokes, ambivalence, internal contradictions, and deeply questionable politics around sexism, racism, and any of the other things that disrupt the sterling identities of Timeless Poets as well as Supreme Court Justices—two of our most precious ideological commodities. For it is only by occluding the disruptive symptoms in authoritative cultural texts, like Simpson's elimination of Iago's racist and misogynist presence in *Othello,* and Thomas' denial of Anita Hill's accusations, that they can achieve their status as icons of moral authority.

Perhaps more than any other event in recent memory, the Thomas/Hill hearings demonstrated (among other things) the extent to which "Shakespeare" has come to function as the commodity fetish whose name provides instant authoritative cachet. It is precisely Shakespeare's prior high-cultural "history" that is the "thing" dragged along underfoot, effaced but never forgotten, in his transformation into the transcendental cultural signifier. Proving Warhol's thesis that "more than anything people just want stars" (*The Philosophy of Andy Warhol*, p. 85), Shakespeare's name has been "up in lights" all over the surface of popular culture, helping to foster an artificial sense of cultural continuity and unified "history" in a society composed of chafing subcultures, one that denies at its own peril the ongoing existence of racism, sexism, and other unconscionable inequities.

In terms of the place "Shakespeare" has come to occupy in the current processes of symbolization, the fetish of the name circulates in a symbolic economy similar to that which circulates around money. In Baudrillard's terms, "what is fascinating about money is neither its materiality, nor even that it might be the intercepted equivalent of a certain force (e.g., of labour) or of a certain potential power: it is its *systematic nature*, the potential enclosed in the material for total commutability of all values, thanks to their definitive abstraction."[5] In his cultural ascension to notorious identity, Shakespeare "himself" has been definitively abstracted: minted into what is presumed to be the "closed perfection of [his] system," frozen into the "universal" Bard whose name "means" the values that we all presumably subscribe to, even if we're no longer sure what they really are. It is just this assumption that authorizes Alan Simpson to read Iago's dissembled views as if they were Shakespeare's own; it is this that authorizes the exclusion of the "golden calf," which is immaterial.

In making Shakespeare "himself" a legend, we have imposed the same identity politics on the "author" as the legend plays impose on their notorious figures. The difference, however, is that Shakespeare's plays interrogated the function of such narratives by simultaneously deploying and deconstructing them, suggesting that even in the most overdetermined versions of identity, names never "say it all." Whether the traffic in Shakespeare's name will continue to benefit the Alan Simpsons and Clarence Thomases of the world, or will allow for some strategic poaching by those who have not hitherto been the beneficiaries of the "Bard's" surplus value, remains to be seen. Notorious identity can turn names into currency; or it can reify names into tombstones—markers of a past identity that can only be memorialized. In either case, the jury is still out on whether or not the gap it attempts to close between signifier and signified can be manipulated for a new kind of noncanonical identity politics, one in which subjects are neither bricked into nor out of, neither falsely shored up by nor subsumed beneath, the fetishized "authority" of names. If all identity, no matter how notorious, is a constitutive fiction, a local habitation, a contingent site that we move in and out of, then we all negotiate with versions of ourselves to which we are never identical, no matter how much others may attempt to determine, and enforce, our "characters." And if this bargain is successful, we can hear, in the words that for Troilus meant only bitter confusion, the blueprint for something considerably more hopeful. We can say with perfect accuracy—even of the notorious Bard—this is, and is not, Shakespeare.

Notes

Introduction

1. See Leo Braudy's broad-ranging and learned study *The Frenzy of Renown: Fame and Its History* (Oxford: Oxford University Press, 1986). The main and major difference between Braudy's approach to the topic of fame and my own is in the way we regard its cultural origins and uses, and in the way we conceptualize psychological "individuals." For Braudy, fame is something that is universally longed for, at some level or other, by everyone. Famous persons (Braudy deals only with "real" famous persons, not famous fictional figures) "represent" through the record of their achievements a kind of immortality for which, according to Braudy, we all long. Famous persons transcend death and oblivion and achieve universal remembrance through their ever-renewed significance in public discourse.

Braudy's project ranges from antiquity to the present, and his concern is to show the historical development of the notion, construction, and significance of fame in its changes as well as its continuities. But while he argues for a different kind of fame under the greatly expanded communication technologies of modernity, a fame that is increasingly coveted for its own sake rather than for what it might mean, the fundamental assumption beneath what he characterizes as an "urge for uniqueness" remains, in his view, a need for a certain kind of self-confirmation: a use of fame as a way to corroborate one's existence to oneself as much as to others. Braudy's focus on the direction of fame, then, is literally inside out: it originates in the individual's desire for "distinction" (a term Braudy uses in theoretically unreflective ways) and radiates out into successful reception and consolidation as fame in the world. I, on the contrary, am arguing for an imposition of fame from the outside in: a cultural requirement, produced through reproduction, that figures "live up to" the mandates of their own notorious identities.

2. For my purposes it doesn't matter whether such figures "really existed" or existed only in literary or legendary texts. For I am talking about not the "originals" but their multiple representations; and once we move into the realm of representation, famous figures operate similarly in a culture whether they once had protoplasmic existence or not. (For example, it is bizarrely difficult to assess the possible differences in cultural impact and use between, say, Madonna and Bart Simpson. And what about a figure such as Marilyn Monroe, who at once

existed and was always totally fictitious?) In a way, the very phrase "real historical persons" signals the tendency we have to want to gesture toward something more substantial or "real" about figures who "really lived" as opposed to those who exist solely in cultural texts of one kind or another. But the critical and theoretical developments of poststructuralism and post-Marxism, and the contributions of deconstruction and feminist psychoanalysis in challenging notions of fixed essences, whether of human nature, class, race, or gender, have led to a different understanding of what it means to be "a person," as well as what history "itself" means. It is now a theoretical truism to say that there is no notion of history that is not fictional. No historicization without representation. "Real" persons become historical figures only via representation in the texts, oral or written, of others. It makes no difference whether we are talking about "real" historical persons, then, or "literary" figures; for there is no identity apart from representation. No one, fictional or real, anonymous or infamous, exists socially (and that includes in self-representations) without mediation through the symbolic codes that enable us to think ourselves and others.

3. I should point out that what I assert is the naturalizing tendency of the legendary Roland Barthes claims is a similar characteristic of myth: "Myth consists in overturning culture into nature, or, at least, the social, the cultural, the ideological, the historical into the 'natural.'" See *Image-Music-Text*, trans. Stephen Heath (New York: Hill and Wang, 1977), p. 165. But there is, I would argue, a crucial difference between myth and legend, a difference of transmissibility. By etymology, legends are transmitted in writing in order to be read *(legere, legendum)*; they are stories that began in local, oral forms but that have been given the transmissible authority—the artificial "thingness"—of history. Myths, on the other hand, are defined as beliefs, popular notions, attitudes. Less "concretized" by their mode of reproduction (as well as the relations of production), myths are not so easily relegated to or located in the written; they are less the province of print culture.

Although both myths and legends share an epistemology that conflates fiction and history, and although both may be taken as "representative" simultaneously of historical events and the significance of those events, the difference resides in how that significance is encoded, transmitted, and applied. The legendary has a political and historical weight that the mythic never quite attains. As Barthes has said in *Mythologies* (trans. Annette Lavers [New York: Hill and Wang, 1972]): "Myth is a type of speech . . . myth cannot possibly be an object, a concept, or an idea; it is a mode of signification, a form . . . Myth is not defined by the object of its message, but by the way in which it utters its message: there are formal limits to myth, there are no substantial ones" (p. 110). The legendary, we might say, is myth reified. For a legend is precisely defined by the "object of its message," and there are "substantial" political and social limits to what does, and does not, become legendary.

4. *Webster's New Collegiate Dictionary* (Springfield, Mass.: G. and C. Merriam Company, 1976).

5. Jean-Joseph Goux, *Symbolic Economies: After Marx and Freud*, trans. Jennifer Curtiss Gage (Ithaca, N.Y.: Cornell University Press, 1990), pp. 83–85.

6. See *Worlds Apart: The Market and the Theater in Anglo-American Thought,*

1550–1750 (Cambridge: Cambridge University Press, 1986), p. 59. The competition of market forces was certainly felt in the activities of the playwrights of sixteenth and seventeenth century London, as they worked to produce plays that would draw larger audiences and longer runs to their theater companies than those their competitors could attract. Even before the commodification of the product appeared in the form of copyright law and ownership rights as a result of this burgeoning competition, anxiety around the uses of and rights to certain kinds of cultural products (and, in turn, their meanings) was evident in legal codes (for example, the sumptuary laws governing permissible modes of dress on the basis of social standing).

An ever-growing awareness of commodification in the process of symbolic and material exchange appeared in many ways before early modern England could be said to have fully instituted a capitalist economy. Or rather, a nascently "capitalist" *symbolic* economy was already operating during the emergence of mercantile and financial capitalism in England in the sixteenth century—evident, for one thing, in the courtier literature of the period, both English and continental. Such texts adumbrate an economy of social "free enterprise" for aspiring courtiers and would-be aristocrats. The politics of decorum that a text such as Castiglione's *Book of the Courtier* elaborates relies upon the realization and understanding of the social as an arena for marketing "selves," which are then "purchased" (patronage) by those with the resources of status, land, and capital. It is, in effect, a manual of upward mobility through self-commodification. What Stephen Greenblatt calls Renaissance "self-fashioning" (see *Renaissance Self-Fashioning: From More to Shakespeare* [Chicago: University of Chicago Press, 1980]) had in fact, by the late sixteenth and early seventeenth centuries, become Renaissance self-marketing—an entrepreneurship of identity that was (when successful) directly productive of material gain.

As Agnew and many other cultural historians have thoroughly and convincingly argued, early modern England was starting to register in every aspect of life what Agnew calls "the antagonism of market relations." These shifts were viewed as threatening not just the social privileges of the aristocracy but the ideological underpinnings of gender, class, and power. New markets were being generated by voyages to the Americas, the East and West Indies, Russia, and elsewhere; the Royal Exchange in London had been completed; massive amounts of gold and silver were flowing into the European marketplace; and inflationary prices were acting in concert with the booming import-export trade conducted by merchants. With these developments, a moneyed middle class began visibly to emerge in England, and wealth increasingly was understood in terms of capital rather than inherited property, since the latter could no longer bring the landed gentry an income competitive with rising prices in the marketplace. Economic power was rapidly becoming the prerogative of "middle-class" and "masterless" men; and their upwardly mobile social ambitions impinged upon the "integrity" of the aristocracy, who found themselves spending increasing sums of money in shows of ostentation aimed at, among other things, maintaining their sense of distinction from such men. Ironically, the landed gentry had to borrow money from the merchant class in order to finance this staging of "distinction"; consequently, they found themselves in debt to—

and therefore imbricated with—the very class of people they decried. Encouraged by Tudor policy (which after a century of civil wars was concerned to avoid the economic empowering of dangerous aristocratic ambition), the plenitude of capital at the middle class's disposal, as well as the mode and relations of production it encouraged, was enormously influential in every aspect of English life.

While the middle class increasingly had the power of monetary capital, the stakes rose around the production of symbolic capital, which was still located largely in the technologies of meaning-production. With the invention of the printing press, the production of texts, once almost entirely the province of the aristocracy (with the exception of the clergy), became possible for those who could afford to pay for it; and the combination of increasing middle-class literacy and middle-class money generated an ever-growing market for the consumption of texts. Although printing was still an expensive undertaking, many people who hitherto had had little or no opportunity to produce and to consume texts could now afford to do both. A wide range of texts addressed to an economically and socially variegated audience was now being produced, and a battle between "high" cultural texts (produced for the court and represented by, for example, the aristocratic literary undertaking of Sidney's sonnets) and "popular" texts (produced for sale and distribution in St. Paul's, and represented by the pamphlets of middle-class "wits" such as Nashe) opened up for contestation the textual production of cultural "authority." The imbrication of these two marketplaces, the economic and the textual—their influences upon each other and the rifts that they generated—affected not only how new kinds of meanings were authored but how the "lessons" of history and the "legendary" were *reconceived as well as reproduced* under, and in terms of, these new market conditions.

See Christopher Hill, *The Century of Revolution, 1603–1714* (New York: W. W. Norton, 1980); idem, *The World Turned Upside Down* (New York: Penguin, 1975); William Bouwsma, "Anxiety and the Formation of Early Modern Culture," in *After the Reformation: Essays in Honor of J. H. Hexter*, ed. Barbara C. Malament (Philadelphia: University of Pennsylvania Press, 1980), pp. 215–246; G. R. Hibbard, ed., *Three Elizabethan Pamphlets* (London: George G. Harrap, 1951); R. H. Tawney, *Religion and the Rise of Capitalism* (London, 1926); Walter Cohen, *Drama of a Nation: Public Theatre in Renaissance England and Spain* (Ithaca, N.Y.: Cornell University Press, 1985); Peter Burke, *Popular Culture in Early Modern Europe* (London: Temple Smith, 1978); Alan MacFarlane, *The Origins of English Individualism: The Family, Property and Social Transition* (London: Basil Blackwell, 1978); Norbert Elias, *The Civilizing Process*, vol. I: *The History of Manners*, trans. E. Jephcott (New York: Pantheon, 1978); Lawrence Stone, *The Causes of the English Revolution, 1529–1642* (London: Routledge, 1972); idem, *The Crisis of the Aristocracy, 1558–1641* (London: Oxford University Press, 1967).

7. Ed. George Burton Hotchkiss (New York: New York University Press, 1931), p. 316.

8. Bruce Robbins, "The Politics of Theory," *Social Text: Theory/Culture/Ideology* 6, no. 3 (1987): 3–18, esp. 10.

9. See Louis Althusser's well-known essay "Ideology and Ideological State Apparatuses," in *Lenin and Philosophy and Other Essays*, trans. Ben Brewster

(New York: Monthly Review Press, 1971), pp. 127–186. I refer here to Althusser's notion of the "interpellation" of subjects by preexisting ideological vectors, which then "determine" both the nature of that subjectivity and the experience of the "individual." This conception has come under much critical fire among postmarxists over the last ten years, partly because of Althusser's tendency to hypostatize Ideology as an overwhelmingly monolithic, monological, and unidirectional force. But his famous dictum that "Ideology interpellates individuals as subjects" (p. 160) has recently been ingeniously revised by Peter Stallybrass, who argues that "within the capitalist mode of production, ideology inter-pellated, not the individual as a subject, but the *subject* as an *individual*. For the individual is not the simple given of bourgeois social formations. On the contrary, he/she is a laborious construction in the political defeat of absolutism, when political freedom is gained at the expense of the occlusion of economic independence. To put it crudely: historically the subject precedes the individual." See "Shakespeare, the Individual, and the Text," in *Cultural Studies*, ed. Lawrence Grossberg, Cary Nelson, and Paula Treichler (London: Routledge, 1992), pp. 593–612, esp. 593. Concerned to show how the specific term "individual" is "deployed in England in the seventeenth century," Stallybrass argues that it was rarely used in the sense in which we tend to use it now. The "individual" is an ideological product of the advancement of capitalism and of capitalism's economic and social relations. For the particular problem I have articulated as notorious identity, however, both paradigms of interpellation— Althusser's formulation and Stallybrass's revision—are relevant. For the plays do investigate "unique" figures' relations to preexisting determinant forces— legendary figures *are* culturally constructed as unique, extraordinary individuals—and therefore the ideology of their identities interpellates them as subjects. But insofar as they are reproductions of earlier versions of "themselves," they are not "unique" at all; rather, in order to reproduce them as legends, their notorious identities must be effective at "rehailing" them as the "individuals" that they can no longer be (and never "really" were). Consequently, while I find Althusser's views too reductive of the possibility of disruptive agency and resistance, there is much that is still useful and right in his work. As a paradigm for how absolute *identity* attempts—and I stress "attempts"—to operate, his theory of ideological "hailing" is theoretically useful to my argument and powerfully convincing to me in general.

For more recent and theoretically inclusive studies of the problem of the "subject," see Paul Smith, *Discerning the Subject* (Minneapolis: University of Minnesota Press, 1987); and Judith Butler, *Gender Trouble: Feminism and the Subversion of Identity* (New York: Routledge, 1990). According to Butler, "The question of 'the subject' is crucial for politics, and for feminist politics in particular, because juridical subjects are invariably produced through certain exclusionary practices that do not 'show' once the juridical structure of politics has been established" (p. 2). There are echoes of Althusser here, as well as of Foucault, whom Butler criticizes for being insensitive to gender politics. Butler also says something similar to my formulation about the difference between identity and subjectivity when she asks, "To what extent is 'identity' a normative ideal rather than a descriptive feature of experience?" (p. 16).

10. See Elizabeth Freund, "'Ariachne's Broken Woof': The Rhetoric of Citation in *Troilus and Cressida*," in *Shakespeare and the Question of Theory*, ed. Patricia Parker and Geoffrey Hartman (New York: Methuen, 1985), pp. 19–36, esp. 21.

11. In *The Frenzy of Renown*, Braudy locates the origins of fame in the impulses of the "individual" for recognition. Beginning with this as a first principle and then attempting to map its development, Braudy, in an effort to acknowledge the importance of historical specificity, goes no farther than to account (albeit with enormous skill and great attention to detail) for the familiar public-self/private-self debate that has been so prominent in Western texts. Universalizing and transhistoricizing the "individual's" impulse for widespread social recognition (almost a Jungian archetype), Braudy assumes that the fundamental tension within fame is between an impulse to be publicly recognized as "unique" and an impulse to remain "private" (a false opposition, since the impulse to "privacy" is itself a historical development and can just as frequently be seen as an effort to protect one's sense of "uniqueness").

Advancing a history of fame that is deeply positivist, Braudy, while acknowledging the different meanings famous figures may have over centuries, claims that "such people are vehicles of cultural memory and cohesion. They allow us to identify what's present with what's past. By preserving their names, we create a self-conscious grammar of feeling and action that allows us to connect where we have been as a society and where we are going" (p. 15). This remark is accurate, I think, but not quite in the way Braudy intends. It romanticizes both fame and its history by positing cultural memory and cohesion as unproblematic, uncontested, unfragmented. It will be my argument that legendary figures—at least in Shakespeare but perhaps even more generally—are necessary precisely to *overcome* contestation in versions of history, as a way of consolidating the hegemony of *particular* interests. In Braudy's view, fame is what enables us to recognize who we are and where we are going, what our collective values and fantasies are. The problem with this view is its unreflective use of the term "we," as if a culture were a "we" before a certain group consolidates itself as dominant. I agree with Braudy that fame does help provide the cement that holds historiographic narratives together; famous figures embody ideologies that cannot be advanced without them. But to assert that individuals in a culture "preserve" famous names in order to light the way to self-knowledge is to speak from within the very ideology that notoriety helps administer and secure: it is to take in a *unself conscious* way the "self-conscious grammar of feeling and action" that Braudy claims is so historically enlightening.

Far from saying that fame is something that enlightens us about "ourselves," I wish to argue that in its fetishized forms (which include what I've described as "notorious identity") it ensures a failure of illumination, a certain refusal to fall in fully with the positivist narratives that consolidate Western historiography. What characterizes the difference between "mere" fame and notorious identity is the success or failure of the paradigmatism: the degree to which it produces "self-recognition" as cultural *misrecognition.* However thoroughly detailed and full of rich anecdotes and examples Braudy's study may be, his universalist notion of fame and his use of the humanist "we" (as if a culture's famous figures were nominated and appropriable by everyone, male and female, of every race

and class, in a timeless utopian democracy) seems naive at best and patriarch-
ally and imperially reinscriptive at worst. Assuming that people are just "naturally" interested in the exploits of the famous, "naturally" fascinated with fame
rather than *made* to be so by systems which make such interest profitable,
Braudy asserts that "fame is made up of four elements: a person and an accom-
plishment, their immediate publicity, and what posterity has thought about
them ever since" (p. 15). My project will take up the issues that this simplistic
genealogy leaves out: which figures and whose accomplishments get targeted
for "immediate" publicity, and why and by whom; the nature of this "posterity," whose it is, and whose interests are served; and the ideological conditions
that are enabled, reproduced, and underwritten by the production and reproduction of "publicity"—the manufacturing of notorious identity.

12. To elaborate: Lacan's thesis that the unconscious is structured like a language is powerfully useful. Insofar as the subject's relation to the symbolic is
built on a fundamental misrecognition of "lack" as "loss," it allows for powerful
readings of *representations* of desire, displacement, and hysteria. And Lacan's
formulation of the symbolic as the law of the father provides an accurate description—not prescription—of representation in phallogocentric patriarchal
culture. See Jacques Lacan, *The Four Fundamental Concepts of Psycho-Analysis*,
trans. Alan Sheridan (New York: W. W. Norton, 1981). Even more useful, perhaps, than Lacan's own formulations are the revisions of his work by feminist-
psychoanalytic, feminist-materialist, and deconstructionist theorists. For example, see Jane Gallop, *Reading Lacan* (Ithaca, N.Y.: Cornell University Press, 1985);
Shoshana Felman, *Jacques Lacan and the Adventure of Insight* (Cambridge, Mass.:
Harvard University Press, 1987); Jacqueline Rose, *Sexuality in the Field of Vision*
(London: Verso, 1987); and Butler, *Gender Trouble*, esp. pp. 1–34. See also Susan
David Bernstein's discussion of various appropriations of Lacan as well as of
his "style" in Bernstein, "Confessing Lacan," in *Seduction and Theory: Readings
of Gender, Representation, and Rhetoric,* ed. Dianne Hunter (Urbana: University
of Illinois Press, 1989), pp. 195–213. I rely throughout on Althusser's discussion
of how "ideology interpellates individuals as subjects." While I disagree with
his monolithic sense of the effectiveness of ideological state apparatuses, his formulation is highly relevant to the phenomenon of notorious identity, insofar as
both explore how ideological prescriptedness always precedes "persons."

I rely upon the deconstructionism of Derrida for its critique of the "metaphysics of presence" and his analysis of the diacritical displacement inherent in the
way language operates (the way signifiers displace signifieds as they slide along
the metonymic chain and consequently destabilize "absolute" significations). In
eliminating the stable, centered subject by laying bare the shifting signifiers on
which it builds its fictions of unitary presence, Derridean deconstruction has
much in common with Lacan's analysis of the split subject of desire/lack who is
constituted as such only through language. Both analyze the misrecognition involved in rewriting originary absence as either "presence" or as "loss." It is
Derrida who "coins" the term "phallogocentrism" by arguing an identity between an inherently unstable "logocentrism" and Western culture's obsession
with the phallus as absolute signifier in "the erection of a paternal logos." See
Jacques Derrida, *Writing and Difference,* trans. Alan Bass (Chicago: University of

Chicago Press, 1978). See also Jonathan Culler, *On Deconstruction: Theory and Criticism after Structuralism* (Ithaca, N.Y.: Cornell University Press, 1982), p. 172.

I have found very persuasive Pierre Bourdieu's sophisticated elaboration of the concept of "habitus:" the structures of regulated practice within specific social formations that in turn structure and make "objective" "consensual" sense of every aspect of subjective and social experience, however "personal," "contingent," or "arbitrary" such experience might seem. See Pierre Bourdieu, *Outline of a Theory of Practice* (Cambridge: Cambridge University Press, 1977). Throughout *Outline,* Bourdieu keeps defining and redefining what he means by "habitus." The following passage most intelligibly represents the meaning and function of the concept: "The structures constitutive of a particular type of environment (e.g. the material conditions of existence characteristic of a class condition) produce *habitus,* systems of durable, transposable *dispositions,* structured structures predisposed to function as structuring structures, that is, as principles of the generation and structuring of practices and representations which can be objectively "regulated" and "regular" without in any way being the product of obedience to rules, objectively adapted to their goals without presupposing a conscious aiming at ends or an express mastery of the operations necessary to attain them and, being all this, *collectively orchestrated without being the product of the orchestrating action of a conductor"* (p. 72, italics added in last line).

What is intriguing about this concept is the way it describes the apparatus that enables the making of "sense" without requiring the individual per se to "make sense." We make sense, but we don't have to *make* it: sense is already sensible in the habitus; and we are structured by this collective "sense," which produces us and which we in turn reproduce. The habitus is that which allows us to understand others within the same habitus without consciously having to strive to do so. Our "points of view," "like-mindedness," the way we just "know" what we mean—all are products of the habitus. This is useful for the way in which it breaks down absolute distinctions between the subjective and the objective, seeing them as literally continuous with each other. It suggests that the very notion of agency "itself" cannot be located solely within individuals but, rather, must be seen as a certain "given" in the interactions between the "individual" and the habitus.

However, like Althusser's theory of Ideology, Bourdieu's formulation runs a serious risk of totalizing social relations. Michel de Certeau, in *The Practice of Everyday Life* (trans. Steven Rendall [Berkeley: University of California Press, 1984]), critiques Bourdieu for just this kind of "dogmatism" (p. 59), for the way his theory of practice subjects everything to the law of reproduction, and pretends to render everything visible and apprehensible through the application of the notion of the habitus, eliminating altogether any agency that does not originate in the habitus itself. The habitus becomes the massively variegated and complex but sole determinant of what people believe to be their own "choices."

Certeau criticizes Bourdieu's theory of the habitus along with Foucault's theory of discourse (after carefully laying out the differences between them) for the way both presume to function "panoptically," allowing the theorist to believe that he is "seeing everything" (p. 63).

My use of the concept of habitus, as well as my use of the Foucauldian notion of "discourse," is similar to my use of Althusser's "interpellation": in all three instances the powerful determining force of the cultural "surround" on the construction of identity and subjectivity is directly relevant to notorious identity; and especially the formulations of Althusser and Bourdieu, since notorious identity *is* belated and reiterative identity and therefore is subject to, although not fully contained by, the "law of reproduction." But even within the context of notorious identity, these theories are too rigid, totalizing, and counterintuitive in their overdeterminism. They are useful insofar as they help establish the cultural paradigms that are attempting to impose their norms of apperception and perception (Bourdieu, *Distinction: A Social Critique of the Judgement of Taste*, trans. Richard Nice [Cambridge, Mass.: Harvard University Press, 1984]) on subjects. But I emphasize the *attempt* here rather than its uncontested and complete success. For I shall also argue that the "habitus" of notorious identity—its ideological "interpellations," its incitement to "discourse"—produces the very symptoms of resistance that render the success of this identity questionable.

The "numismatic" theory of Jean-Joseph Goux is useful, in limited ways, for the structural homology it posits between apparently different "symbolic economies": the relationship he argues between the "general equivalent" forms of money in the economic, the phallus in the psychoanalytic, the name of the father in linguistic and cultural patriarchy, and the kinds of symbolic exchanges each enables. See Goux, *Symbolic Economies.*

I am especially indebted to Slavoj Žižek, a provocative postmarxist neo-Hegelian Lacanian, for his discussion of the way the Real is "intercalated" or caught up in the network of symbolic representation and retroactively "recognized" (as a function of *necessary* misrecognition) in the "sublime objects of ideology." Žižek's master trope is "back to the future," a phrase that evokes not only the retroactively constituted nature of all historical experience (including individual memory) but, more importantly, the strangeness of this movement—the way it produces a sense of the uncanny. Žižek's formulations help render legible the appearance of symptoms in all representational fields, whether literary, theoretical, subjective, or historical. See Slavoj Žižek, *The Sublime Object of Ideology* (London: Verso, 1989). Analyzing how the uncanny is denied or repressed in historiography, Žižek points to the way originary absence is covered over by fantasies of plenitude and presence (metaphysical authority, the father's phallus, and so on)—fantasies that are always belied, somewhere, in the fabric of the symbolic, which (according to Žižek) knits whatever has been permanently, originally, and inevitably rent into a semblance of consistency.

In other words, symptom is the way we—the subjects—"'avoid madness,' the way we 'choose something (the symptom-formation) instead of nothing (radical psychotic autism, the destruction of the symbolic universe)' through the binding of our enjoyment to a certain signifying, symbolic formation which assures a minimum of consistency to our being-in-the-world" (p. 75).

Knowledge of this "choosing" may be displaced, may even be disowned, but is never entirely un-known: "what was foreclosed from the Symbolic returns in the *Real of the symptom*" (p. 73, italics added). Suggesting that what we are accustomed to regard as "neurotic" or pathological may in fact be the subject's *only possible engagement with the Real,* Žižek implies that only in the symptom does one discover the means of disrupting ideological overdetermination and the misrecognition it produces and requires. In historiography it may be precisely those ruptures, those events and figures which resist historically productive narrative, that signal the presence of something "true," however "anamorphic" they may appear.

Finally, the work of feminist materialist and feminist psychoanalytic critics and scholars has been enormously helpful, and the list is very long indeed. Many whose work has been directly influential in my particular readings of Shakespeare's plays will be cited in subsequent chapters. But for a few whose work has been useful to me in formulating theoretical overviews, see Jacqueline Rose, *Sexuality in the Field of Vision* (London: Verso, 1987); Gayle Rubin, "The Traffic in Women: Notes on the 'Political Economy' of Sex," in *Toward an Anthropology of Women,* ed. Rayna Reiter (New York: Monthly Review Press, 1975); Eve Kosofsky Sedgwick, *Between Men: English Literature and Male Homosocial Desire* (New York: Columbia University Press, 1985); Catherine Belsey, *Critical Practice* (New York: Methuen, 1980); Laura Mulvey, "Visual Pleasure and Narrative Cinema," *Screen* 16 (1975): 6–18; and Annette Kuhn, *The Power of the Image: Essays on Representation and Sexuality* (London: Routledge, 1985).

13. See Gilles Deleuze and Félix Guattari, *Anti-Oedipus: Capitalism and Schizophrenia,* trans. Robert Hurley, Mark Seem, and Helen R. Lane (Minneapolis: University of Minnesota Press, 1983); and idem, *A Thousand Plateaus: Capitalism and Schizophrenia,* trans. Brian Massumi (Minneapolis: University of Minnesota Press, 1987).

14. As Catherine Belsey has asked about Foucault, "where [is] the evidence of resistance here? Where [is] the symptomatic textual analysis which would betray as precarious, as unstable, the regimes of self-discipline the book [is] concerned to analyze?" See Catherine Belsey, "Towards Cultural History—in Theory and Practice," *Textual Practice* 3, no. 3 (Summer 1989): 169. Belsey is referring to Foucault, *The Use of Pleasure,* vol. 2 of *The History of Sexuality* (London: Viking, 1986).

15. See the interview with Avital Ronell in *Angry Women,* ed. Andrea Juno and V. Vale, *Re/Search,* vol. 13 (San Francisco: Re/Search Publications, 1991), pp. 127–153, esp. 131. Ronell is referring to Hélène Cixous' views on the power of hysteria.

16. I quote Ronell rather than Cixous because I want to invoke a notion of *productive* hysteria that is not necessarily linked to *"écriture féminine"*: I do not think that hysteria is a specifically feminine or ultimately feminized form of cultural resistance (a view that to my mind, however it may be appropriated, ultimately reinforces the fascism of phallogocentrism). And while I do agree with Cixous that in patriarchal culture there is no doubt that woman is the repressed Other, I don't think it is necessarily true that "when 'The Repressed' of their culture and society come back, it is an explosive return, which is absolutely shattering, staggering, overturning, with a force never let loose before." See Sandra Gilbert's introduction to Hélène Cixous and Catherine Clément, *The Newly Born Woman,* trans. Betsy Wing (Minneapolis: University of Minnesota Press, 1986), pp. ix, 14–15.

1. Belaboring the Obvious

1. Franz Kafka, *"The Metamorphosis," "In the Penal Colony," and Other Short Stories,* trans. Willa Muir and Edwin Muir (New York: Schocken, 1975), p. 197.

2. Leslie Fiedler, *Freaks: Myths and Images of the Secret Self* (New York: Simon and Schuster, 1978), p. 13.

3. Erving Goffman, *Stigma: Notes on the Management of Spoiled Identity* (Englewood Cliffs, N.J.: Prentice-Hall, 1963), p. 2.

4. Of course, over the last decade many critics have argued that the "Elizabethan world picture," like the "Medieval world view," was neither as monolithic nor as homogeneous as many historians of the nineteenth and early twentieth centuries made them out to be. Such versions of medieval and Renaissance culture had as much to do with how they constituted institutional fields of study and current politics as with the materials they were presumably meant to organize and interpret. R. Howard Bloch, for example, in his critique of the category of the "medieval," argues that "a significant sector of the field of medieval studies still labors under the century-old attempt to shed the yoke of the Romantic *mysterium,* an attempt that rests upon the following assumptions: . . . The medieval world is somehow simpler than that of the early-modern era. A spontaneous period, a happy period, the Middle Ages participates in the fantasy of an elementary beginning, a world of innocence analogous to the lost paradise of childhood." See Bloch, "New Philology and Old French," *Speculum* 65, no. 1 (1990): 38–58, 42. And critiques of the Tillyardian view of the Renaissance have been so fundamental in constituting the grounds of "new historicism" that they are now commonplace—although it is worth pointing out, *pace* Bloch's argument about all claims for the "new" (whether or not they precede terms like "philology" or "medievalism"), that the "process of declaring oneself 'new' is indeed very old" (p. 38), and that the "new historicism" itself relies heavily on the kind of work that the German historian Norbert Elias was producing in the 1930s and 1940s.

However, it is likely that by the later sixteenth century the increase in literacy among a growing middle class, the structural changes in governmental-theological politics brought about during the Reformation, the economic, social, and theological debates manifest in the pamphlet wars, as well as voyages to the "New World" and scientific "discoveries" enabled an unprecedented number of radically different views to infiltrate popular cultural discourses. That these views achieved voice, however, didn't necessarily mean that Elizabethans became more comfortable with ambiguity and uncertainty. On the contrary. For example, see William Bouwsma, "Anxiety and the Formation of Early Modern Culture," in *After the Reformation: Essays in Honor of J. H. Hexter,* ed. Barbara C. Malament (Philadelphia: University of Pennsylvania Press, 1980); Ernst Cassirer, *The Individual and the Cosmos in Renaissance Philosophy,* trans. Mario Domandi (New York: Barnes and Noble, 1963); Alexandre Koyré, *From the Closed World to the Infinite Universe* (Baltimore: Johns Hopkins University Press, 1957); Lucien Febvre, *The Problem of Unbelief in the Sixteenth Century: The Religion of Rabelais,* trans. Beatrice Gottlieb (Cambridge, Mass.: Harvard University Press, 1982); Lawrence Stone, *The Crisis of the Aristocracy, 1558–1641* (London: Oxford University Press, 1967); David Underdown, *Revel, Riot and Rebellion: Popular Politics and Culture in England, 1603–1660* (Oxford: Oxford University Press, 1985); Christopher Hill, *The World Turned Upside Down* (New York: Penguin, 1975); Alan MacFarlane, *The Origins of English Individualism* (Oxford: Basil Blackwell, 1978); and Norbert Elias, *The Civilizing Process,* vol.I: *The History of Manners,* trans. E. Jephcott (New York: Pantheon, 1978).

5. Keith Thomas still provides one of the best and most thorough discussions of early modern attitudes toward prodigious events; see Thomas, *Religion and the Decline of Magic* (New York: Scribners, 1971).

6. As Bouwsma explains in "Anxiety and the Formation of Early Modern Culture," the sixteenth century did inherit from the preceding two centuries its *penchant* for attempting to categorize all forms of cultural experience; but as the "accumulating social changes of the later Middle Ages eventually exceeded the flexibility of the inherited culture and forced men increasingly to violate the old boundaries" (p. 230), boundaries of all sorts seemed increasingly fragile. If, as Bouwsma asserts, "as a fully articulated system of boundaries, medieval culture was admirably suited to the management of anxiety," then the "psychological boundaries by which the old culture had sought to understand the nature of man and predict his behavior were useless when he was no longer inhibited by the pressures of traditional community; and experienced concretely in a more complex setting, human acts proved too ambiguous for neat ethical classification. Even the boundaries of the physical universe, so intimately linked to those in society and the human personality, were collapsing. No objective system of boundaries could now supply either security or effective guidance" (p. 230).

7. Ambroise Paré, *Of Monsters and Marvels,* trans. Janis L. Pallister (Chicago: University of Chicago Press, 1982), p. 5. Paré's work was originally published in 1573 by André Wechel of Paris. See also Alan G. R. Smith, *Science and Society in the Sixteenth and Seventeenth Centuries* (London: Thames and Hudson, 1972); and Katherine Parks, "Unnatural Conceptions: The Study of Monsters in Sixteenth- and Seventeenth-Century France and England," in *Past and Present,* ed. T. H. Aston (Oxford: Past and Present Society, 1981). Parks notes that "characteristically, monsters appear most frequently in the context of a whole group of related natural phenomena: earthquakes, floods, volcanic eruptions, celestial apparitions, and rains of blood, stones, and other miscellanea. The interpretation of this canon of phenomena underwent a series of metamorphoses in the years after 1500. In the most popular literature such events were originally treated as divine prodigies, and popular interest in them was sparked and fuelled by the religious conflicts of the Reformation" (p. 5).

8. Parks, "Unnatural Conceptions," p. 23. And even the level-headed Montaigne took an interest in monstrous births. In his essay "Of a Monstrous Child" (in *The Complete Essays of Montaigne,* trans. Donald Frame [Stanford: Stanford University Press, 1957]), Montaigne reminds us that "what we call monsters are not so to God, who sees in the immensity of his work the infinity of forms that he has comprised in it; and it is for us to believe that this figure that astonishes us is related and linked to some other figure of the same kind unknown to man. From his infinite wisdom there proceeds nothing but that is good and ordinary and regular; but we do not see its arrangement and relationship" (p. 538). Here

Montaigne anticipates Fiedler's point about the defining relation between deformity and conformity and Goffman's point about a larger language of relationships; Goffman stresses that we must see the larger "arrangement."

9. See Georges Vigarello, "The Upward Training of the Body from the Age of Chivalry to Courtly Civility," in *Zone: Fragments for a History of the Human Body*, part II, Michel Feher, ed. (New York: Urzone Press, 1989), pp. 148–192 and passim, esp. pp. 153–155.

10. Paré's journals acutely reveal his own failure of disinterestedness in his views on the power of the female imagination in teratogenesis. It had long been argued that pregnant women could influence the shape of the fetus by the force of a powerful imagination, or by looking at things that women were not supposed to look upon. In a chapter entitled "An Example of Monsters that are Created through the Imagination," Paré gives several examples of women who gave birth to monstrous children (one white woman gave birth to a black child after gazing at a portrait of a Moor that hung by her bed; another woman delivered a child with the face of a frog, caused by the fact that she had had in her bed, for medicinal purposes, a frog on the night that the child was conceived), and declares that "it is necessary that women—at the hour of conception and when the child is not yet formed (which takes from thirty to thirty five days for males, and forty or forty two, as Hippocrates says, for females)—not be forced to look at, or to imagine monstrous things" (pp. 39–40). Paré claims Aristotle, Hippocrates, Empedocles, Heliodorus, and Damoscene as his "authoritative" sources for this theory.

And Ian Maclean, in *The Renaissance Notion of Woman* (Cambridge: Cambridge University Press, 1980), reports that "the alleged effect of the imagination (the 'power to generate mental images') on the uterus, especially during pregnancy, causing birthmarks and deformities, is also noted. Paracelsus and other occult philosophers make much of this. Some doctors comment on this belief; its most comprehensive refutation does not occur until 1727" (p. 41). Fiedler tells us that this notion was passed along by Aristotle (who eventually came to reject it) to the Middle Ages and the Renaissance; and later scholars and theologians "amalgamated" his scientific theories of teratogenesis with their own theological theories, creating a "standard teratology at once teleological and etiological" (*Freaks*, p. 231). This theory is significant for the way it locates both the power and the responsibility for monstrous births in women and how they use their eyes—literally or in imagination.

But looking was not the only way a woman could deform a fetus. "Incorrect" sexual behavior also determined shape. Jacob Rueff, a Swiss obstetrician, wrote on monsters and deformed fetuses with a similar combination of the "scientific" and the theological. In the 1637 English translation of his work "The Expert Midwife, or An Excellent and Most Necessary Treatise of the Generation and Birth of Man," Rueff chronicles a "monster" born of the "detestable sinne of Sodomie": "In the yeere 1512 at Ravenna (a City in Italy) a Monster was borne, which had a horne on his head, two wings, no armes, a crooked foot with talons, like a ravenous bird, an eye on his knee, of both sex" (Lilly Library, Indiana University, Bloomington, Lib. 5, p. 158). Intriguing in this formulation is the way "Sodomie" (usually condemned precisely for being abortive or nonrepro-

174 Notes to Pages 26–29

ductive) here produces a creature "like a ravenous" animal, with misplaced (eye on knee) and bisexual organs. "Unnatural" conception leads to a *failure in the syntax of body parts.* Like the ways in which other kinds of negative "determinations" are displaced onto (and into) women, female imagination and sexual agency—when granted at all—is figured as at once passive (presumably the "Sodomie" was practiced upon the woman) and monstrous in its effects.

11. Hayden White, *Tropics of Discourse: Essays in Cultural Criticism* (Baltimore: Johns Hopkins University Press, 1978), p. 87, italics added.

12. Phyllis Rackin, *Stages of History: Shakespeare's English Chronicles* (Ithaca, New York: Cornell University Press, 1990): p. 27. While I don't agree with Rackin's characterization of Richard III as a "single strong character," I find most of her discussion of the first tetralogy to be very persuasive on its own terms; and in her first chapter, "Making History," she provides an excellent discussion on the relationship of current critical approaches to the projects of early modern historiographers themselves. She gives a useful critical overview of what constitutes current efforts to "reconstruct" the Renaissance.

13. The whole notion of the "first tetralogy" is itself proleptic, insofar as Shakespeare has written later historical events into his earlier chronicle plays, and earlier historical events into his "second tetralogy." The legitimacy and authority of the Tudor claim to the throne is, then, problematized at the point of its inception—namely, in Bolingbroke's usurpation of Richard II's crown, in a play written *after* the same claim has already been "justified" by the earlier (but historically later) "monstrosity" of Richard III. In other words, the positivist telos of the first tetralogy is undercut by its revision as questionable epistemology in the second tetralogy.

14. I mean this term to echo Joel Fineman's usage, which consists of a series of exploratory (necessarily, because of his untimely death) speculations about the relationship between subjectivity and specifically linguistic forms of representation. Fineman uses the term "subjectivity effect" to assert that subjects are the effects of linguistic representations, in the Lacanian sense that language—which constitutes entrance into the symbolic—is necessarily structured on lack; and subjects, who become such only by their entrance into the symbolic, are therefore always subjects of desire-in-lack. Fineman argues, *pace* Lacan, that since the unconscious is structured "like a language," specifically literary forms of linguistic representation are capable of producing the most pronounced subjectivity effects—both as literary representation and as subjective experience. Literary texts, in this view, more than other kinds of cultural texts, become contiguous with the structures of the unconscious. This is not too far from Althusser's notion of how successful interpellation operates (Althusser himself borrowing from Lacan while for the most part neglecting the complex and active psychoanalytic technology of the "unconscious"), insofar as distinctions between ideological production and subjective "interiority" are recognized as forms of misrecognition of the nature of the real (which for Althusser, finally, is always political rather than psychological).

Fineman counters what he sees as an increasingly second-class theoretical citizenship assigned to literary texts by the "institutionalization" of critical emphases on their social and cultural contexts. His critical aim is to recognize those contexts while still making a case for the literary as a special and particularly powerful kind of cultural intervention and, more crucially, *invention*. At the risk of oversimplifying his complex approach, one might say that his stance emphasizes a particular direction in cultural influence—not in a simple binary way (since the "new historicism," which he was directly and indirectly targeting in his literary theory, does not argue a unidirectional epistemology) but by relentlessly insisting on the etiological *priority* of the linguistic to the material: the way literary texts precede and change the nature, and structure, of historical contexts and subjectivities.

In *Shakespeare's Perjur'd Eye* (Berkeley: University of California Press, 1986), Fineman argues for the centrality of Shakespeare's sonnets in producing a new "version" of desiring subjectivity as specifically poetic, as the desire *for* language itself (at bottom, I suspect, the subject's desire for himself-as-author). And in *The Subjectivity Effect in Western Literary Tradition: Essays toward the Release of Shakespeare's Will* (Cambridge, Mass.: MIT Press, 1991), Fineman's essays address in various texts the transition to a dominantly verbal, rather than visual, form of desire that he argues originated in Shakespeare's sonnets; they also examine the development of this new kind of "poetic subjectivity" in the plays, and in the texts, of other Western authors.

I mean my use of the term "subjectivity effect" to be haunted, and not defined by, Fineman's work; for I am not convinced by his efforts to locate a historically new form of subjectivity—his own "recuperative originology"—in Shakespeare's sonnets. Like my hesitations around Foucault's isolation, in the eighteenth and nineteenth centuries, of bourgeois subjectivity, my response to Fineman is guided by a conviction that subjectivities, like other historical phenomena, develop over extended periods of time in less mappable, less determinable, and more variegated ways. Put simply, I don't believe in epistemological "breaks," whether conceived as versions of history or as versions of persons. This is not, however, to argue for positivist continuity, for a "developmental" or, conversely, timeless or unchanging subjectivity. Quite the reverse. To posit any radical shift in the epistemology of the subject—whether literary, as Fineman does, or institutional, as Foucault does—is precisely to posit what can only be a fictional construct: an imagined prior firm ground that is then radically destabilized by its new "priorities."

At the same time, there is little doubt that something different does emerge in the textual production of early modern England; something that becomes increasingly legible (in senses both of reading and of writing) around the problem of subjectivity. The result of political, theological, ideological, economic, material, *and* literary changes, subjectivity becomes, as other critics have observed, as much an effect of its fissures and discontinuities (Jonathan Dollimore, Peter Stallybrass, Catherine Belsey) as of its efforts to refashion identities through power (Stephen Greenblatt, Louis Montrose, Jonathan Goldberg, Stephen Orgel); as much a function of heightened gender debates and anxieties (Coppélia Kahn, Janet Adelman, Madelon Sprengnether, Valerie Traub, Lisa Jardine) as of shifting class status and a growing mercantile-capitalist economy (Frank Whigham, Jean-Christophe Agnew, Walter Cohen).

When I use the term "subjectivity effect," then, I direct it toward a locus that is not firmly "locatable" and yet is quite specific: the space between textual and material efforts to consolidate "identities" and the incommensurabilities and excesses that frustrate those operations. In other words, subjectivity *is* an effect: not solely of linguistic representation or solely of "real" material conditions but, rather, of the conflict between what representation falsely promises at the level of stable signification—identity—and what it materially produces, at the level of symptomology, by the *imposition* of that identity. Thus, the subjectivity effect in Shakespeare, as I define it, is an effect of the inability and/or unwillingness fully to inhabit one's required identity, whether it is social or, in the case of the legend plays, intertextual. Furthermore, in the legend plays, social identity is represented *as the mandate* of intertextual identity. By figuring subjects as by-products of resistance to notorious identity, Shakespeare renders the subjectivity effect at once pathologically pronounced and pronounceable as pathology: the simultaneous deviation from, and capitulation to, the mandate to "be oneself."

15. See Coppélia Kahn, *Man's Estate: Masculine Identity in Shakespeare* (Berkeley: University of California Press, 1981); Robert N. Watson, *Shakespeare and the Hazards of Ambition* (Cambridge, Mass.: Harvard University Press, 1984); C. L. Barber and Richard P. Wheeler, *The Whole Journey: Shakespeare's Power of Development* (Berkeley: University of California Press, 1986); Richard P. Wheeler, "History, Character and Conscience in *Richard III*," *Comparative Drama* 5 (1971–1972); and Michael Neill, "Shakespeare's Halle of Mirrors: Play, Politics, and Psychology in *Richard III*," *Shakespeare Studies* 8 (1975).

This argument has been made most recently and persuasively by Janet Adelman, who concentrates on the figure of Richard III as "the point of origin for my exploration of masculinity and the maternal body in Shakespeare because the origin that Richard imagines for himself turns crucially on that body: if he speaks fully for the first time here [*King Henry VI, Part 3:* 3.2.153–168 are the lines cited], what he speaks about is the origin of his aggression in the problematic maternal body. Misshapen in the womb by a triply maternal figure—Mother, Love, and Nature combined—he considers his deformed body and its consequences her 'monstrous fault.'" See Adelman, *Suffocating Mothers: Fantasies of Maternal Origin in Shakespeare's Plays, "Hamlet" to "The Tempest"* (New York: Routledge, 1992), p. 2. Adelman also hears in Richard's words "the voice of a fully developed subjectivity, the characteristically Shakespearean illusion that a stage person has interior being, including motives that he himself does not fully understand" (p. 1). But as I will argue elsewhere in this chapter, the fact that Richard "himself" makes the mother's body the locus of blame renders this placement suspicious: Richard may fantasize the maternal body as the origin of his aggression; but to my mind this is a function of how he continually misplaces blame, finding female figures who will serve as vehicles to carry displaced aggressions (of the playwright as well as of Richard) that originate in political and historiographic imperatives, imperatives that continually localize themselves in female bodies that can then be burned, murdered, blamed, reviled, contained, or simply eliminated. I am not convinced that the *origin* of his masculine anxiety is the maternal body, especially since he is so quick to identify it as the source of his "motivation." This alone signals that behind this maternal motive lies yet another motive that Richard "himself does not fully understand."

16. Critics who concentrate on the problem of Tudor propaganda in Shakespeare's representation of Richard tend to line up between this position and one that seeks to "vindicate" Richard from his ignominy. Andrew and Gina MacDonald, for instance, argue that "Shakespeare's dramatic problem in *Richard III* is to make credible the Tudor myth to an audience for whom stories of the historical Richard were still fresh, even though second or third hand . . . Thus Shakespeare is faced with the same problems with which Morton and More had to deal: despite the Elizabethan horror at usurpation as a literal attack on God's rightful ordering of the universe, he must justify Henry VII's usurpation of Richard's throne, and in so doing be careful not to extend his attack to the whole York line and so offend his present absolute monarch, who proudly emphasized her personal union of 'red' and 'white.'" This was obviously no easy task, since "the question of Richard remained open long after More." See "The Necessity of Evil: Shakespeare's Rhetorical Strategy in *Richard III*," in *Shakespeare Studies* 19 (1980–1981): 55–69. The general thrust of the MacDonald's argument is that Shakespeare had to walk a fine line between depicting Richard as too monstrous and depicting him as too admirable. He resolves this by giving him admirable traits which are put to monstrous use.

But the "question" of Richard was open prior to Tudor "historians" as well, as Desmond Seward argues. He points to the Crowland chronicler and to the testimony of John Russell, Bishop of Lincoln and Richard's contemporary, among others, and emphasizes what seems to be their genuine horror at Richard's viciousness and subsequent lack of remorse. According to Seward, even Charles Ross's "magisterial" 1981 study of Richard III "admits that his contemporaries believed that [Richard] had murdered his nephews, that the black legend is of pre-Tudor origin and dates from Richard's lifetime." See *Richard III: England's Black Legend* (Country Life Books, 1983), pp. 19–20. Seward argues that Richard was "certainly not a monster, but a peculiarly grim young English precursor of Machiavelli's Prince" (p. 21). He sees the generation of the Richard-as-monster myth as an expression of the increasing Renaissance disillusionment with politics and political figures. "Richard was by no means an isolated phenomenon, let alone a freak. He belongs to the same ferociously ruthless company as Louis XI, Ferdinand of Aragon, and Cesare Borgia—and Edward IV and Henry VII" (p. 21).

Larry Champion, on the other hand, describes the evolution of the Richard myth through the Tudor historians Rous, Vergil, More, Halle, and Holinshed, asserting that "in such a manner we see the construction of a detailed certainty of crime on a foundation of rumor which first appeared some twenty years after Richard's death and over thirty years after the incidents described." See "Myth and Counter-Myth: The Many Faces of *Richard III*," in *A Fair Day in the Affections: Literary Essays in Honor of Robert B. White, Jr.*, ed. Jack D. Durant and M. Thomas Hester (Raleigh, N.C.: Winston Press, 1980). In this essay, Champion describes the manipulation of the Richard myth, beginning with contemporary accounts, and following their embellishments through Tudor historians into a twisted form masquerading as certainty.

The list of books and articles addressing the history of the Richard legend is almost endless. Here are a few of the works that give accounts of the "evolution" of and the debates over the Richard story: Roxanne Murph, *Richard III: The Making of a Legend* (Metuchen, N.J.: Scarecrow Press, 1977); Charles Ross, *Richard III* (Berkeley: University of California Press, 1981); Peter Saccio, *Shakespeare's English Kings* (New York: Oxford University Press, 1977); and Paul M. Kendall, *Richard the Third* (New York: Doubleday, 1956).

Discussions of whether Richard was the victim of Tudor propaganda or an unusually depraved historical figure are by now so commonplace and so undecidable that they seem only to beg more important questions. That the figure of Richard was colored by Tudor interests is beyond question. But even Tudor propagandists could not totally alter the shape of a king whose exploits and accomplishments were still relatively fresh in national memory. However, to concentrate on these matters is to substitute abortive debates over historical "truth claims" for what I would argue is the play's more invested interest in *representational* politics and the way they break down distinctions between historical "fact" and "fiction" at the very site at which subjectivity is constructed.

17. According to Žižek, this Lacanian big Other is "the symbolic order itself." See *The Sublime Object of Ideology* (London: Verso, 1989), p. 93.

In less theorized terms, Ronald Levao, in *Renaissance Minds and Their Fictions: Cusanus, Sidney, Shakespeare* (Berkeley: University of California Press, 1985), has remarked that "Richard's animosity is strangely philosophical, directed not merely against political rivals, but toward a suffocating and sinister cosmos" (p. 295). I would add, however, that this "cosmos" must be theorized precisely because it is a textual one. Levao argues that "for most of *Richard III*, Richard's obsession is more joyful than it is tormenting" (p. 295). Although I disagree with Levao's notion that Richard glories in his difference, I find much of his brief section on *Richard III* interesting and intelligent. Particularly astute is his notion that "Richard is just as surely a demonic parody of Renaissance man's most optimistic self-image. He is the paragon of a world where malevolent desire replaces the *amor platonicus*, and where the bestiality of 'this breathing world' replaces the *anima mundi*. His self-fashioning compulsively overreaches its models: he *adds* colors to the chameleon, is *more* versatile than Proteus" (p. 296).

Marjorie Garber, in "Descanting on Deformity: *Richard III* and the Shape of History" (in *Shakespeare's Ghost Writers: Literature and Uncanny Causality* [New York: Methuen, 1987], pp. 28–51), shares Levao's view of Richard's obsession as joyful: "In Shakespeare's play Richard's physical appearance, his ill-design, perversely glories in its difference from the usual, the uniform, the fully formed" (p. 49). And yet, while the thrust of this point is that Richard revels in his "exceptionality," there is some uneasiness here, as we can detect in the syntax of Garber's sentence, which makes a split between Richard and "Richard's physical appearance."

18. All citations from the play are taken from the Arden edition of *King Richard III*, ed. Antony Hammond (London: Methuen, 1981).

19. For the most complete exposition of the medieval legal and theological doctrine of the "King's Two Bodies," see Ernst H. Kantorowicz's seminal work

The King's Two Bodies: A Study in Medieval Political Theology (Princeton: Princeton University Press, 1957). This powerful notion of the correspondence of the king's human body with its eternal, unimpeachable, and divine counterpart, the "King's" royal body, was still operative (although rapidly becoming demystified in post-Machiavellian England) in somewhat secularized form in Shakespeare's day; and thus would have been doubly appropriate in application to Richard. Since Richard III ruled in the Middle Ages, the doctrine can logically be considered a part of Richard's world within the play. And the secularizing of the doctrine under Elizabeth, as well as its increasingly obvious use as ideological mechanism, would have opened up for a playwright as astute as Shakespeare its histrionic possibilities. Shakespeare plays with the notion of the King's Two Bodies with the only other figure in English history who needed an "authoritative" king's body even more than Elizabeth: the "monstrous" Duke of Gloucester.

See also Clifford Geertz, "Centers, Kings, and Charisma: Reflections on the Symbolics of Power," in *Culture and Its Creators: Essays in Honor of Edward Shils*, ed. Joseph Ben David and Terry Nichols Clark (Chicago: University of Chicago Press, 1977). Geertz describes Elizabeth's appropriation of the doctrine of the King's Two Bodies, and the charisma she was able to fashion for herself out of the ingenious use of "rites and images" (p. 152): "[Britain's political imagination] was allegorical, Protestant, didactic and pictorial; it lived on moral abstractions cast into emblems. Elizabeth was Chastity, Wisdom, Peace, Perfect Beauty, and Pure Religion as well as queen . . . and being queen she was these things. Her whole public life—or, more exactly, the part of her life the public saw—was transformed into a kind of philosophical masque in which everything stood for some vast idea and nothing took place unburdened with parable" (p. 156).

And Leah Marcus discusses the ways Elizabeth manipulated both the discourses of gender and the ideology of the King's Body in her own self-staging and rhetorical self-references. By emphasizing Elizabeth's reliance on the doctrine of the King's Body, Marcus sublates the fact that Elizabeth's human body was a "weak woman's" body to the "fact" that she also possessed the symbolically masculine King's Body through her link to her father, Henry VIII. Marcus connects this practice to Shakespeare's representations of cross-dressed, rhetorically cross-gendered comic heroines such as Portia, Viola, and Rosalind. See "Shakespeare's Comic Heroines: The Political Uses of Androgyny," in *Women in the Middle Ages and the Renaissance: Literary and Historical Perspectives*, ed. Mary Beth Rose (Syracuse, N.Y.: Syracuse University Press, 1986), pp. 135–154.

20. My use of the terms "center" and "periphery" is influenced by but ultimately independent of the larger model Edward Shils constructs in his chapter "Center and Periphery," in *Essays in Macrosociology* (Chicago: University of Chicago Press, 1975), pp. 3–16. Some mention of that model is relevant here, however. One of Shils's defining characteristics of the "center" of a society is that its "central value system is constituted by the values which are pursued and affirmed by the elites of the constituent subsystems and of the organizations which are comprised in the subsystems. By their possession of authority, they attribute to themselves an essential affinity with the sacred elements of their society, of which they regard themselves as the custodians . . . One of the major

elements in any central value system is an affirmative attitude toward established authority . . . Authority enjoys appreciation because it arouses sentiments of sacredness. Sacredness by its nature is authoritative. Those persons, offices, or symbols endowed with it, however indirectly and remotely, are therewith endowed with some measure of authoritativeness" (p. 5).

Shils's theory is germane in connection with my assertion that Richard's desire is to acquire the value attributed to the sacred perfection of the "King's body." If, as Shils claims, sacredness inheres within authoritativeness, and both together form the originary point from which all other values are derived, then we can regard Richard's desire to be king as his desire to make himself the *episteme* of all values (or, in other terms, the arbiter of all signification) in the play. This desire, however, must be pitted against the fact that Richard "recognizes" no sacred authority behind the kingship of others, notably Henry VI and his own brother Edward. In a classic circuit of willful misrecognition, he seeks to realize the symbolic capital that comes from being "round impaled with a glorious crown" (*King Henry VI, Part 3:* 3.2.171), capital that he scornfully denies to others. This is in keeping with his general attempt to render commutable the value of all signification only if it originates in his own person.

21. Geertz, in "Centers, Kings, and Charisma," discusses Shils's conception of charisma as "the connection between the symbolic value individuals possess and their relation to the active centers of the social order" (p. 151).

22. Pierre Bourdieu, *Distinction: A Social Critique of the Judgement of Taste,* trans. Richard Nice (Cambridge, Mass.: Harvard University Press, 1984), p. 208.

23. Marjorie Garber's exploration, in *Shakespeare's Ghost Writers,* of the way Shakespeare uses the "historicity" of the figure of Richard pushes beyond the usual bounds of the Tudor-propaganda debate into the deconstructive politics of historiography. Garber argues that all history writing is essentially propagandistic insofar as it is "deformed" by the invested, "authorized" writing hand; and that the amplification of Richard's deformity over time signifies the inevitable deformations of history itself. Richard's character "marks the inevitability of deformation in the registers of the political and historiographical" (p. 33). Thus, the writing of history, like the writing of Richard, exemplifies "the dangers of re-membering, of history as an artifact of memory" (p. 44). Garber eloquently asserts that to remember is to re-member, to re-assemble, to assign new members to something; and that the figure of Richard is just such a "re-membering": "Richard is not only deformed, his deformity is itself a deformation. His twisted and misshapen body encodes the whole strategy of history as a necessary deforming and unforming—with the object of re-forming—the past" (p. 36). The suggestion here is that Richard *is* History: both are prodigious, both are untimely (in the sense of being constructed after the fact), both are misshapen by authorized and authorizing hands.

In what I take to be the central point of her argument, Garber asserts that, like history, and "created by a similar process of ideological and polemical distortion, Richard's deformity is a figment of rhetoric, a figure of abuse, a catachresis masquerading as a metaphor. In a viciously circular manifestation of neo-Platonic determinism, Richard is made villainous in appearance to match the desired villainy of his reputation, and then is given a personality warped and bent to compensate for his physical shape" (p. 36). While I agree with Garber's characterization of the vicious circle of historiography Richard finds himself in, and finds in himself, her exposition seems haunted by what it leaves out, forecloses on something about Richard that, however anamorphically, demands to be seen. As Garber herself points out early in her argument, "no account of Shakespeare's literary or political motivations in foregrounding his protagonist's deformity is adequate to explain the power and seductiveness of Richard's presence in the plays. Indeed, the very fascination exerted by the historical Richard III seems to grow in direct proportion to an increase in emphasis on his deformity" (p. 31). But emphasizing his deformity as standing solely for the process of writing a history play also seems inadequate "to explain the power and seductiveness of Richard's presence in the play." In her understandable concern not to essentialize "character," Garber ends an otherwise convincing discussion almost where one wants it to begin. Accepting the *play's* legerdemain by reinscribing the deformed figure of Richard as a "catachresis masquerading as metaphor," her account misses the way that Shakespeare is representing a *subjective identity between* metaphor and catachresis: the fact that anyone who is made to "stand for" him or herself will feel "incorrect" or warped, like a bad facsimile of some more "authentic" "original"—that the identity *coerced* by metaphor is always itself a "masquerade," always itself purchased *by* catachresis. In subsuming the figure of Richard under the larger conceptual carapace of "Shakespeare's ghost writers," Garber's account doesn't explain the "power and seductiveness of Richard's presence in the play" because it leaves out the ghost in the machine.

24. *The Curious Perspective: Literary and Pictorial Wit in the Seventeenth Century* (New Haven: Yale University Press, 1978), p. 22.

25. That the history of criticism of this scene is largely one of incredulity is evident in the vehemence of the criticism that argues for its psychological verisimilitude. Donald Shupe, in "The Wooing of Lady Anne: A Psychological Inquiry," *Shakespeare Quarterly* 29 (1978): 28–36, argues that Richard's Machiavellian skill at manipulation makes the scene psychologically believable; and Denzell Smith, in "The Credibility of the Wooing of Anne in *Richard III*," *Papers on Language and Literature* 7 (1971): 199–202, argues for the psychological "realism" of the scene as well. However, for an interesting analysis of why the scene doesn't work for Richard precisely because he *does* accomplish his aim, see Marguerite Waller, "Usurpation, Seduction, and the Problematics of the Proper: A 'Deconstructive,' 'Feminist' Rereading of the Seductions of Richard and Anne in Shakespeare's *Richard III*," in *Rewriting the Renaissance: The Discourses of Sexual Difference in Early Modern Europe*, ed. Margaret W. Ferguson, Maureen Quilligan, and Nancy J. Vickers (Chicago: University of Chicago Press, 1986), pp. 159–174. Dolores Burton, in "Discourse and Decorum in the First Act of *Richard III*" (*Shakespeare Studies* 14 [1981]: 55–84), analyzes the wooing of Anne in terms of classical rhetoric, noting that Richard triumphs over Anne because of his skill with forensic or judicial oratory: "Because this oratory of the courtroom attempts to defend or to blame a person's behavior, it looks back to the past, develops arguments from the special topics of justice and injustice, and employs as its means accusation and defense" (p. 62). It is a rhetoric of disputa-

tion, and Richard wins because "despite [Anne's] ability to match Gloucester's language word for word and phrase for phrase, [she] is no match for his logic" (p. 65). Although Burton's interpretation is splendid in its attention to the details and nuances of the language, I don't agree with her sense of what is at stake in the scene. For Burton, the many references to eyes and sight must be understood in the sonnet tradition, the language of which Richard deploys against Anne. She makes no connection between Anne's plea for proper vision in this scene and the larger politics of visual evidence in the play.

26. I refer here to a paper Goldberg read at the meeting of the English Institute at Harvard University, August 1991. Brilliantly linking the historical and legal construction of "sodomy laws" (in which the "crimes" are never uniformly defined in, as Goldberg puns, "fundamental" terms) with representations of Saddam Hussein during the Persian Gulf war, Goldberg argued the way in which constructions of "sodomy" and homosexuality are grafted onto figures that a culture wishes to demonize by coding as "unnatural." Focusing his discussion on an advertisement for a T-shirt that depicted Saddam's face on the rear end of a camel ("in place of" the animal's anus), Goldberg asserted that through such strategies Saddam's "monstrousness" was visually and discursively driven home, and that justification of the war synecdochized the moral imperatives of heterosexism with those of national sovereignty. The paper, entitled "Sodometries," is now part of *Sodometries: Renaissance Texts, Modern Sexualities* (Stanford, Calif.: Stanford University Press, 1992).

Patricia Parker, in *Literary Fat Ladies: Rhetoric, Gender, Property* (London: Methuen, 1987), also discusses the "preposterous" as a "rhetorical figure or trope—hysteron proteron, routinely Englished in the Renaissance as 'The Preposterous.' Puttenham and others described it as a form of verbal reversal, one which sets 'that before which should be behind' (Puttenham) or 'that which ought to be in the first place . . . in the second' (Angell Day)" (p. 67). Parker skillfully analyzes this figure in terms of the politics of gender and role reversals and the threat they pose to the ideological syntax of "proper order"—whether of history, inheritance laws, or gender relations.

And Joel B. Altman, in "'Preposterous Conclusions': Eros, *Enargeia,* and the Composition of *Othello*" (*Representations* 18 [Spring 1987]: 129–157), uses the figure of *hysteron proteron* to argue that Shakespeare's characters in general, and in *Othello* in particular, deploy it in their attempts to construct "probability" out of what the playwright himself represented as "radical improbability" (p. 132). Arguing that the trope of the preposterous operates for characters when, "under the sway of passion, effects precede causes (rationally construed) and ends precede means" (p. 133), Altman persuasively demonstrates in his sophisticated rhetorical analysis that Shakespeare "would seem to have had considerable purchase upon a probabilism that was beginning to acquire the dangerous features of an ideology in his time" (p. 133).

27. David Holbrook, *Sex and Dehumanization in Art, Thought and Life and Life in Our Time* (London: Pitman Publishing, 1972), p. 24.

28. Richard's skill at the Latin rhetorical form *insinuatio* is manifest. In this one scene he fulfills seven out of the eight criteria of the form elaborated by Edward Corbett in *Classical Rhetoric for the Modern Student* (New York: Oxford Univer-

sity Press, 1971), p. 310. Richard (1) denies the charges that have created prejudices against him, (2) admits the charges but denies their alleged magnitude, (3) cites a compensating virtue or action, (4) attributes the discrediting action to an inescapable compulsion, (5) cites others who were guilty of the same thing but were not charged, (6) substitutes a different motive or cause for the one alleged, (7) inveighs against calumny and malicious insinuation in general.

29. Jean Baudrillard, *The Ecstasy of Communication,* trans. Bernard Schutze and Caroline Schutze (New York: Semiotext(e), 1988), pp. 67, 69–70.

30. I borrow the term "homosocial" from Eve Sedgwick's powerful account of the representational strategies and structures of male bonding within a "heterosexual," homophobic culture; see Sedgwick, *Between Men: English Literature and Male Homosocial Desire* (New York: Columbia University Press, 1985). In defining her use of the term, Sedgwick says that "'homosocial' is a word occasionally used in history and the social sciences, where it describes social bonds between persons of the same sex; it is a neologism, obviously formed by analogy with 'homosexual,' and just as obviously meant to be distinguished from 'homosexual.' In fact, it is applied to such activities as 'male bonding,' which may, as in our society, be characterized by intense homophobia, fear and hatred of homosexuality. To draw the 'homosocial' back into the orbit of 'desire,' of the potentially erotic, then, is to hypothesize the potential unbrokenness of a continuum between homosocial and homosexual" (p. 1). Relying heavily on the concept of triangulated desire developed by René Girard in *Deceit, Desire, and the Novel,* Sedgwick articulates the structure relevant to my use of the term here: "What is most interesting . . . in his study is his insistence that, in any erotic rivalry, the bond that links the two rivals is as intense and potent as the bond that links either of the two rivals to the beloved: that the bonds of 'rivalry' and 'love,' differently as they are experienced, are equally powerful and in many senses equivalent" (p. 21).

31. See Peter Travis, "The Social Body of the Dramatic Christ in Medieval England," *Early Drama to 1600, Acta* 13 (1985): 17–36.

32. Perhaps three of the most important and influential works on the shifting historical standards of what one might call orificial decorum are Elias, *The History of Manners;* Mikhail Bakhtin, *Rabelais and His World,* trans. H. Iswolsky (Cambridge, Mass.: MIT Press, 1968); and Mary Douglas, *Purity and Danger: An Analysis of the Concepts of Pollution and Taboo* (London: Routledge, 1966). For a brilliant critical synthesis and theoretical analysis of representations of and debates around the body and its apertures in early modern England, see Peter Stallybrass and Allon White, *The Politics and Poetics of Transgression* (Ithaca, N.Y.: Cornell University Press, 1986), esp. pp. 1–26.

33. Stanbury, "The Virgin's Gaze: Spectacle and Transgression in Middle English Lyrics of the Passion," *PMLA* 106, no. 5 (October 1991): 1083–1093, esp. 1085. Women are supposed to be objects, not subjects, of the gaze; and as Stanbury puts it, the key question is "Why does Mary seem exempted in this setting from taboos against a woman's gaze, particularly one focused on the male body?"(p. 1086). She argues that "medieval passional lyrics present a drama of transgression," but that "Mary is not prohibited from looking . . . because a nearly dead body is hardly an erotic spectacle; moreover, her gaze is

maternal and compassionate, entitled by a mother's right. Yet, I would counter, these categories—what is maternal, what is erotic—are not that simply fixed . . . What we do not see when we look at a tableau as familiar as, for example, Giotto's *Lamentation* are its transgressions, its violations of ordinary boundaries through gestures that conflate Eros, Thanatos, and maternal power" (p. 1086).

Stanbury is right that the categories above, as well as others, are not simply fixed and that they exceed their own boundaries as well as overlap the boundaries of other codes of "decorum" all the time. Such transgression is, I would add, precisely what gives these representations their power of fascination: they represent less fully their own subject matter than they do what's involved, evoked, and conjured in the act of "apprehending" it.

34. See Michel Foucault, *Discipline and Punish: The Birth of the Prison*, trans. Alan Sheridan (New York: Vintage, 1977); and idem, *The History of Sexuality*, vol. 1: *An Introduction*, trans. Robert Hurley (New York: Vintage, 1980). Dianne Hunter, editor of *Seduction and Theory* (Chicago: University of Chicago Press, 1989), argues in her introduction (pp. 1–10) that masculine subjectivity in patriarchal Western culture depends on its ability to dominate and subjugate others (most notably women) with and to the gaze. Norman Bryson, in *Vision and Painting: The Logic of the Gaze* (New Haven: Yale University Press, 1983), argues that the gaze enacts "a certain violence (penetrating, piercing, fixing)" and that it "actively seeks to confine what is always on the point of escaping or slipping out of bounds" (p. 93).

Barbara Freedman, in her fine study *Staging the Gaze: Postmodernism, Psychoanalysis, and Shakespearean Comedy* (Ithaca, N.Y.: Cornell University Press, 1991), has argued that the Renaissance stage in particular, and theatricality in general, are site and trope respectively for representations of the gaze that are best illuminated by Lacan's theory of subjectivity. Freedman points out the ways Shakespearean drama fetishizes the observed and the observing. And she asserts that its requirement that the audience identify with the performative acts, as well as physical outlines, of the figures on stage reproduces the conditions of subject formation charted in Lacanian psychoanalysis: "*Méconnaissance* is Lacan's term for the misrecognitions through which the ego is constructed and the illusory identifications, whether of gender or ideology, through which it is sustained. The term reminds us that Lacan's mirror stage has broader implications, especially because the mirror stage need not rely on a physical mirror per se . . . For Lacan, self-identification is based on a representation that alienates as it procures: 'Man becomes aware of this reflection from the point of view of the other; he is an other for himself'. . . . Desire and aggressivity mark the distance between subject and its ideal image, termed *ideal* because it can never be fully assimilated" (p. 53). It is just such a "procurement" that the gaze establishes: one that constitutes the gazing observer as subject precisely by "alienating" as "Other" the object of the gaze.

35. Stephen Greenblatt argues that discrepancies between gender roles, conceptions of the male and female bodies, and the conditions of cross-dressing in Shakespearean comedy generate a "chafing" or "friction" that produces erotic "heat," both within the play and for the audience as well. Using a masturbatory image as the central trope for an allegory of theater-as-foreplay, Greenblatt's

"case" is more persuasive for courtship in the comedies than for courtship in the tragedies, where the "friction" of "foreplay" (which is where the comedies tend to end—with preconsummated nuptials) usually leads to an eroticism that inevitably invokes male sexual anxiety and violence. See "Fiction and Friction," in *Shakespearean Negotiations* (Berkeley: University of California Press, 1988), esp. pp. 88–93. Interestingly, I discovered after writing this chapter that Greenblatt amplifies his statement that "erotic chafing is the central means by which characters in [comedies] realize their identities and form loving unions" (p. 88) with a footnote in which he confesses, "I think Shakespeare first realized the erotic energy of chafing in the wooing scene in *Richard III* " (p. 183). If Richard and Anne Neville generate this kind of erotic "friction," it is the result of a temporary suspension of their "proper" gender roles as they jockey for position and power over Henry's feminized corpse, a suspension that will quickly be canceled once Anne capitulates to the frictional eroticism that can be celebrated in the comedies only because it is always, ultimately, under male control.

36. See Peter Stallybrass, "Patriarchal Territories: The Body Enclosed," in *Rewriting the Renaissance: The Discourses of Sexual Difference in Early Modern Europe*, ed. Margaret W. Ferguson, Maureen Quilligan, and Nancy Vickers (Chicago: University of Chicago Press, 1986), pp. 123–142.

37. Georges Bataille, *Visions of Excess: Selected Writings, 1927–1939*, ed. and trans. Allan Stoekl, with Carl R. Lovitt and Donald M. Leslie, Jr. (Minneapolis: University of Minnesota Press, 1985), p. 140.

38. Lewis Hyde, *The Gift: Imagination and the Erotic Life of Property* (New York: Vintage, 1979), p. xiv.

39. Marcel Mauss has described the way gift exchange binds all involved in the obligation to give, to receive, and to reciprocate and consequently weaves them into a fabric of social constraints that have little to do with the individual "wills" of the participants. The obligation is especially compelling for the recipient, who is "free" neither to refuse a gift nor to extricate herself from the "debt" incurred. See *The Gift: The Form and Reason for Exchange in Archaic Societies*, trans. W. D. Hall (New York: Routledge, 1990), p. 39.

One could object that what we are seeing between Anne and Richard is merely political strategy and sexual dissembling, and therefore that there is nothing "genuinely" erotic about the scene. And certainly one could argue that within the patriarchal relations that structure all relations in the play, we see only the hobbled kind of eroticism that a habitus structured around murderous phallic aggression is capable of producing. But these objections would be more interesting for what they tend to assume rather than point up about the erotic. To say that there could not be any genuine erotic attraction between Richard and Anne would be to assume (1) that eroticism is always based on a *benevolent* libidinal investment, and (2) that it is a fixed category that does not shift shape, target, and configuration. It would be to assume, mistakenly, that there is nothing erotic about *dissembling itself.* (Whatever we might think of them, figures such as Kierkegaard's "seducer" Johannes, Choderlos de Laclos' Valmont and Merteuil, Richardson's Lovelace, not to mention the more recent success of a cultural figure like Madonna, give the lie to this.) It is to repeat the mistake that medieval church censors made when they failed to see erotic transgression in the gaze of the Virgin: to assume that the matter being represented (the ostensible *object* of desire) is more "authentic" than the process involved in representing and apprehending it—more real than what gets set in motion around the object "itself." Such an assumption posits an absolute division between forms of desire, such as ambition, lust, envy, competition, love—a division that is ideological rather than essential. In terms of the erotic *effect* of the scene, it little matters what Richard's "real" aims are or what his "darker purpose" is.

40. See Jacqueline Rose, "*Hamlet:* The Mona Lisa of Literature," in *Sexuality in the Field of Vision* (London: Verso, 1986), pp. 124–125.

41. *The Politics and Poetics of Transgression* (Ithaca, N.Y.: Cornell University Press, 1986), p. 141. Of course, Richard's body is not yet the "bourgeois body," with its repression of the "lower bodily stratum"; there is not yet the full stratification and policing of acceptable/unacceptable bodily spheres as they make their way into discourse (and as discourse makes its way into bodily spheres).

And yet Francis Barker, in *The Tremulous Private Body: Essays in Subjection* (London: Methuen, 1984), is wrong to assert that there were in the sixteenth and early seventeenth centuries no distinctions between the individual's physical person and the bodily stratum of the social, which he terms "the plenum." Throughout the first tetralogy, particular bodies are very much in the way. They "obstruct" unauthorized political movement; and they do so because they belong to persons who stand in a "legitimate" or illegitimate relationship to accession to royal power by virtue of bloodlines. Richard's body is discreditable because it "reveals" Richard's "true" relation to the social and political, a relation which is designated monstrous and perverse. But it is no mere metaphor. The tension between the body as metaphor and as all-too-concrete is precisely what constitutes Richard's identity; others produce figurative material out of a body that has condensed around Richard like a shell, disqualifying him from utterances of metaphorical signification because of inevitable and literal self-implication.

42. Sir Thomas More, *History of King Richard III* ; this passage is taken from Appendix 3 in the Arden edition of the play, p. 350.

43. In an earlier essay (parts of which comprise a section of her book chapter "*Macbeth* and *Coriolanus*"), Adelman briefly mentions Shakespeare's concern with maternal power in *Richard III,* and argues that "Richard constructs his own desire for the crown specifically as compensation for his failure at the sexual game." See "Born of Women: Fantasies of Maternal Power in *Macbeth*," in *Cannibals, Witches and Divorce: Estranging the Renaissance,* ed. Marjorie Garber (Baltimore: Johns Hopkins University Press, 1987), pp. 91–92. I would argue that Richard is less like Macbeth (who, as Adelman demonstrates, wishes to escape altogether the agency of the womb) than he is like Coriolanus, who Adelman argues wants "to become the author of his mother . . . to have power over her" (*Suffocating Mothers,* p. 159). If in *Macbeth* the fantasy is a world without women in which men can give birth to themselves, and if in *Coriolanus* the fantasy is a world in which men can be "author of themselves," in *Richard III* the fantasy is a world in which men are born of women but in which women are no more than the passive vessels for the "re-imprinting" of male imagination. The fantasy

compensates for the Renaissance view that women could, through the power of their imaginations, affect the shape of the fetus in the womb. This view finds both its expression and its denial in Richard's "revision" of prenatal experience. This "revision" includes Richard's remarks in the play's opening lines about being "sent before [his] time," "scarce half made-up"; the play's "other Richard" was two years in the womb, and born with teeth and shaggy hair. But it also permits the politics of authorship and the "anxiety of influence" *between men* to be displaced onto and into women's bodies, which can then be reviled, rejected, or, in this instance, rewritten by the playwright as well as by the play's male figures.

44. "'Neither Mother, Wife, nor England's Queen': The Roles of Women in *Richard III,*" in *The Woman's Part: Feminist Criticism of Shakespeare,* ed. Carolyn Ruth Swift Lenz, Gayle Greene, and Carol Thomas Neely (Chicago: University of Illinois Press, 1980), pp. 35–54, 45.

45. *The Prince,* ch. 18; in *The Portable Machiavelli,* ed. and trans. Peter Bondanella and Mark Musa (New York: Penguin, 1979).

46. *Sublime Object of Ideology,* p. 34.

47. Harry Berger, Jr., coins this term in *Imaginary Audition: Shakespeare on Stage and Page* (Berkeley: University of California Press, 1989). Many scholars have discussed the performativity of sixteenth and seventeenth century culture, both within the fishbowl world of the court and in the social arena of middle-class upward mobility. Early modern texts address it variously as wicked (the "antitheatrical prejudice" of Stubbes, Gosson, and Nashe) and as something that can be prescribed (the courtesy and conduct books of Castiglione, Elyot, Colet, Guazzo, Pettie, Brathwait, and many others). For critical discussions, see Greenblatt, *Renaissance Self-Fashioning;* Weimann, *Shakespeare and the Popular Tradition;* Steven Mullaney, *The Place of the Stage: License, Play, and Power in Renaissance England* (Chicago: University of Chicago Press, 1988); and Whigham, *Ambition and Privilege.*

48. Mary Douglas describes this as a form of symbolic power known as *baraka* in Somali culture; see *Purity and Danger,* pp. 110–111. See also idem, *Natural Symbols: Explorations in Cosmology* (Harmondsworth: Penguin, 1973).

49. *Purity and Danger,* p. 165.

50. See Žižek, *Sublime Object,* p. 87.

51. This is not to say, however, that Richard is entirely deconstructed in this scene. On the contrary, he is consolidated into the reified text that has been the play's relentless ideological telos. Other critics disagree, however, about what this moment in the play achieves. Janet Adelman argues that "even while Shakespeare suggests the etiology of Richard's transformation into an actor, he participates in the erasure of Richard's intolerable selfhood: in *Richard III,* our attention is directed more to Richard's theatrical machinations than to any imagined subjectivity behind his roles; even in Richard's spectacular final soliloquy (5.3.178–204), the effect is less of a psyche than of diverse roles confronting themselves across the void where a self should be" (*Suffocating Mothers,* p. 9).

As I have argued earlier, it is precisely in those moments when the figure becomes aware of the gap between a notorious identity being foisted upon it and the possibility of or yearning for something "else" that subjectivity is represented; and it is precisely at this moment in the play when Richard materializes most fully as a subject. Not, to be sure, as a "psyche" (with its connotations of substantial inwardness and unity of self), but, rather, as an entity all of a sudden fully and horribly aware of the intolerable mandates of his social identity, a role that demands that he play the monster, a role that one finally senses, if only for a moment, he does not want to play. In this soliloquy Richard is not "the perfect actor who has no being except in the roles he plays" (p. 9) but the subject grown exhausted by the resistance these roles simultaneously require and break down. This scene doesn't "erase" Richard's "intolerable selfhood" (p. 9); it *produces* it in the face-off between the two versions of Richard the play has been advancing along convergent paths.

52. The psychological notion of Richard's feeling licensed by his exceptionality, "exempt" from normal codes of moral behavior, derives from Freud's famous essay "Some Character-Types Met with in Psychoanalytic Work," section 1: "The Exceptions," in *Character and Culture*, ed. Philip Rieff (New York: Macmillan, 1963). Freud describes Shakespeare's Richard as a figure "in whose character the claim to be an exception is closely bound up with and motivated by the circumstance of congenital injury" (p. 160). But the relationship between a wounded bodily image and the will to power was articulated long before Freud in Francis Bacon's essay "Of Deformity": "Deformed persons are commonly even with nature, for, as nature hath done ill by them so do they by nature, being, for the most part (as the Scripture saith) *void of natural affection*, and so they have their revenge of nature. Certainly there is a consent between the body and the mind, and where nature erreth in the one she ventureth in the other . . . Whosoever hath anything fixed in his person that doth induce contempt, hath also a perpetual spur in himself to rescue and deliver himself from scorn; therefore, all deformed persons are extreme bold. First, as in their own defence, as being exposed to scorn; but in the process of time, by a general habit. Also it stirreth in them industry, and especially of this kind, to watch and observe the weakness of others, that they may have somewhat to repay." See *Francis Bacon: A Selection of His Work*, ed. Sidney Warhaft (Indianapolis: Bobbs-Merrill, 1965), pp. 158–159.

Although Bacon's essay wasn't published until 1623, and *Richard III* was being performed regularly as early as 1594, the idea of a "consent between the body and the mind" was a commonplace, evident in the popularity of Renaissance physiognomies. Bacon's essay articulates the reversal Richard attempts: the logical entanglement involved in trying to deliver oneself from the scorn attending something that is "fixed" in one's person—to be, in Freud's terms, the "exception" to the exception one already is. The "industry" Bacon alludes to is applied, therefore, toward claiming as personal agency, as "boldness," what is already attributed to one as prodigality—as contemptibility. A form of belaboring the obvious, it is to call attention to oneself as a "monster" of one's own design.

53. René Girard, *Violence and the Sacred*, trans. Patrick Gregory (Baltimore: Johns Hopkins University Press, 1977), p. 39.

54. See Žižek, *Sublime Object*, pp. 169–171. Putting spins on various definitions of the real in philosophical, linguistic, and psychoanalytic theory,

Žižek brilliantly formulates how the real manifests its presence precisely through its "interventions" in the symbolic. This formulation posits the real not as something from which subjects are forever "barred," but as something present in "the distortions it produces in the symbolic universe of the subject." In other words, the real is present in its *symptoms*: "The Real is therefore simultaneously both the hard, impenetrable kernel resisting symbolization *and* a pure chimerical entity which has in itself no ontological consistency. To use Kripkean terminology, the Real is the rock upon which every attempt at symbolization stumbles, the hard core which remains the same in all possible worlds (symbolic universes); but at the same time its status is thoroughly precarious; it is something that persists only as failed, missed, in a shadow, and dissolves itself as soon as we try to grasp it in its positive nature . . . We have the Real as the starting point, the basis, the foundation of the process of symbolization . . . that is, the Real which in a sense precedes the symbolic order and is subsequently structured by it when it gets caught in its network" (p. 169).

55. Mikkel Borch-Jacobsen, *The Freudian Subject,* trans. Catherine Porter (Stanford: Stanford University Press, 1988), p. 28.

56. I am loosely paraphrasing Žižek's definition of the Hitchcockian "MacGuffin" (see *Sublime Object,* pp. 182–185).

57. Jonathan Dollimore, "The Cultural Politics of Perversion: Augustine, Shakespeare, Freud, Foucault," *Textual Practice* 4, no. 2 (Summer 1990): 182, 184.

58. See Lacan, "Desire and the Interpretation of Desire in Hamlet," in *Literature and Psychoanalysis,* ed. Shoshana Felman (Baltimore: Johns Hopkins University Press, 1982). I am quoting Avital Ronell's description of Cixous' definition of the uses of hysteria as an effective stratagem of a revolutionary feminism. See the interview with Ronell in *Angry Women: Re/Search 13,* ed. Andrea Juno and V. Vale (San Francisco: Re/Search Publications, 1991), p. 131. I apply this definition of hysteria as productive disruption to *Richard III* with a heavy dose of caution and irony, since whatever its effects may be within the play, it serves finally to secure the agenda of Tudor politics, which were (Queen Elizabeth notwithstanding) deeply antifeminist; and the agenda of patriarchal culture, which was and remains deeply misogynist.

59. On Lacan's neologism "l'extimité" and its relation to the subject and to the symbolic order, see Žižek, *Sublime Object,* pp. 130–132, 180–181.

60. Peter Stallybrass' work on the word "individual" in Renaissance texts (and specifically with regard to Shakespeare and Milton) has been suggestive in my formulating a sense of how Richard is being "singled out" as part of a larger social process. See "Shakespeare, the Individual, and the Text," in *Cultural Studies,* ed. Lawrence Grossberg, Cary Nelson, and Paula Treichler (New York: Routledge, 1992), pp. 593–612. Although Stallybrass argues convincingly that in the Renaissance the word "individual" was almost always used in its original sense of "indivisible from," I disagree with the extent to which he interprets this as evidence that there was little or no representation of early forms of the individualism that centuries of "modern" scholars and critics have overread into the "Renaissance." Whether or not the specific word was used, there is textual evidence that the concept of self as autonomous agency—however fantasized, however ideological, however fictional a construct it might have been—was

being fabricated and "tried on" at this time, whether or not it was experienced as a subjective "truth." Stallybrass' deconstruction of "individualism" is part of the larger project of cultural materialism, represented in the work of Raymond Williams, Terry Eagleton, Jonathan Dollimore, Lisa Jardine, Alan Sinfield, and Catherine Belsey, among others, who aim at radically shifting focus away from the "sovereign individual" of Renaissance humanism toward the historical processes that generated ideologies of individual freedom, full choice, and autonomy as productive elements in those aspects of Western culture that are most explicitly racist, classist, sexist, and imperialist.

2. "So Unsecret to Ourselves"

1. All quotations are from the Arden edition of *Troilus and Cressida*, ed. Kenneth Palmer (London: Methuen, 1982).

2. C. G. Jung, *Psychological Reflections: A New Anthology, 1905–1961*, ed. Jolande Jacobi (Princeton: Princeton University Press, 1953), p. 207.

3. Louis Althusser, "A Letter on Art," in *Lenin and Philosophy and Other Essays*, trans. Ben Brewster (New York: Monthly Review Press, 1971), p. 222.

4. See Leo Braudy, *The Frenzy of Renown: Fame and Its History* (New York: Oxford University Press, 1986), for a meditation on the historical impulse to locate a "better, more perfect self" (p. 8) in the past.

5. Sigmund Freud, in *Sexuality and the Psychology of Love*, ed. Philip Rieff (New York: MacMillan, 1963), p. 29.

6. See Montaigne, "Of the Most Outstanding Men." This and all other Montaigne passages are taken from *The Complete Essays of Montaigne*, trans. Donald M. Frame (Stanford: Stanford University Press, 1965). See p. 570.

7. I am grateful to Doug Bruster, who said to me in conversation that my argument about notorious identity reminded him of "that line from 'Penny Lane.'"

8. See Bertolt Brecht, "What Is Epic Theatre? (Second Version)," in *Understanding Brecht*, trans. Anna Bostock (London: New Left Books, 1973). I loosely paraphrase Benjamin, who quotes Brecht: "The actor must show an event, and he must show himself. He naturally shows the event by showing himself; and he shows himself by showing the event." Benjamin goes on to say that "the actor must reserve the right to act skillfully out of character. He must be free, at the right moment, to act himself thinking [about his part]" (p. 21).

9. Elizabeth Freund says something similar in "The Rhetoric of Citation in *Troilus and Cressida*," in *Shakespeare and the Question of Theory*, ed. Patricia Parker and Geoffrey Hartman (New York: Methuen, 1985): "The play also persistently calls attention to its intertextuality, its anachronicity, its dependence upon a prodigious literary and rhetorical legacy" (p. 21). But for Freund, the play's citationality renders it merely "derivative," and empties the characters entirely of any signifying presence that is not merely "referential." I would say, however, that while the figures in *Troilus and Cressida* may be permanently "identified," insofar as their names encode their legends, as dramatic characters they exist as "versions" of themselves, as what Marjorie Garber would call (referring to Derrida and to Benjamin) "multiplications of 'the original.'" See the

introduction to Garber, *Shakespeare's Ghost Writers: Literature as Uncanny Causality* (New York: Methuen, 1987), p. 15. Consequently, the very fact of claiming physical ground and space through the medium of theater generates something that cannot be erased. The ghost of a subject persists.

10. Of course, in the sixteenth and seventeenth centuries, "monsters" were not just aberrations but *significant* aberrations, "portents" of miraculous or disastrous events. The word "monstrous" has as its roots both the Latin *monére*, to warn or admonish, and *monstrare*, to show, point out, or demonstrate. The "monstruosity in love" for Cressida resides in what it simultaneously points to and warns of: the "end" of her love for Troilus.

11. Janet Adelman, Gayle Greene, Stephen J. Lynch, and René Girard, while advancing significantly different arguments about the representation of Cressida, all say something similar about this scene. For all four critics, Cressida panics because she has shown her "hand" to Troilus in an erotic world in which playing "hard to get" generates and sustains desire. See Adelman, "'This Is and Is not Cressid': The Characterization of Cressida," in *The (M)Other Tongue: Essays in Feminist Psychoanalytic Interpretation,* ed. Shirley Nelson Garner, Claire Kahane, and Madelon Sprengnether (Ithaca, N.Y.: Cornell University Press, 1985), p. 121; Girard, "The Politics of Desire in *Troilus and Cressida,*" in *Shakespeare and the Question of Theory,* p. 190; Greene, "Shakespeare's Cressida: 'A Kind of Self,'" in *The Woman's Part: Feminist Criticism of Shakespeare,* ed. Carolyn Ruth Swift Lenz, Gayle Greene, and Carol Thomas Neely (Urbana: University of Illinois Press, 1980), p. 139; and Lynch, "Shakespeare's Cressida: 'A Woman of Quick Sense,'" in *Philological Quarterly* 63, no. 3 (Summer 1984): 359.

12. As Franco Moretti has said, "To persuade is the opposite of to convince. The aim is not to ascertain an intersubjective truth but to enlist support for a *particular* system of values. In the seventeenth century—which witnessed the first great flowering of empirical science, and *at the same time* the collapse of all social 'organicity' in the fight to the death between opposing faiths and interest—the perception of this contrast was extremely acute." See *Signs Taken for Wonders,* trans. Susan Fischer, David Forgacs, and David Miller (London: Verso, 1983), p. 13.

13. The following works provide useful extended discussions of some of the political, rhetorical, economic, psychological, and demographic circumstances contributing to the ideological upheavals of the early seventeenth century: Jonathan Dollimore, *Radical Tragedy: Religion, Ideology and Power in the Drama of Shakespeare and His Contemporaries* (Chicago: University of Chicago Press, 1984); Joel B. Altman, *The Tudor Play of Mind: Rhetorical Inquiry and the Development of Elizabethan Drama* (Berkeley: University of California Press, 1978); William Bouwsma, "Anxiety and the Formation of Early Modern Culture," in *After the Reformation: Essays in Honor of J. H. Hexter,* ed. Barbara C. Malament (Philadelphia: University of Pennsylvania Press, 1980); Christopher Hill, *The Century of Revolution, 1603–1714* (New York: W.W. Norton, 1980); and Stephen Greenblatt, *Renaissance Self-Fashioning: From More to Shakespeare* (Chicago: University of Chicago Press, 1980).

14. See Eve Kosofsky Sedgwick, *Between Men: English Literature and Male Homosocial Desire* (New York: Columbia University Press, 1985).

15. Carol Cook says something very similar in a powerful essay entitled "Unbodied Figures of Desire," *Theatre Journal* 38 (1986). Seeing desire in the play as something that exceeds the characters' abilities to represent it, Cook argues that "the *idea* of Helen . . . serves, notwithstanding its attendant ironies, to rationalize the play of drives" (p. 40). Though I agree with Cook's description of Helen as a "cypher," I would reverse the terms of her statement and say that the "idea" of Helen serves not to "rationalize the play of drives" but to drive the rationale of the play.

16. Francis Barker, *The Tremulous Private Body: Essays in Subjection* (London: Methuen, 1984), p. 34.

17. Dollimore, *Radical Tragedy*, p. 39.

18. Troilus' "idealism" is, from the beginning, far from constant—constructed as it is through a language that splits women into "pearls" and "plackets." The fact that Cressida is compared to Helen, the play's paradigmatic "placket," contaminates Troilus' attempts to idealize her. When Troilus rhetorically asks "Apollo" to tell him "what Cressid is" (1.1.99), he answers his own question: "Her bed is India; there she lies, a pearl" (1.1.100). Presumably she lies there for the taking. Troilus' fantasized idealization of Cressida as "pearl" is at its very inception contaminated by sexual, mercantile, even colonial allusions built into the language he deploys to "worship" her.

Dollimore is not the only antiessentialist critic to reproduce Troilus' mistake. Thomas Cartelli, for instance, claims that "Troilus' association of one woman with all women . . . derives from an attitude toward sexual relations as pristine and pure as naive idealization of parental love." See "Ideology and Subversion in the Shakespearean Set Speech," *ELH* 53 (1986): 1–25, esp. 14. While Cartelli suggests here that a "naive" idealization of parental love subvents Troilus' desire for Cressida, he assumes that even this idealization can be "pure." Janet Adelman, on the other hand, has remarked on what is threatening and dangerous about maternal idealization: its capacity to inflict the "dangerous fusion of infancy" ("'This Is and Is not Cressid,'" p. 131). Adelman recognizes the intense "nostalgia" that permeates the play and Troilus' desire, and she sees this as "the power of a nostalgic longing for union with an overwhelmingly maternal figure; from the first [Troilus] associates his love with his own infantilization" (ibid., p. 130). Although both Cartelli and Adelman properly identify the "association of one woman with all women" that occurs in the play, I would propose a different genesis to this association. Troilus first and foremost associates Cressida not with the "purity" (or danger) of mothers but with the sexual and social "value" of Helen. Troilus' problem is not that he has idealized Cressida; it is that he has tried and failed to idealize her, and *failed from the beginning*. Troilus would like, at the play's opening, to be "true" to his "role" and idealize Cressida, but he cannot: the very terms he exchanges with Pandarus belie her with false compare (to the unfaithful Helen). Troilus' dreamy rhetoric is, then, a sign of nostalgia for an idealization that is no longer possible, an idealization foreclosed upon not only by the textual force of the story's proleptic outcome but, on a metadramatic level, by the cynicism and worldliness that pervade the lyric "idealization" of women in seventeenth century poetry generally. If Troilus is a "lyric poet," he shares the problem (but not the conscious awareness) of the poet of the dark-lady sonnets—the irrecuperability of the Petrarchan beloved and hence the impossibility of constructing a poetic subjectivity in relation to it.

19. Suspicion of the subversive function of theater was, of course, rampant in the late sixteenth and early seventeenth centuries. Antitheatrical polemics flourished, as writers such as Philip Stubbes (*Anatomie of Abuses,* 1583) and Stephen Gosson, to name just two, "railed at the theatre for its idolatry and its impiety," while "the State, even as it patronized the actors, feared their potential for sedition and subversion"; see Peter Stallybrass and Allon White, *The Politics and Poetics of Transgression* (Ithaca, N.Y.: Cornell University Press, 1986), p. 61. We might imagine Shakespeare's Ulysses agreeing with Gosson, who argues (in *Playes Confuted in Five Actions,* 1582) that "plays are no images of trueth, because sometime they handle such thinges as never were, sometime they runne upon truethes, but make them seeme longer, or shorter, or greater, or lesse than they were, according as the Poet blowes them up." For useful treatments of Renaissance antitheatricality, see Jonas Barish, *The Antitheatrical Prejudice* (Berkeley: University of California Press, 1981); Jean Howard, "Renaissance Antitheatricality and the Politics of Gender and Rank in *Much Ado about Nothing,*" in *Shakespeare Reproduced,* ed. Jean E. Howard and Marion F. O'Connor (New York: Methuen, 1987), pp. 163–187; and Stallybrass and White, *The Politics and Poetics of Transgression,* pp. 59–66.

20. This quote is taken from Braudy, *The Frenzy of Renown,* p. 548.

21. See Laura Mulvey, "Visual Pleasure and Narrative Cinema," in *Screen* 16, no. 3 (Autumn 1975): 6–18.

22. Louis Althusser, "Freud and Lacan," in *Lenin and Philosophy,* p. 210.

23. René Girard, "The Politics of Desire in *Troilus and Cressida,*" in *Shakespeare and the Question of Theory,* p. 199.

24. This phrase has been "coined," as it were, by Gayle Rubin in her influential essay "The Traffic in Women: Notes on the 'Political Economy' of Sex," in *Toward an Anthropology of Women,* ed. Rayna Reiter (New York: Monthly Review Press, 1975), pp. 157–210.

25. For three different methodological and theoretical approaches to representations of desire in *Troilus and Cressida,* see Cook, "Unbodied Figures of Desire"; Eric Mallin, "Emulous Factions and the Collapse of Chivalry: *Troilus and Cressida,*" *Representations* 29 (Winter 1990): 145–179; and Gregory Bredbeck, *Sodomy and Interpretation: Marlowe to Milton* (Ithaca, N.Y.: Cornell University Press, 1991), esp. pp. 33–48. Cook's continental feminist-psychoanalytic approach sees the intersection of the war/love plots in terms of what Irigaray has called "hom(m)o-sexuality" (Cook, p. 42). Mallin, whose approach is largely "new historical," cites, as I do, Sedgwick's discussion of the homosocial; he argues that the play interrogates through its representations of homosocial desire (with its attendant misogyny) the breakdown of chivalric ideology within the Tudor court. My account differs from both of these, insofar as I argue that *all* forms of desire in the play are ideological—both *heterosocial* and *homosocial*—and always already so: that is, the representation of desire is not a function or mediation of psychosexual "drives" but, rather, a representational strategy on the part of the playwright, designed to "convincingly" motivate textual and theatrical repro-

duction. And Bredbeck argues persuasively that Thersites' satirical construction of Patroclus as "catamite" reveals that Renaissance satire's "recourse to homoeroticism is part of a larger strategy of social exclusion" (p. 35).

26. See Louis Althusser, "Ideology and the Ideological State Apparatus," pp. 154, 162. Desire in the play corresponds to Althusser's definition of ideology as a "representation of the imaginary relationship of individuals to their real conditions of existence" (p. 162), insofar as it repackages practices that have publicly oriented, ideological aims (the activity and commerce of warfare, the reproduction of "reputation" and "honor") as motivations that are "private," and psychosexually derived.

27. Nancy Vickers, "'This Heraldry in Lucrece' Face,'" in *The Female Body in Western Culture*, ed. Susan Rubin Suleiman (Cambridge, Mass.: Harvard University Press, 1986), p. 220.

28. Braudy, *The Frenzy of Renown*, p. 123.

29. Gilles Deleuze and Félix Guattari, *Anti-Oedipus: Capitalism and Schizophrenia*, trans. Robert Hurley, Mark Seem, and Helen R. Lane (Minneapolis: University of Minnesota Press, 1983). I slightly paraphrase Deleuze and Guattari, who assert: "We maintain that the social field is immediately invested by desire, that it is the historically determined product of desire, and that libido has no need of any mediation or sublimation, any psychic operation, any transformation, in order to invade and invest the productive forces and relations of production. *There is only desire and the social, and nothing else*" (p. 29). In this formulation (and in their argument in general) there is something called "desire" that exists independently of, and prior to, its "social forms"; something that circulates about on its own, with the power to "invade and invest" the social. While I agree that the social field is "immediately invested by desire," I would argue that desire is also immediately invested by social forms, and that we should understand the term "immediately" to mean "originally."

30. I have been arguing throughout this book for subjectivity as a sense of disruptive and multiple self-presence in conflicted relation to one's name, and not, as is more typical, subjectivity as conscious agency or "inwardness." Janet Adelman takes issue with my analysis of Cressida on the grounds that "it obscures gender differences as they are played out in literary representation, obscuring specifically here the extent to which Cressida's reduction to her name is much more final than Troilus's. Perhaps we are all equally iterable citations; but Shakespearean representation tends frequently—particularly in the tragedies— to create the illusion that men are subjects, and women citations." See *Suffocating Mothers: Fantasies of Maternal Origin in Shakespeare's Plays, "Hamlet" to "The Tempest"* (London: Routledge, 1992), p. 263, n. 18. In terms of how I am defining the paradoxical subject of notorious identity, Cressida is *all the more* a subject than Troilus because she is all the more *aware* of being finished by her name. In this play it is Troilus, and not Cressida, who actively strives to be a "citation." And it is not surprising, since his citation is so salutary ("as true as Troilus") while hers is so condemnatory ("as false as Cressid").

31. Barbara Everett, "The Inaction of *Troilus and Cressida*," *Essays in Criticism* 32 (1982).

3. Spies and Whispers

1. This quote is taken from Mark Crispin Miller, *Boxed In: The Culture of TV* (Evanston: Northwestern University Press, 1988), p. 106.

2. Miller's chapter on the role of the television newscaster is trenchant and thought provoking. Miller describes the coverage of this convention, with its particular focus on the events going on around Moscone Center: "On the regular evening newscasts early in the week, there were prominent stories highlighting the assemblage, all around Moscone Convention Center, of many gung-ho deviants—crusading potsmokers, a pallid clown named Zippy the Pinhead, hookers, punks, and tree worshippers. Ostensibly a chuckling evocation of American diversity, each of these stories was in fact calculated to heat the audience up with glimpses of wild weirdos about to go berserk . . . Thus, in advance, the convention was subtly advertised as a grotesque and shameless rampage, just the sort of orgy you expect whenever Democrats convene, and especially in San Francisco" (*Boxed In*, p. 105).

3. Janet Adelman, *The Common Liar: An Essay on Antony and Cleopatra* (New Haven: Yale University Press, 1973), pp. 31, 39. Other critics have also remarked on the play's foregrounding of the role of messengers. Ronald R. MacDonald, for instance, has called this "a play swarming with messengers, perhaps forty or fifty of them, depending on how elastic the definition of messengers is." See "Playing Till Doomsday: Interpreting *Antony and Cleopatra*," *ELR* 15 (1985): 78–99, esp. 85.

4. Many critics have noted the play's apparent ethical and imagistic binarism. For some of the best discussions, see Adelman, *The Common Liar*, esp. ch. 3; Jonas Barish, *The Antitheatrical Prejudice* (Berkeley: University of California Press, 1981); and Rosalie Colie's powerful chapter "The Significance of Style," in *Shakespeare's Living Art* (Princeton: Princeton University Press, 1974). Carol Cook, in an unpublished manuscript entitled "The Fatal Cleopatra," astutely notes that in this play "binariness itself . . . is offered to our attention" (p. 18).

5. Other critics have noticed this tension as well, without necessarily seeing it, as I do, as the *primum mobile* of all other constructions of difference in the play. W. B. Worthen, however, in a wonderful discussion of the play, has characterized one of its major representational themes as "a contest between narrative and drama, text and performance." See "The Weight of Antony: Staging 'Character' in *Antony and Cleopatra*," *SEL 1500–1900* 26, no. 2 (1986): 297.

6. Worthen's discussion anticipates mine on several fronts, insofar as we are both interested in the way the play foregrounds its own staginess, and plays theatricality against narrative fixity. Worthen says that Shakespeare "brings the histrionic surface of the actors' performances sharply into view, dramatizing the double vision that the theater requires of its audience as part of our experience of the play" ("The Weight of Antony," p. 296). But Worthen's discussion remains focused on the staging of "character" in the play, the way the play foregrounds the *actors' bodies*. For Worthen, the play's two modes of characterization are both paradigmatic of theater generally. On the other hand, I am claiming that these two modes of "characterization" (a term I want, finally, to avoid)

are best explored in the medium of theater because that medium most analogously replicates how subjects are constructed in life. In other words, in the Renaissance, the trope of life-as-theater means that interrogations of how "character" is constructed within theater are necessarily interrogations of how "subjects" are constructed within a culture. I am concerned here to analyze how Shakespeare represents the effects of such staging as they are internalized as subjectivation.

R. R. MacDonald has remarked on the way Cleopatra demonstrates Shakespeare's conception of character "as performance" (p. 92). See also Phyllis Rackin, "Shakespeare's Boy Cleopatra, the Decorum of Nature, and the Golden World of Poetry," *PMLA* 87 (1972); idem, "Anti-Historians: Women's Roles in Shakespeare's Histories," *Theatre Journal* 37 (1985): 329–344; Barish, *The Antitheatrical Prejudice;* Cook, "The Fatal Cleopatra"; Colie, *Shakespeare's Living Art.* Jyotsna Singh argues that the theatricality of Cleopatra represents the general alignment of femininity with the theatrical in Renaissance antifeminist and antitheatrical discourse; see "Renaissance Antitheatricality, Antifeminism, and Shakespeare's *Antony and Cleopatra,*" in *Renaissance Drama,* n.s., vol. 20 (Evanston: Northwestern University Press, 1990), pp. 99–121.

7. All references are to the Arden edition, ed. M. R. Ridley (London: Methuen, 1965).

8. Not that this relationship between authority and authorship was stable or unconflicted. The writings of Virgil, Horace, and, obviously, Ovid are fraught with conflict and ambivalence about Augustan power and ideology. I am indebted here to Janet Adelman's chapter "The Common Liar: Tradition as Source in *Antony and Cleopatra,*" in *The Common Liar,* pp. 53–60; and to Leo Braudy's chapter "The Authority of Augustus," in *The Frenzy of Renown: Fame and Its History* (Oxford: Oxford University Press, 1986), pp. 90–111.

9. Braudy, *The Frenzy of Renown,* p. 127.

10. Michel de Certeau, *The Practice of Everyday Life,* trans. Steven Rendall (Berkeley: University of California Press, 1984), pp. 36–37. Certeau goes on to say of tactics: "This nowhere gives a tactic mobility, to be sure, but a mobility that must accept the chance offerings of the moment, and seize on the wing the possibilities that offer themselves at any given moment. It must vigilantly make use of the cracks that particular conjunctions open in the surveillance of the proprietary powers. It poaches in them. It creates surprises in them. It can be where it is least expected. It is a guileful ruse. In short, a tactic is an art of the weak" (p. 37).

11. "Desire and the Interpretation of Desire in *Hamlet,*" in *Literature and Psychoanalysis: The Question of Reading: Otherwise,* ed. Shoshana Felman (Baltimore: Johns Hopkins University Press, 1982), pp. 11–52, esp. p. 25.

12. Both Egypt and Rome can be regarded as "habitus" in Bourdieu's sense, insofar as they represent not just particular dwellings, local habitations, but also sets of interiorized structures, *habits of mind* that reproduce those structures and their accompanying values. Bourdieu's "habitus" is, according to Certeau, "the acquired" (p. 43); synomyms are: "ethos," "modus operandi," "second nature," "common sense" (p. 58). The habitus is the total space—physical, ethical, class-stratified, ideological, practical, habitual—inhabited by the subject, who is in

turn determined by that space and who in turn helps reproduce it. It is the mise-en-scène, as it were, of everyday life, and determines both the range and limitations of possible "improvisations" within its bounds. As Bourdieu himself puts it in *Outline of a Theory of Practice* (Cambridge: Cambridge University Press, 1977): "The habitus [is] the durably installed generative principle of regulated improvisations . . . In practice, it is the habitus, history turned into nature, i.e. denied as such, which accomplishes the . . . production of practice" (p. 78). A structured structure which is also a structuring structure, the habitus determines the range and possibilities of the "thinkable" itself.

13. See Ania Loomba, *Gender, Race, Renaissance Drama* (Manchester: Manchester University Press, 1989), esp. pp. 75–78. Loomba's feminist-materialist analysis of Cleopatra's "power" reveals what is in fact an amalgamation, in the figure of exoticized "woman," of stereotypical patriarchal male fears about female governance, class status, racial difference and sexuality. Loomba argues that in this play, as in *Othello*, "colonialist, racist and sexist discourses are mutually dependent" (p. 78).

14. Worthen has remarked on the extent to which "Caesar relies on narrative—the 'news' of Alexandria, Antony's 'reported' (1.iv.67) exploits in the Alps, perhaps even in the 'writings' he offers in his defense after Antony's death (V.i.9–10)—to characterize his general" ("The Weight of Antony," p. 299).

15. Adelman has talked about the importance of "deciding the meaning of a *known* narrative" in affective rather than merely genetic terms (*The Common Liar*, p. 53); and Worthen has noted how "Caesar demands a thorough identification between the moral 'abstract' of Antony's character and the aging soldier who must continue to play the part" ("The Weight of Antony," p. 299).

16. See Louis Althusser, "Ideology and Ideological State Apparatuses," in *Lenin and Philosophy*, trans. Ben Brewster (New York: Monthly Review Press, 1971), esp. pp. 170–177.

17. Richard P. Wheeler says something very similar in *Shakespeare's Development and the Problem Comedies: Turn and Counter-Turn* (Berkeley: University of California Press, 1981): "Antony's bond to Cleopatra expresses a longing denied by the Roman ideal of manly honor and autonomy. Once he has been ensnared by Cleopatra's 'strong toil of grace' (V.ii.346), Antony can neither retrieve full rapport with that ideal nor fully articulate an identity for himself independent of it. When he fails to live up to a Roman ego-ideal he cannot abandon or qualify, the essential imagery of self-experience becomes for him as 'indistinct/ As water is in water' (IV.xiv.10–11)" (p. 208).

While there are several convergences in our discussions of the play ("To be Cleopatra's 'man of men' [I.v.72] is to be enmeshed in the contradictory imperatives realized as paradox in Antony's death" [p. 209]), Wheeler sees it as exploring structures that are ultimately deeply interpersonal and psychological: "The longing for this union [with Cleopatra] is the most powerful need driving Antony: it at once allows him to achieve a richer, more inclusive humanity and estranges him from political resources established by Caesar's deflection of all human impulse into the quest for power" (p. 209). Wheeler's discussion of the play—especially in the context of the need for mutuality and trust that he sees Shakespeare's later plays developing—is powerful and sophisticated. But I think his focus on the intrapsychic and interpersonal relations charted in the plays, as well as his sense of how these represent Shakespeare's "development," leads his discussion in very different directions from mine. To my mind Shakespeare is concerned more to explore the representational and social politics that move these figures than to explore psychological needs or drives; and although Wheeler acknowledges that "they are incompatible with the structures of sustained life as they are understood in this play" (p. 210), I am not convinced that the structures of power that "stand for" the Roman world do not obtain in the Egyptian one.

18. Ronald R. MacDonald has noted the extent to which "Rome speaks in Antony" ("Playing Till Doomsday," p. 92); in his fine article, he analyzes how not only Antony and Cleopatra but Shakespeare as well must struggle to speak "through their sources" rather than have their sources speak through them (p. 99). But while I find myself in close sympathy with his discussion throughout, it is finally too celebratory of their freedom: "Antony and Cleopatra *are* in a compelling sense free to create themselves, to refuse the cultural representations that would reduce them or rob them of their reality. And Shakespeare is similarly free to imagine them creating themselves, for in doing so he is not blindly or naively resisting an irreducible reality. He is inserting his own version into what has been revealed as a collection of competing interpretations" (p. 98). While Shakespeare is certainly "inserting his own version into this collection of competing interpretations," I would argue that the effects of such "competition" on his protagonists are different. While MacDonald asserts that Antony and Cleopatra are "free to refuse" their cultural representations, the crucial point to make is that they do not refuse them. And, I would add, they do not (and cannot) precisely because they are more than just competing representations of "history"—they are competing representations that have been amalgamated into "historical necessity": legend.

19. Helmut Kuzmics lists these tenets as central to Goffman's "tacit precondition[s] for successful interaction"; see Kuzmics, "Embarrassment and Civilization: On Some Similarities and Differences in the Work of Goffman and Elias," *Theory, Culture & Society* 8 (1991): 1–30; 1–2.

20. Ibid., pp. 2–3.

21. We see this operate most notably in *Othello* (see Loomba, *Gender, Race, Renaissance Drama,* esp. p. 59), between Iago and Roderigo, Othello, and Cassio. But it can be clearly seen in many other plays; *Richard III, King Lear, All's Well,* and *Much Ado* provide memorable examples.

22. In contrast to this, Bourdieu adds that "ease, a sort of indifference to the objectifying gaze of others which neutralizes its powers, presupposes the self-assurance which comes from the certainty of being able to objectify that objectification, appropriate that appropriation, of being capable of imposing the norms of apperception of one's own body." See Pierre Bourdieu, *Distinction: A Social Critique of the Judgement of Taste,* trans. Richard Nice (Cambridge, Mass.: Harvard University Press, 1984), pp. 207–208. Norbert Elias, in *The Civilizing Process,* vol. I: *The History of Manners,* likewise talks extensively of the "changes in affect" that accompanied a massively increased level of social self-consciousness in the Renaissance. See also Georges Vigarello, "The Upward Training of the Body."

23. I take this quote by Burke from Frank Whigham, *Ambition and Privilege: The Social Tropes of Elizabethan Courtesy Theory* (Berkeley: University of California Press, 1984), p. 64.

24. "It derives its force," Whigham tells us, "from its resistance to assimilation by the familiar world. Objections to the glamourous can be written off as uncomprehending, and Annibale elsewhere argues that such incompetence frequently has an affiliation with 'the idle, the ignorant, the unfortunate, and bankerupts, which have no good success in their own affaires" (*Ambition and Privilege*, p. 64). Whigham's skillful analysis of the sublety of rhetorical competition and social strategy among the up and coming middle classes in the sixteenth and seventeenth centuries has been helpful to me in analyzing the various rhetorical performances that occur in this play.

25. Kenneth Burke, quoted in Whigham, *Ambition and Privilege*, p. 63.

26. Walter Benjamin, "The Work of Art in the Age of Mechanical Reproduction," in *Illuminations: Essays and Reflections*, ed. Hannah Arendt (New York: Schocken, 1969).

27. Steven Mullaney, *The Place of the Stage: License, Play, and Power in Renaissance England* (Chicago: University of Chicago Press, 1988), p. 8.

28. Other critics have remarked on the way Cleopatra seems to represent a certain kind of theatricality: see Adelman, Barish, Colie, MacDonald, Rackin, Worthen, and Carol Cook, all cited above. Michael Shapiro has said that the emphasis on Cleopatra's histrionicism underlines a "dual consciousness" in which the audience is asked to see Cleopatra simultaneously as a boy actor and as a female "character" (see "Boying her Greatness: Shakespeare's Use of Coterie Drama in *Antony and Cleopatra*," *Modern Language Review*, 77, no. 1 (1982): 1–15, esp. 11–14). Carol Cook addresses the way Cleopatra "plays" different roles; but Cook sees Cleopatra finally as a "figure for a certain kind of *textual* operation" (p. 26, italics added) rather than, as I would argue, a figure for a certain kind of *theatrical* operation. See also Jyotsna Singh, "Antitheatricality and *Antony and Cleopatra*," pp. 100–101. These critics, as well as many others, have remarked on Cleopatra's histrionic manipulations; but to my knowledge, none has regarded this histrionicism as a remapping of identity itself—a theatrical principle of identity in which subjectivity is posited as a kind of theater.

29. Annette Kuhn, *The Power of the Image: Essays on Representation and Sexuality* (London: Routledge and Kegan Paul, 1985), p. 52.

30. The idea of Cleopatra as a female principle of fluidity has been remarked by Barish (*Antitheatrical Prejudice*, p. 130); Adelman (*The Common Liar*); and Colie, *Shakespeare's Living Art*; and Carol Cook has argued that "Cleopatra seems an apt figure for a larger principle at work in the play, a fluid principle which destabilizes principles, overflowing the confines of categories as the Nile overflows its banks" ("The Fatal Cleopatra," p. 10). Cook is right in saying that Cleopatra refuses the kind of stability that can be made property to serve Rome. But Cleopatra does not refuse the kind of stability that can be made property to serve *Egypt*. And although Cook claims that Cleopatra refuses "essence," her argument draws upon the same terminology of gender binarism (although now appropriated for the *jouissance* of continental feminist psychoanalysis) that has in the past produced a female "essence" of mystery, the "unrepresentable" against the phallocentric unity of masculinist representation. To my mind such

an argument does, paradoxically, produce a "female principle" as essence. For Cook, Cleopatra stands for whatever Shakespeare felt was "unrepresentable" about "woman."

Janet Adelman, however, in her recent discussion of the play in *Suffocating Mothers: Fantasies of Maternal Origin in Shakespeare's Plays, "Hamlet" to "The Tempest"* (London: Routledge, 1992), sees a clear and pervasive representation of another kind of female principle at work (admittedly tenuously) in the play, that of the bounteous mother whose amplitude redeems ("for one fragile moment," p. 191) Antony (and Shakespeare) from the masculine economy of "withholding": "Bounty and scarcity continue to be the key terms in Antony and Cleopatra" (p. 176); and these are aligned with, respectively, the infinitely fertile world of Egypt, Cleopatra, and the benevolent, enabling mother versus the punitive and Oedipal male world of Rome (see esp. pp. 174–192). As compelling as these formulations are in their attention to the language of the play, I remain uneasy with what seems to me a risk of recapitulating the structures of gender binarism these arguments otherwise critique. In my view, Cleopatra has to do with the playwright's fantasy of the representational possibilities offered by a fundamentally performative subjectivity rather than something fundamentally female in general (Cook's position) or maternal in specific (Adelman's).

31. Joel Altman has also noticed Shakespeare's more general investigation of this relationship in terms of his own plays as "texts." See "The Practice of Shakespeare's Text," in *Style* 23, no. 3 (Fall 1989): 466–500, for a convincing and subtle analysis of Shakespeare's texts as blueprints for practices rather than as reified products; and in particular p. 493, on the relationship of "textual practice" to "textual identity."

32. The deliberate cultivation of this kind of erotic cognitive dissonance—one in which the female object is more alluring because she is unaware of being watched—is formulated explicitly in Castiglione, *The Book of the Courtier*, trans. Charles Singleton (New York: Anchor Books, 1959), bk. 1, pp. 64–66. In fact, the woman is instructed to cultivate a performance in which she reveals her ankles, her face, so as to appear to the viewer completely unaware of the fact that she is viewed.

33. Jean Baudrillard, *The Ecstasy of Communication*, trans. Bernard Schutze and Caroline Schutze (Brooklyn: Semiotext(e), 1988), p. 63.

34. Robert Weimann, "Towards a Literary Theory of Ideology: Mimesis, Representation, Authority," in *Shakespeare Reproduced: The Text in History and Ideology*, ed. Jean E. Howard and Marion F. O'Connor (New York: Methuen, 1987), p. 270.

35. Adelman has discussed this in terms of "multiplicity" (*The Common Liar*, pp. 45–49); Cook, in terms of the way both the play and Cleopatra "gesture toward something beyond the play's scene of representation" ("The Fatal Cleopatra," p. 10). Barbara Bono, in *Literary Transvaluation: From Vergilian Epic to Shakespearean Tragicomedy* (Berkeley: University of California Press, 1984), has described this in terms of the "'motion' Cleopatra induces in Antony as a dissolution of his nature" (p. 169).

36. John Fiske, *Television Culture* (New York: Routledge, 1986), p. 253.

37. I refer to a paper that Stallybrass read at the 1990 meeting of the Shake-

speare Association of America in Philadelphia. The paper, "Transvestism and the 'Body Beneath': Speculating on the Boy Actor," appears in *Erotic Politics: Desire on the Renaissance Stage,* ed. Susan Zimmerman (London: Routledge 1992).

38. For some fine feminist and theoretical discussions of cross-dressing, androgyny, and gender roles in Shakespeare, Renaissance drama, and Western culture, see Rackin, "Shakespeare's Boy Cleopatra"; Carol Thomas Neely, *Broken Nuptials in Shakespeare's Plays* (New Haven: Yale University Press, 1985), esp. pp. 138–139; Catherine Belsey, *The Subject of Tragedy* (London: Methuen, 1988); Jean E. Howard, "Crossdressing, The Theatre, and Gender Struggle in Early Modern England," in *Shakespeare Quarterly* 39, no. 4 (Winter 1988): 418–440; Lisa Jardine, *Still Harping on Daughters: Women and Drama in the Age of Shakespeare* (Sussex: Harvester Press, 1983); Leah Marcus, "Shakespeare's Comic Heroines: Elizabeth I and the Political Uses of Androgyny," in *Women in the Middle Ages and the Renaissance: Literary and Historical Perspectives,* ed. Mary Beth Rose (Syracuse, N.Y.: Syracuse University Press, 1986), pp. 135–153; and Marjorie Garber, *Vested Interests: Cross-Dressing and Cultural Anxiety* (London: Routledge, 1992). Madelon Sprengnether approaches Cleopatra's cross-dressing in a way I find persuasive: "the boy actor is fundamental not only to Shakespeare's stage but also to his equivocal representations of femininity, allowing him to portray women as both 'other' and 'not other.'" See "The Boy Actor and Femininity in *Antony and Cleopatra,*" in *Shakespeare's Personality,* ed. Norman Holland, Sidney Homan, and Bernard Paris (Berkeley: University of California Press, 1989), p. 192.

39. This is, of course, only an effect. By foregrounding the Chinese-box syndrome in the representation of Cleopatra, the playwright deconstructs the trope of identity—which is, finally, self-referential, revealing nothing at the "heart" of Cleopatra but the process of staging itself. Anticipating Brechtian theater, such lines produce the *Verfremdungseffekt,* or "alienation effect," around not only the notion of gender but the "metaphysics of presence" as well. Demanding at this moment that the "theatre audience learn to see 'character' as an effect of acting"– (Worthen, "The Weight of Antony," p. 298), these lines also require the audience to see gender as an effect of acting. As Elin Diamond has remarked about cross-dressing in contemporary theater, "gender is exposed as a sexual costume, a sign of a role, not evidence of identity. Recalling such performances should remind us of the rigorous self-consciousness that goes into even the most playful gender-bending . . . When gender is 'alienated' or foregrounded, the spectator is enabled to see a sign system *as* a sign system—the appearance, words, gestures, ideas, attitudes, etc., that comprise the gender lexicon become so many illusionistic trappings to be put on or shed at will." See Diamond, "Brechtian Theory/ Feminist Theory: Toward a Gestic Feminist Criticism," *TDR* 32 (Spring 1988): 82–94, esp. 85 (I am grateful to Timothy Wiles for bringing this article to my attention).

Thus, Cleopatra's lines function doubly: they demystify the conditions of performance, exposing the mise-en-scène to remind us that the actor playing Cleopatra is not female, and is also not Cleopatra "herself." But within the context of the play they produce the "A-effect," conjuring a mise-en-abyme in which we are also asked to imagine a "real" Cleopatra who exists separately from the Roman actors who would boy her greatness. In order to preserve the illusion of the "something secret in appearances," Cleopatra must preserve the *illegibility* of her appearance.

40. Laura Mulvey, "Visual Pleasure and Narrative Cinema," *Screen* 16 (1975): 6–18.

41. See Joel Altman, "The Practice of Shakespeare's Text," n. 14, p. 495.

42. Parts of this section of the chapter appear, in different form, in Linda Charnes, "'What's Love Got to Do with It?': Reading the Liberal Humanist Romance in Shakespeare's *Antony and Cleopatra,*" *Textual Practice* 6, no. 1 (1992): 5–20. I thank Routledge for permission to use these portions, in revised form, here.

43. I refer to the 1967 Warner Brothers film *Bonnie and Clyde;* and to the 1986 Zenith production *Sid and Nancy,* the story of "Sid Vicious" and his American girlfriend Nancy Spungen, whom he murdered in a drug-induced rage. As for Ron and Nancy, their narrative is still undergoing revisions, the latest offering being Kitty Kelley's "unauthorized" biography of Nancy Reagan (New York: Simon and Schuster, 1991).

44. Hayden White, *Tropics of Discourse: Essays in Cultural Criticism* (Baltimore: Johns Hopkins University Press, 1978), p. 59.

45. William Kerrigan, "The Personal Shakespeare: Three Clues," in *Shakespeare's Personality* (Berkeley: University of California Press, 1989), esp. pp. 188–189.

46. Michael Steppat, *The Critical Reception of Shakespeare's Antony and Cleopatra, from 1607 to 1905* (Amsterdam: Verlag B. R. Gruner, 1980), pp. 1–2.

47. Ibid., p. 2. It is no accident that the play caught the interest of "the Romantics"; for writers like Coleridge, Hazlitt, and Shelley, no matter what their professed social and political concerns, contributed above all to the notion of "great individuals." Proleptically reading their own cause into the play's effects, "the Romantics" foregrounded the very aspects of the play that Shakespeare's audience would probably have found most indecorous (Antony and Cleopatra's apparent indulgence of "self" and sensuality over public duty, desire over public honor and reputation), and, like many critics since, regarded them as liberatory.

48. Dryden's 1678 version of the story doesn't have the strongly individualist romance ethos which I would claim isn't fully developed or ideologically operative until the late eighteenth century. But in *All for Love,* the force and scale of the political does recede under the foregrounding of a more domesticated vision of the problems of love, jealousy, and fidelity. And as in *Truth Found Too Late* (Dryden's revision of the Troilus and Cressida story, in which Cressida isn't "really" false to Troilus—she's just misunderstood, and Troilus' character is restored to its proper dignity), love may not conquer all at the level of plot, but it certainly does at the level of didacticism. Dryden is able to achieve this in *All for Love* partly because he removes most of the incommensurable elements of Shakespeare's play that make it impossible for love to knit together what time, place, and culture have put asunder. We see Dryden's Antony only on his last day, and only in one place—Alexandria. (See Brice Harris, introduction to *Restoration Plays* [New York: Random House, 1953], p. ix.) And Dryden's Cleopatra

is explicitly "white" (see Antony's first lines in Act 3), not, like Shakespeare's, "with Phoebus' amorous pinches black/And wrinkled deep in time."

49. I am aware that questioning the love of Antony and Cleopatra is in certain circles tantamount to slaughtering one of Shakespeare criticism's most sacred cows; but I for one have never found the play's rhetoric of love convincing. However, unlike critics who reject their love as being morally offensive or untenable—for instance, critics who believe such an attachment between two figures couldn't be "real love" (usually alongside claims that he is misogynistic and she is manipulative)—I don't have an alternative vision of what else love might mean in this play. Critics who view the love story favorably usually see this play as an example of Shakespeare's meditation on the pleasures of "mature love," a ripened version of the passion we see in Romeo and Juliet, the "triumph" of Antony and Cleopatra's love over their mutual suspicions and political obstacles, etc. There is much critical work on the play that regards love in such terms, as anyone familiar with Shakespeare criticism knows; but this kind of celebratory rhetoric even makes its way into the work of critics who, while critiquing the play's patriarchalism and misogyny, still manage to hold love up as something that will, to quote Antony, "stand up peerless."

50. Antony's posture would have been recognizable to a Renaissance audience familiar with Aristotle's definition of magnificence: "A magnificent man is like a skilled artist: he has the capacity to observe what is suitable and to spend large sums with good taste. For as we said at the outset, a characteristic is defined by its activities and by its objects. Therefore, the expenses of a magnificent man are great and suitable, and so are, consequently, the results which he produces . . . Accordingly, a result must be worth the expense and the expense worth the result or even exceed the result. A magnificenct man will spend amounts of this kind because it is noble to do so; for this motive is common to all the virtues. Moreover, he will spend with pleasure and with a free hand, for exact bookkeeping is niggardly." See *Nichomachean Ethics*, trans. Martin Ostwald (Indianapolis: Liberal Arts Press, 1962), p. 90. Noteworthy in this description of the magnificent man vis-à-vis Antony is that while Antony invokes its rhetoric insofar as he will not "reckon" his expenditure of love, he has also, at least in Roman terms, lost the "capacity to observe what is suitable" and "to spend with good taste." In the Egyptian habitus he is "magnificent," whereas in the Roman habitus he is seen as "excessive."

For Castiglione's definition of *sprezzatura* as the art of appearing artless, see *The Book of the Courtier*, trans. Charles Singleton (New York: Anchor Books, 1959), p. 43.

51. Critics differ widely about the effectiveness and effects of both Antony's and Cleopatra's death scenes. While many have noted Antony's clumsy execution of his, most still feel that it achieves a certain transcendence or, at the very least, a grandeur. Michael Shapiro argues that "the remarkable thing about Antony's death scene is his refusal to blame Cleopatra for tricking him into killing himself: there are no accusations in his dying words" ("Boying her Greatness," p. 10). Shapiro addresses the difficulty that the protagonists' rhetoric of suicide-for-love entails, asking if Antony and Cleopatra aren't "merely attempting to evade the humiliation of capture by Caesar rather than refusing to remain

alive in a world barren of the beloved?" (p. 10). He then asserts that to remain in such a position "might be considered perverse" (p. 10), since by the end of the play even the most skeptical characters (including, presumably, Octavius) have been "converted" to and by the authenticity of their love. Jyotsna Singh says that "Antony dies by imaginatively evoking the values of love" ("Anti-theatricality and *Antony and Cleopatra*," p. 116). And on Cleopatra's suicide being as much an act of rhetorical self-creation as an act of self-immolation, see Thomas Van Laan, *Role-Playing in Shakespeare* (Toronto: University of Toronto Press, 1978), p. 220. For Janet Adelman, Cleopatra's suicide secures the re-creation not only of herself but, more importantly, of Antony: "Cleopatra must, in particular, die for the right reason: she can become the repository of Antony's new masculinity only insofar as she is willing to die specifically for him, simultaneously validating their love and her vision of him" (*Suffocating Mothers*, p. 190).

What I find disturbing about these accounts (each masterful on its own terms) is the way each makes the triumph of love somehow dependent on death. In these accounts, Antony and Cleopatra's love for each other is redeemed, secured, elevated, and ennobled, in the last instance, only by the rhetoric of their suicides. What makes me uneasy with such an interpretation is that it doesn't require much of a leap to connect the transcendentalizing rhetoric of suicide-for-love with that of murder-for-love. After Othello kills Desdemona, he deploys the rhetoric of love as explanation for her death by instructing others to "speak of one that loved not wisely, but too well." Death becomes the sign by which transcendent Love renders itself "beyond question."

52. But there is another important reason for this revisionist epistemology. With Octavius' translation of what he earlier characterized as "shames" into "high events," Antony's masculinity, his "dignity" as a legendary warrior-lover, is recuperated. This is of course necessary in order for Caesar to cash in the glory voucher that comes only from having defeated a "worthy" opponent. As part of this project, Cleopatra must also be recuperated as the "great cause" that would keep a great general from the great business of Rome. And it is Cleopatra's suicide, the act that within the play enables her to escape the "censure" of Rome as harlot-on-parade, that enables Octavius' new construction of her as a woman who dies "for love." What makes Antony and Cleopatra recuperable as a legendary love story is the fact that Cleopatra does finally "do the right female thing" and commit suicide. And with this final act, she inscribes herself into the time-worn literary tradition of women who kill themselves for love, providing for Octavius, the audience, and centuries of critics the glue needed to reestablish the "proper" gender decorum that Antony and Cleopatra have throughout the play been disrupting. For Octavius, such a recuperation ensures a *political* and symbolic, as well as a martial, victory.

Conclusion

1. I am grateful to Jeffrey Martinek, who provided me with the Warhol quote in the epigram and who lent me his bedside bible copy of *The Philosophy of Andy Warhol* (San Diego: Harcourt, Brace, Jovanovich, 1975).

2. Peter Sloterdijk, *A Critique of Cynical Reason*, trans. Michael Eldred (Minneapolis: University of Minnesota Press, 1987), p. 24

3. See Walter Benjamin, "The Work of Art in the Age of Mechanical Reproduction," *Illuminations: Essays and Reflections*, ed. Hannah Arendt, trans. Harry Zohn (New York: Schocken, 1969), pp. 217–252, esp. 220–221.

Epilogue

1. It makes little difference whether or not Shakespeare is treated humorously in ads and movies. Even when an image of "Shakespeare" produces comic effect by being juxtaposed with something "low" (like mufflers or underwear), his status as both high- and mass-cultural icon is reinforced by the incongruity. In the parody of the graveyard scene from *Hamlet* in the recent film *L.A. Story* (in which Rick Moranis, of *Honey I Shrunk the Kids* fame, plays the gravedigger), Steve Martin's character (an overeducated weather announcer with a doctorate in "Arts and Humanities," too attached to Mother and alienated by the rottenness of the state of Los Angeles) knows that he is in love with his romantic object (played by the British actress Victoria Tennant) when she recognizes the allusion and recites the proper lines from the play. Unlike the Valley Girl shop clerk he has been having casual sex with, this is someone he can take to meet Mother: this girl knows "her Shakespeare."

2. Which is not to say that during the past two centuries the construction of Shakespeare the Author has been any less ideological, either in conception or administration. Quite the contrary. The work of editors of Shakespeare, for most of the last two centuries, has consisted of deciding what distinguishes a "true" Shakespearean text from a "corrupt" one, in an effort to preserve/posit the "integrity" of Shakespeare as individual genius and sole author. There has been fine recent scholarship (by Jonathan Goldberg, Elizabeth Pittinger, Peter Stallybrass, Randall McLeod, Michael Warren, Margreta DeGrazia, and Gary Taylor, among others) on the editorial strategies that have gone into constructing the Shakespearean "corpus."

3. In *Star Trek VI* it is the treacherous Soviet-*manqué* Klingon, General Chang, who declares a Shakespearean quotation war with that defender of intergalactic democracy (with his credo of "no interference unless the natives are seriously restless"), Captain Kirk: "You haven't really read Shakespeare, Captain, until you've read him in the original Klingon." Both Captain Kirk and the Klingon general are using Shakespeare as spokesman for their respective nationalist agendas. For Kirk, a card-carrying member of "The United Federation of Planets," the agenda corresponds to George Bush's "New World Order." For General Chang the agenda is openly imperialistic. In making "doubles" of its protagonist and antagonist through the "joint" of Shakespeare, the movie reveals (probably inadvertently) the appropriateness and appropriability of much of Shakespeare for nationalist, masculinist, racial, and imperialist politics. It is also interesting to note that the more the Klingon quotes Shakespeare, the more Kirk refrains from quoting (presumably in an effort to dissociate himself from Chang—in the way that Antonio, say, dissociates himself from Shylock), suggesting that the "level" ideological ground or equality that the racially exotic

Klingon believes he can share with Kirk through the "universal" medium of Shakespeare is fantasmatic (no matter how the movie ends).

4. See the Arden edition of *Othello,* edited by M. R. Ridley (London: Methuen, 1958), 3.3.161–165.

5. Jean Baudrillard, *For a Critique of the Political Economy of the Sign,* trans. Charles Levin (St. Louis, Mo.: Telos Press, 1981), p. 93. He adds that "what is fetishized is the closed perfection of a system, not the 'golden calf,' or the treasure" (p. 93). In postmodern culture we are accustomed to fetishizing names. But this kind of fetishism is closer in the way it operates to Baudrillard's critique of the term than it is to the Marxian definition. As Baudrillard points out, "the term 'fetish' has undergone a curious semantic distortion. Today it refers to a force, a supernatural property of the object and hence to a similar magical potential in the subject, through schemas of projection and capture, alienation and reappropriation. But originally it signified exactly the opposite: a *fabrication*, an artifact, a labor of appearances and signs" (p. 91).

Discussing the history of the term and its embeddedness in notions both of manufacture and of embellishment, Baudrillard stresses the literal *artificiality* that etymologically constitutes the fetish: "In the 'fetishist' theory of consumption, in the view of marketing strategists as well as of consumers, objects are given and received everywhere as force dispensers (happiness, health, security, prestige, etc.). This magical substance having been spread about so liberally, one forgets that what we are dealing with first is signs: a generalized code of signs, a totally arbitrary code of differences, *and that it is on this basis, and not at all on account of their use values or innate 'virtues,' that objects exercise their fascination*" (p. 91). While I agree with Baudrillard's criticism that Marxist theories of the fetish "forget" that "what we are dealing with first is signs," he is wrong in asserting that what produces an object as fetish is merely "a totally arbitrary code of differences." There are, to echo what Barthes says about myths, "substantial limits" to what can be produced as fetish, just as there are substantial limits to what can be produced as "legend."

Index